J
973.3
REV   The Revolutionaries

DUE DATE

THE REVOLUTIONARIES

THE AMERICAN STORY

THE REVOLUTIONARIES

by the Editors of Time-Life Books, Alexandria, Virginia

CONTENTS

An Air of Independence

According to the strait-laced John Adams, a delegate to the First Continental Congress, some of the guests at Thomas Mifflin's Philadelphia town house on September 3, 1774, were "very high." The Virginian Richard Henry Lee, for one, was showing the effects of an afternoon of drinking Burgundy with fellow delegate John Dickinson of Pennsylvania. After polishing off what Adams described as an "elegant supper," the guests began drinking toasts. Considering their boisterous spirits and their grievances—the congress had been called by Britain's American colonies in response to a long series of arbitrary taxes and restrictions imposed by the English Parliament—the toasting was remarkably restrained. Said Massachusetts delegate Robert Treat Paine, raising his glass: "May the collision of British flint and American steel produce that spark of liberty which shall illumine the latest posterity." Another guest proposed: "Union of Britain and the Colonies on a constitutional foundation."

Just four years before, a squad of red-coated British regulars had gunned down six protesting Bostonians in a confrontation quickly dubbed the Boston Massacre, and only eight months had passed since colonists responded to a new tea tax by disguising themselves as Mohawk Indians and dumping a shipload of choice British tea into Boston Harbor. But despite their strong resentment at being governed and taxed from afar without direct representation in the chambers of Parliament, the delegates sought only to assert their full rights as free-born Englishmen, as American subjects of the British Crown. Indeed, the idea that the 13 colonies might combine as a new and sovereign nation would have seemed rather far-fetched. For the differences among the colonists sometimes seemed greater than those between England and the colonies. In the main, citizens were loyal to their respective colonies and to England. And sizable numbers of colonists, known as Tories, were so faithful to the king that they opposed even the mildest resistance to royal rule.

In the 1750s provincial militias fought alongside British regular troops in the Seven Years' War, whose American phase was known as the French and Indian War. Their victory gave Canada to Britain and extended British dominion from the Atlantic to the Mississippi. But the war also left the Crown deeply in debt, and many of the British soldiers who had crossed the Atlantic to fight stayed on to protect what they had won for their king. To raise revenue to support them, the ministers turned naturally enough to the American colonists—most of whom believed that their homegrown volunteer militias were protection enough against any conceivable enemy. And some citizens suspected that the king's redcoats were in America not to protect the people from enemies, but from themselves—or rather, from what they were becoming. For even though most colonists were probably only dimly aware of it, they had changed considerably from the first loyal dependents who had stepped ashore in the New World a century and more before. Life on the American frontier had proved harder than the old life in Europe, but also richer in every kind of opportunity—including that of independent action. Gradually, political power in the colonies had shifted largely from royal officials to provincial ones, and each colony had its own parliament that was dominant on purely domestic matters. Far from the home country, the British settlers had become, almost unconsciously, culturally distinct. English in name, in fact they were Americans.

Still, the 13 colonies remained loyal. More than halfway through the 18th century, a citizen of any one of them would have flinched from open talk of full independence. Such stuff was treason. But a rash of unprecedented tax measures—the Sugar Act, the Currency Act, the Stamp Act—had collided with the colonists' growing notions of autonomy. When the First Continental Congress adjourned at the end of October 1774, John Adams and his fellow delegates declared that the principles of English liberty entitled them to decide for themselves what taxes should be levied in America. Advising the colonies to boycott British tea and to stop exporting goods to Great Britain, the congress agreed to hold another session in May 1775 if their grievances remained unresolved.

By the time of the second meeting, however, British soldiers and Massachusetts volunteer militiamen had exchanged fire at Lexington and Concord, leaving many dead and wounded on both sides. Now the Continental Congress was mounting a rapidly growing armed campaign against all the forces of imperial Great Britain. At first the hostilities were seen by most participants as a civil war. But within little more than a year it would become something more: a full-scale war for American independence.

CHAPTER 1

"THE REGULARS ARE COMING OUT!"

"I know what you are after, and have alarmed the country all the way up."

PAUL REVERE, APRIL 19, 1775

Breathing hard after his dash through the narrow, bustling streets of Boston, the young stableboy stood in the doorway of Paul Revere's house in the town's North End. Revere listened intently as the boy told his story. A friend of his, he said, worked in a livery stable where British army officers boarded their horses. Earlier that day some officers had come to the stable to check their saddles and bridles, and the boy's friend had overheard bits and pieces of their quiet conversation. One phrase had stuck in his mind, something ominous, something about "hell to pay tomorrow."

It was only natural that the boy had come to Revere with this forbidding tale. The silversmith was one of about 30 townsmen who met regularly at places like Boston's Green Dragon Tavern to discuss the latest British movements, which they reported to such freedom-minded men as John Hancock, Samuel Adams, and Joseph Warren. Stocky and businesslike at 40, with the burly arms of a woodcutter and the graceful hands of a sculptor, Revere was one of Boston's leading mechanics, as artisans called themselves at the time. He was also an accomplished horseman, highly regarded for the speed with which he carried secret messages across the colony. With a cohort of Boston mechanics,

Revere had established a "committee for the purpose of watching the movements of the British soldiers, and gaining every intelligence of the movements of the Tories." This committee, in turn, had arranged an elaborate system for spreading word of that intelligence across the colony.

Revere was not surprised by the stableboy's report. It was April 18, 1775, and all of Boston already knew that something big was afoot. Three days before, Lieutenant General Thomas Gage, the royal governor of Massachusetts and commander in chief of all British forces in America, had ordered his elite light infantry and grenadiers relieved of routine duties until further notice. The light infantry were the swift, fit soldiers who protected the long exposed flanks of columns on the march. The grenadiers, originally named for their specialty of heaving hand grenades at the enemy, were a brawny species of infantry used like a bludgeon to breach fortified positions. As word of Gage's order spread, it seemed obvious that these regulars—as the king's troops were called—were being readied for an important action.

When the boy finished his story Revere thanked him and informed him that he was not the first to have brought such news. Indeed, Revere had heard reports of similar conversations from two other

Metalsmith, engraver, and rebel, Paul Revere holds an unfinished silver teapot in this portrait done by John Singleton Copley around 1765. The energetic, colorful Revere organized a network of more than 60 fellow artisans that formed the secret heart of Boston's Revolutionary movement.

informants. And now he knew that the crisis that he and his colleagues had long prepared for was probably at hand, that the simmering disputes between the 13 colonies and their mother country were about to erupt into armed conflict.

Discord had been brewing for a dozen years, ever since the end of the Seven Years' War in 1763, when the British Parliament had sought to cover its huge war debt by imposing on the American colonies a series of unprecedented taxes. To be sure, Parliament repealed most of the measures in the face of colonial resistance, but American resentment of new imperial policies remained high. A breaking point of sorts had come in 1773, after the government imposed a tax on tea. As usual, objections were loudest in Boston, and on the night of December 16 a group of colonists disguised with Indian feathers and blackened faces dumped a shipload of British tea into Boston Harbor.

When efforts to punish the culprits came to nothing, and when the colonists refused to pay for the tea that was destroyed, King George III and Parliament settled into a mood to suppress Massachusetts. A series of Coercive Acts, which the colonists referred to as the Intolerables, imposed British-appointed courts of justice, closed Boston to shipping, and allowed colonists to be deported to Canada or England to stand trial.

New Englanders wasted no time in reacting. In Massachusetts, after issuing a Solemn League and Covenant that boycotted all British goods, the citizens convened their Provincial Assembly, which then called for a congress of all 13 colonies. Responding to that call, the First Continental Congress met in Philadelphia in September of 1774. The delegates, finally pulling together against their British overlords, condemned the so-called Intolerable Acts, declaring their right to pass their own laws and levy their own taxes.

A month later, emboldened by the larger body's cohesion, the Massachusetts Provincial Assembly began calling itself the Provincial Congress—effec-

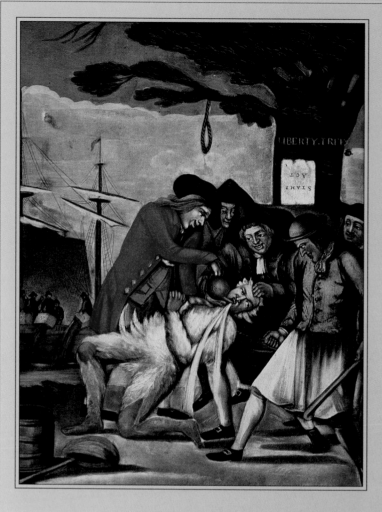

As a protest against British taxes, Bostonians pour tea down the throat of tarred and feathered customs officer John Malcolm in January 1775. In the background, men dump tea into Boston Harbor.

JOHN MALCOLM: "SINGLE KNIGHT OF THE TAR"

Boston customs official John Malcolm claimed the dubious honor of being the first American tarred and feathered for loyalty to England. He endured the treatment in Maine in 1774 and again in Boston in 1775 for his persistence in collecting import taxes and for his prickly demeanor. On the night of January 25, 1775, a mob broke into Malcolm's house, stripped him to his breeches, and covered him in hot pine tar and goose feathers. As a protest against British tea laws, the mob forced 12 bowls of tea down Malcolm's throat, making him toast a different British official each time. After repeated floggings, Malcolm succumbed to demands that he curse the royal governor.

Jokingly called the "Single Knight of the Tar" by Bostonians, Malcolm later sailed to England to gain compensation for his pains, bringing a strip of his tarred and feathered skin as proof. Malcolm was not the only victim of this brutal but popular method of terrorizing Loyalists. One recipe for the act even encouraged the patriots to hold "a lighted candle to the feathers, and try to set it all on Fire."

tively, the Revolutionary government of Massachusetts. The delegates voted to raise an army of some 15,000 men, and to arm six companies of artillery. Should the British march out of Boston with their "artillery and baggage," the congress said, the militia were to "oppose their March, to the last extremity." The congress also sent delegates to Connecticut, New Hampshire, and Rhode Island to enlist their help in raising a northeastern army that, with the Massachusetts troops, would total 30,000. Across New England, militia units spent the winter drilling, with special emphasis given to an elite, uniquely American type of citizen-soldier: the Minuteman, trained to fight at a moment's notice.

Gage, after arriving at his post in Boston in the spring of 1774, had followed these latest alarming events from his palatial home at Province House, where he lived with his wife and kept his headquarters. Gage had served the king in the 13 colonies and Canada for nearly two decades. He was a stern disciplinarian but looked with compassion on the difficult lot of both his officers and his men, and among colleagues he was a convivial, fair-minded kind of man. He was also considered to be very brave and spectacularly lucky under fire. Wounded in action three times, he had come through some ugly fights alive, including Major General Edward Braddock's rout by the French at the Monongahela River in 1755. There, Gage's determined rear-guard defense saved a shattered, retreating British column from destruction—along with a new friend of his, a young Virginia militia officer named George Washington.

Gage had gone on to greater things, both professional and domestic. In 1757 he won command of the 80th Foot, a new kind of light-infantry regiment that was trained to fight in the American wilderness, and the hand of Margaret Kemble, the stunning daughter of a prominent Brunswick, New Jersey, family. Tall and proud, Margaret Kemble Gage was equal parts English, French, Greek, and Dutch—an exquisite rare bird.

After Britain's war against the French, Gage had spent three years as governor of Montreal. Then, in 1763, he and his wife and their two young children had moved on to New York, where Gage served as commander in chief of British forces in America. The general and his "Duchess," as some people called Margaret, were at the center of the New York social whirl. Their large double house on Broad Street became a magnet for the city's distinguished visitors, including Gage's friend from the Braddock debacle—George Washington.

Finally, in June of 1773, the Gages had begun an extended visit to Great Britain. But duty, in the form of an order from His Majesty's government, had quickly intervened, forcing Gage to return to the American colonies—and into the center of a storm that was brewing rapidly.

Gage was convinced that all of America would rise up in rebellion with New England. In a letter to his friend at court, Lord Barrington, he had urged decisive action. "If you resist and not yield, that resistance should be effectual at the beginning," Gage wrote. "If you think ten thousand men sufficient, send twenty, if one million is thought enough, give two; you will save both blood and treasure in the end." His reasoning was precise: "A large force will terrify, and engage many to join you, a middling one will encourage resistance, and gain no friends." He urged evacuating the troops quartered in Boston and strangling the rebellion with a naval blockade. As early as September 1774 he had begun fortifying the town against a colonial invasion. Finally, in mid-December he had written Barrington: "Affairs are at a crisis, and if you give way it is for ever."

To head off this crisis, Gage had from time to time dispatched bodies of his redcoats on marches through the countryside around Boston. Such sorties were intended to hearten the troops and to rattle the provincials with the sight of fully armed regulars. Instead, they had given rise to a fatal misunderstanding. To Gage and his advisers, the marches demonstrated that his troops could go where they wished without a shot's being fired. To the thousands of colonial militiamen who took up their muskets and stood ready to fight, the fact that the regulars had not engaged them on these sorties indicated that British soldiers would give way wherever the colonials held firm.

Then, on April 14, 1775, Gage received a secret document from his superior, Lord Dartmouth. The colonists, the missive said, were committed to open rebellion; force must be countered with force. The Boston garrison was being strengthened, to encourage Gage's use of troops; the "principal actors and abettors" of the rebellion should be arrested forthwith. In short, the general who had kept the lid on the colonial powder keg for almost a year had been ordered to ignite it.

As it happened, Gage thought he might have a project that would satisfy his orders with minimal risk. Indeed, he had been planning the undertaking secretly for weeks. His spies had alerted him that the provincials were storing sizable quantities of gunpowder, cannon, and other military supplies in Concord, about 20 miles from Boston. Now Gage had decided to dispatch a relatively small body of troops to seize these supplies, and he would intentionally arm them too lightly to provoke a fight. There would be no supply wagons and no artillery. The men would take just a day's ration and 36 of the powder-and-ball cartridges used in the musket they affectionately called brown Bess.

Gage's plan seemed simple enough. The town of Boston was then a virtual island, confined to a diamond-shaped peninsula barely a mile wide and two miles long. It was linked to the mainland at its southern point by a narrow strip of land known as Boston Neck. The Back Bay, an expanse of tidal marshes and mud flats, lay on the west, Boston Harbor opened to the Atlantic on the east. On the northern side, the Charles River separated Boston from Charlestown. Rather than send his forces marching in plain sight across Boston Neck, Gage would order them to leave the town secretly, by water. Armed with the element of surprise, they would reach Concord and carry out their mission before the militias could react.

On Saturday, April 15, Gage had set the plan in motion with his order for the grenadiers and light infantry to stand by. On the 18th, knowing that the colonists' express riders would be out to spread the alarm as soon as the movement of regulars was known, he sealed the only road out of town, at Boston Neck, and alerted watches aboard *Somerset*, *Falcon*, and other men-of-war anchored in the Back Bay and the Charles. That morning he had also sent about 20 mounted officers and men into the countryside between Boston and Concord, under the command of the brave but somewhat excitable Major Edward Mitchell. If any colonial messengers broke through, the mounted officers would intercept them. And should the opportunity present itself, Mitchell's party was about the right size to find and arrest John Hancock, leader of the Provincial Congress, and his rabble-rousing colleague, Samuel Adams; the pair had not returned to Boston after the congress recessed on April 15, but had stopped in Lexington as guests of the Reverend Jonas Clarke.

On the evening of April 18, Gage added to his forces some companies of grenadiers and light infantry from the Royal Marines, creating a unit of about 700 officers and men. Leading the troops was Lieutenant Colonel Francis Smith, 52-year-old regimental commander of the 10th Foot; his second in command was Major John Pitcairn, 53, who was the commander of the marine battalion that was as-

FIRING A BROWN BESS

The most effective and popular weapon during the war's early days, the brown Bess musket had a singular advantage over other guns then available—reloading speed. Indeed, its name was a term of endearment, though the exact origin of the phrase is unknown. Even with musket balls whistling past his head, a good infantryman could reload and fire the 42-inch-long brown Bess three times a minute—far faster than those armed with more accurate guns of the time.

At close range, the musket's .75 caliber, one-ounce ball dealt a staggering blow. But the weapon's accuracy deteriorated rapidly with distance. To fire a brown Bess at the enemy from 200 yards, wrote one British officer, a soldier might "just as well fire at the moon."

To maximize the gun's deadliness, soldiers advanced to within 50 yards of the enemy before firing, a feat demanding great courage. Once soldiers were upon each other, they used the bayonet attached to the musket's barrel for hand-to-hand combat, the final test of their mettle.

signed to the Boston garrison and was an experienced combat leader. As was common practice, only Smith knew the night's objective.

By 10 p.m. the companies of red-coated regulars had converged along an empty strand of Back Bay beach. They were met by a flotilla of longboats that ferried them across the Back Bay and the Charles River to Lechmere's Point, a task that took two hours because of a shortage of boats. A rising tide forced the men to debark into the chilly marsh waters. While the infantry regrouped on the beach around midnight, Smith opened his sealed orders. They were to march by way of Lexington to the town of Concord, there to "seize and destroy all Artillery, Ammunition, Provisions, Tents, Small Arms, and all Military Stores whatever." Smith was to be careful that his troops did not "plunder the Inhabitants, or hurt private property." Shivering in their wet uniforms, the men waited more than an hour for their provisions to be delivered.

At last, sometime after 2 a.m., Smith turned his long column into the cold west wind and began the 20-mile march for Concord. Unknown to him or to his soldiers, or to the thousands of provincial militiamen who were already rising to meet them, Concord was a way point on the road to immortality—and what would happen there on the morning of April 19, 1775, would change the world forever.

From the start, Gage had known that it would be impossible to hide his soldiers' preparations from the prying eyes of colonists. Still, he had hoped to keep secret the troops' destination and mission. But even as the expedition against Concord was getting under way, he learned otherwise. Gage had asked Lord Percy, one of his most talented brigade commanders, to visit him in Province House. When Percy arrived near dusk, Gage had confided where the troops were going and why, and urged him to keep the matter strictly confidential. But when Percy stepped into the chilly April night, he was surprised to come upon a group of Bostonians in earnest discussion near a streetlight by the common. Gathering his cloak about him, Percy moved closer to them. "The British troops have marched," said one, "but will miss their aim."

"What aim?" asked Percy.

"Why, the cannon at Concord," was the reply.

Lord Percy hurried back to Province House in order to tell the general that the expedition's destination was common knowledge on the Boston streets. The usually unflappable Gage uttered a howl of anguish; he had told only one other person of his plan, he said. Percy thought that Gage must be referring to his wife.

After Percy left him alone, Gage sent an aide with a message for Captain Thomas Moncrieffe of Lord Percy's First Brigade. He ordered Moncrieffe to have the First Brigade muster at 4 a.m., and stand ready to relieve Colonel Smith along the Concord road. Another letter ordered out the Royal Marines who had not marched with Major Pitcairn earlier. Then the general went to bed, unaware that his calls for reinforcements would be delayed, that the countryside was being warned, and that thousands of Massachusetts men were already on their way to Concord.

A few hours after his visit from the young stableboy, Paul Revere had had another caller, who bore a message from Joseph Warren, a patrician 33-year-old Boston doctor. One of the leaders of Boston's patriot faction, Warren had been hearing rumors of troop movements throughout the day and early evening, but he had wanted more than the word of bystanders before he asked Revere to bring the countryside to an alert. He had decided it was time to play a dangerous ace: a secret query to an informant close to Province House. The answer had soon come back: The troops were going out to seize Samuel Adams and John Hancock in Lexington, then burn the matériel stored at Concord. His worst suspicions confirmed, Warren had sent for William Dawes, a Boston tanner whose work often took him out of the town, and asked him to carry a warning to Concord. Moments before the city was completely sealed the portly Dawes had squeaked through the gate at Boston Neck, where he knew the guard, and on his ungainly horse headed for Cambridge and the Concord road.

Then Warren had sent for Paul Revere, who answered the doctor's summons sometime after nine, hurrying across the dark town from his North

perienced oarsmen who got him safely past the lookouts aboard the British men-of-war.

The silversmith, wrapped in a long duster and wearing riding boots and a cruel-looking pair of silver spurs, was met at the Charlestown ferry slip by Colonel William Conant of that town's militia and several others. As Revere put it, "I told them what was acting," and the men then handed him the reins of Brown Beauty, a swift New England saddle horse. By 11 p.m. Revere and the mare were pounding north along the muddy thoroughfare through Charlestown Neck, then continuing west on the way to Lexington. Brown Beauty eased into a steady canter as she thumped through the shadows that dappled the puddled surface of the road.

Suddenly Brown Beauty's cadence altered slight-

Commander of British forces in the colonies and Massachusetts governor during the war's opening volleys, Lieutenant General Thomas Gage gestures toward drilling troops.

> *"The eyes of all are turned upon Great Britain, waiting for her determination; and it's the opinion of most people, if a respectable force is seen in the Field, the most obnoxious of the Leaders seized, and a Pardon proclaimed for all others, that Government will come off Victorious."* LIEUTENANT GENERAL THOMAS GAGE, JANUARY 18, 1775

End home. Warren, Revere wrote later, "begged that I would immediately set off for Lexington, where Messrs Hancock and Adams were, and acquaint them of the movement, and that it was thought they were the objects."

Before leaving Boston, however, Revere needed to tie up one loose end. The week before, he had met with leaders in Charlestown, across the river, to work out a scheme for signaling British intentions. He had arranged to show lights from the steeple of the Old North Church—one light would signal that the British had marched out through Boston Neck; two meant they had crossed the Charles in boats. At half past ten, the twin lantern flames were flashed to watchers in Charlestown, who immediately sent off a courier to warn Concord. The man galloped straight into the British cordon of mounted troops—and into oblivion, for his name was never written down. By then Revere was crossing the Charles River in a small boat rowed by a pair of ex-

ly as something distracted her; her rider saw her ears come up, attentive. He was just able to discern, a few hundred feet away, two horsemen. Riding closer, Revere made out their military silhouettes—the cockades on the helmets, the long riding cloaks over holstered arms. He was riding into an ambush.

Revere whipped the reins, hauling Beauty's head about, and dug in with his wicked spurs to make her shoot away from the redcoats. The British officers broke from their shadows at a gallop, one circling off to intercept Revere, the other following on the road. In the deceptive moonlight, the flanking officer took his horse into a bog and had to abandon the chase. The other pursuing regular was soon outdistanced by Brown Beauty's powerful stride.

Near midnight—about the time that the British troops were regrouping on the banks of the Charles—Revere arrived at the Reverend Jonas Clarke's house just beyond Lexington Green, his horse lathered and blown and bloody flanked from

his spurs. The frame house fairly bulged with family and guests—the Clarkes and their eight children, Adams, Hancock, and Hancock's fiancée and venerable aunt. Outside, Sergeant William Munro and a squad of comrades from the Lexington militia stood guard. Munro tried to shush the messenger: not so much noise, people were trying to sleep.

"Noise!" Revere retorted. "You'll have noise enough before long! The regulars are coming out!"

Admitted to the presence of Hancock and Adams, Revere told them about the troops and urged them to flee. When Dawes rode up half an hour later, he and Revere rested themselves and their horses for one more hour, then struck out toward Concord.

Before they were quite out of Lexington, they encountered another midnight horseman, young Samuel Prescott, one of a family of physicians in Concord—and, in Revere's words, "a high son of liberty"—who had been in Lexington to court his fiancée. He readily threw in with them. They agreed that, in view of the king's mounted patrols and the risk of capture, they would alert each house along the road. That way, others could continue spreading the word even if Revere and his fellow riders were captured.

About two miles beyond Lexington Green, Dawes and Prescott cantered off into adjacent fields, to warn the Nelson families in their clustered homes. In fact, the Nelsons had already been rudely informed of British intentions. Their patriarch, Josiah Nelson, had come upon Major Mitchell's party setting an ambush not far down the highway, and, thinking they were provincial messengers, called out to them, "Have you heard anything about when the regulars are coming out?" Furious, one of the soldiers had swung his saber at Nelson, slashing him across the head. "We'll let you know when the regulars are coming out."

The stunned Nelson had managed to flee into the night, and after his wife had bandaged his wound, he picked up his musket and powder and headed for Bedford with the alarm—and something more. In giving the farmer an ugly head wound,

The lantern shown above is one of the two hung in the steeple of Boston's Old North Church on the night of April 18, 1775, by artisan Robert Newman and Captain John Pulling to alert patriots of British troop movements. Paul Revere had arranged with them to show two lanterns "if the British went out by water, and if by land, one."

Mitchell had effectively announced British intentions in a language everyone could read.

Now, while his comrades rode to one of the Nelson houses, Revere started on down the road but pulled up suddenly. There, ahead, were two more shadowy figures on horseback. He yelled for Dawes and Prescott, and when they rode up urged that they attack the outnumbered pair. But as the three messengers drew nearer, what had seemed to be just two British officers became four regulars with drawn pistols and sabers. "God damn you," said one, "stop! If you go an inch further you are a dead man!"

The regulars herded the messengers into a field, but a few paces into it Prescott turned to Revere and whispered, "Put on!" and away the two men went, the young doctor to the left, taking his horse over a low stone wall and vanishing in the wooded, boggy countryside he knew like the back of his hand. Revere headed to the right, goading his exhausted mount toward a dark wall of trees—and there it ended. Six more mounted regulars enveloped him and he was forced to yield. The officers leveled their pistols at him and held Brown Beauty by her bridle. For Paul Revere, the midnight ride was over.

Dawes, however, put the moment's distractions to good use, bolting back toward the highway. "Halloo, my boys, I've got two of 'em!" he yelled to confuse any pursuers, and galloped into the darkness between the buildings of a nearby farm. Spooked by the shadows, his horse drew up sharply, pitching Dawes over its neck, then ran off into the night. Shaken and beginning to feel a tickle of fear, he hobbled inconspicuously back toward Lexington.

Behind him, 10 annoyed regulars turned their wrath on the one man they had managed to hold. They made Revere dismount.

"Sir," said one of the officers, "may I crave your name?"

"My name is Revere."

"What? Paul Revere?"

"Yes."

Revere was not the only prisoner. The officers had stopped everyone on the Concord road that night, and had held on to some who were on provincial business: two men sent from Lexington to watch their movements and 18-year-old Solomon Brown, sent out from Lexington in order to warn Concord. Each captive had been interrogated at length, particularly as to the precise whereabouts of John Hancock and Samuel Adams.

"Gentlemen," Revere told the regulars, "you've missed of your aim."

"What of our 'aim'?" sneered one of the officers. Another put in that their aim had been what it generally was, the rounding up of deserters.

"I know better," said Revere. "I know what you are after, and have alarmed the country all the way up." Warming to his task, the pugnacious metalsmith went further. He told them of their comrades' movement across the Charles that night, and about the march for Concord. His warning had called out the Lexington militia, he said, and they would soon have 500 men at arms there.

Troubled, one of the officers went in pursuit of their leader. When Major Mitchell galloped up, he told his men to search Revere for weapons; if his investigators had found any, the silversmith would have died on the spot. Mitchell came closer and put his pistol to Revere's head. "Tell the truth or I shall blow your brains out."

Revere's version of the truth reinforced the illusion of a large army gathering at Lexington and grave danger rising on the early-morning mists. It may be that he wanted only to get these regulars away from Lexington—away, that is, from Hancock and Adams. His tale agitated Mitchell, who ordered the captives to mount. Then the little party, the provincials sur-

One of the most famous and elaborate of Paul Revere's engravings, this print shows the arrival of red-coated British troops at Boston's Long Wharf in 1768 in response to colonial rioting. Revere wrote that the troops "marched with insolent parade, drums beating, fifes playing, up King Street." Revere issued three different versions of this engraving—for propaganda and profit.

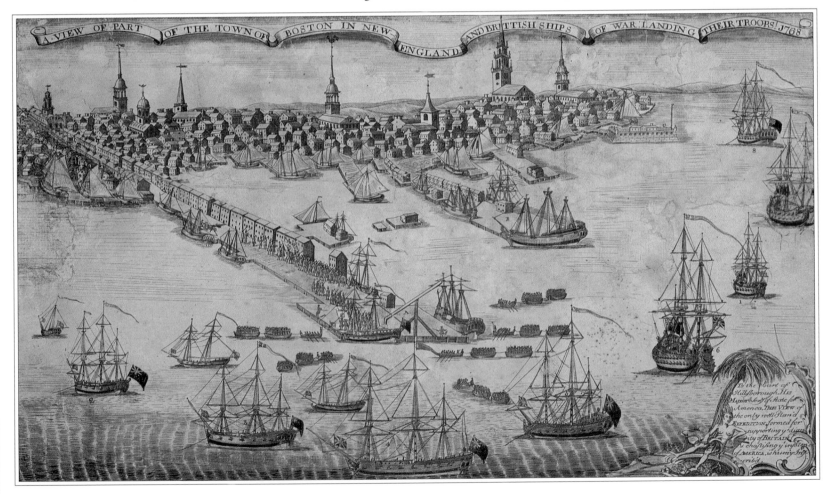

A VIEW OF PART OF THE TOWN OF BOSTON IN NEW ENGLAND AND BRITTISH SHIPS OF WAR LANDING THEIR TROOPS! 1768

THE ENIGMATIC MRS. GAGE

The unusual beauty of Margaret Kemble Gage, the American wife of British lieutenant general Thomas Gage, was obvious to many. John Singleton Copley called his painting of her *(above)* his greatest portrait. But although her beauty was certain, her loyalties were not. After Lexington and Concord, some even suspected she was a spy.

The existence of a traitor in General Gage's inner circle became clear on April 18, 1775, as the British troops marched for Concord. Gage gave an exclamation when he learned his mission had been revealed to the colonists. Only two people had been told of the march—and Margaret Gage may have been one of them. In what might be a reference to her, historian William Gordon wrote that the spy was a "daughter of liberty unequally yoked in point of politics." The question of Margaret Gage's role remains unanswered—no hard evidence condemns or absolves her.

Whether she was a spy or not, one thing is certain about Margaret Gage: She was torn between her loyalties to her husband and her country. In a 1775 letter, Mrs. Gage quoted Blanche of Spain in Shakespeare's *King John* to describe her dilemma: "Which is the side that I must go withal? I am with both: Each army hath a hand; And in their rage, I have holding of both. . . ."

rounded by British regulars, turned back toward Lexington. Revere rode at the front of this circle, but not on his own. When he asked to hold his reins himself, an officer snapped, "God damn you, sir! You are not to ride with reins, I assure you!"

"We are now going toward your friends," cautioned Mitchell, "and if you attempt to run or we are insulted, we will blow your brains out."

With his customary tact, Revere replied: "You may do as you please."

Half a mile from Lexington, the evening quiet was shattered by the sound of a gunshot. Revere told the jittery major that it was an alarm meant to warn the country. Moments later, they heard the unmistakable sound of a full, if ragged, volley of musket fire. It was merely the militia clearing their weapons of gunpowder before entering the Buckman Tavern near Lexington Green, but to the regulars it was the sound of a country in rebellion. The town bell clanged on the night. One of the other captives, following Revere's taunting lead, said to the officers, "The bell's a-ringing! The town's alarmed, and you're all dead men!"

Deciding to jettison their captives, the officers had the prisoners dismount, then cut the reins and saddle girths from the horses and shooed them off into the night—all but Revere's. Brown Beauty, already broken by her exhausting sprint, was handed over to a big grenadier sergeant; some said the worn-out filly died under him before dawn. As the regulars spurred to alert the approaching column of troops, the freed prisoners wandered off to recuperate in the Buckman Tavern.

Revere waited outside. Whatever his state of mind, he must have taken comfort in knowing that the mounted British patrols had not been a match for the warning system he and his mechanics had devised. The province had swarmed with messengers, and now, before 3 a.m., the alarm had been spread from Boston as far away as Tewksbury, 25 miles to the north. Moreover, the riders had not merely galloped down the moonlit roads, yelling that the regulars were coming out, but had gone straight for the military nerve centers of each town to give the individual commanders the word. Thus, everywhere the warning traveled, militia and Minutemen picked up their muskets and started for Concord, ready for a fight.

The British light infantry and grenadiers had by this time traveled nearly an hour from their point of debarkation in the Cambridge marshes. With the light infantry of his own 10th Regiment leading the column, Colonel Francis Smith tried to make up the hours he had lost along the Charles River, driving his troops at the rate of nearly four miles an hour. The night rang with alarm bells and musket shots in the villages ahead of and behind them. The warning fanned out as citizens fled on foot and horseback, and the regulars could almost feel the countryside rising against them. Indeed, within a five-mile circle of their march, 75 companies—more than 2,000 men at

arms—were already in motion, and thousands more were answering the morning's alerts.

A handful of British scouts on foot ranged perhaps half a mile ahead of the main body: Lieutenant William Grant of the artillery; a surgeon's mate named Simms from the 43rd; and two combative infantry lieutenants, William Sutherland of the 38th Regiment and Jesse Adair, an Irishman with the Royal Marines. Smelling adventure when he saw the stealthily mustered troops in Boston, Sutherland had hopped into one of the longboats and reported to Major Pitcairn on the far side of the Charles. By the time the column reached Menotomy, about four miles out, Sutherland had managed to capture two mounted provincials heading out to spread the alarm. Then he and his advance party hurried through the town and up the long hill on the far side.

As they did, an agitated Major Mitchell galloped up to them with his small squadron of horsemen and a tale that could not have been better cal-

Paul Revere's expense report for "self and horse" from April 21 to May 7, 1775, was paid by Massachusetts colonial leaders only after his daily expenses were reduced and 16 people signed off on it. Revere was not paid for his midnight ride.

The British troops that set out early on April 19, 1775, to seize arms at Concord traveled along a 20-mile stretch of the King's Highway. With the countryside alerted, the redcoats found Minutemen and militia ready to meet them. What had been envisioned as an easy sortie into Middlesex became a gantlet of lethal musketry punishing the British column all the way back to Charlestown.

culated to fan the embers of British apprehension. They had captured Revere himself, Mitchell reported, and from this highly credentialed source had learned that they no longer held the advantage of surprise. Revere had warned Hancock and Adams before the troops had even started from the Charles's shore, and the whole countryside teemed with mustering militia. Why, 500 armed men awaited the British column at Lexington: Mitchell himself had heard the sound of a musket volley; his patrol had barely escaped that village alive. Mitchell rode on to give the information to Colonel Smith, reaching his commander back in the column, where he was conferring with Major Pitcairn.

With the day's first light, Smith had become increasingly concerned by the state of the countryside and had just ordered Pitcairn to take six of his 10 light-infantry companies—a total of fewer than 250 men—and hurry with them in order to secure the bridges located on the north and south sides of Concord. Then Smith sent a courier back toward Boston with an urgent message for General Gage: Surprise has been lost; the country is up in arms; send help with all speed.

William Sutherland had meanwhile seized a provincial horse and Jesse Adair a carriage, and the two were ranging far ahead of the rest of the troops. Stopping a wagon with a load of wood, they heard from its driver that 1,000 men waited for the regulars at Lexington. Moreover, they had begun seeing men silhouetted against the early light on every ridgeline, all heading for Lexington.

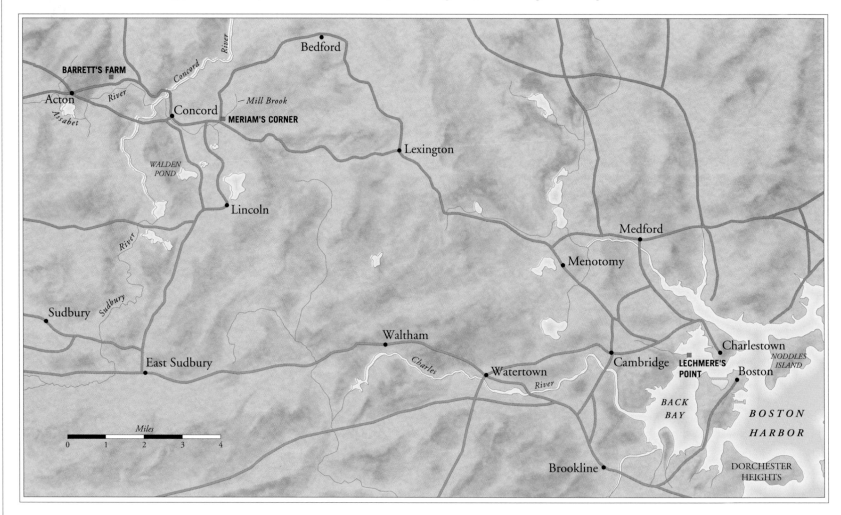

Sutherland and Adair asked Pitcairn to come forward; when he rode up, they reported vast numbers of militia on the move. Just as they were joined by Major Mitchell and others in his mounted squad, a group of provincial riders galloped into view, stopping on the road 100 yards away from Pitcairn's column. "You had better turn back," one of them shouted, "for you shall not enter the town!" Then the riders turned their horses back toward Lexington—but one stayed long enough to raise his musket and fire. It could have been a signal, but Pitcairn did not take any chances. He halted the column and had his soldiers load their brown Besses. Then, with flanking parties out and the aggressive marine lieutenant Adair at point, he marched them toward the village where, as far as Pitcairn knew, 1,000 men waited to fight him.

Standing on the broad expanse of Lexington Green, John Parker peered into the sunrise toward the thin ribbon of the Cambridge road, which split around the green into two roads that surrounded the center of the town. At the fork in the road the meeting house stood against the lightening sky and blocked the view for most of the 70 or so men who stood behind Parker. These men had elected Parker their captain, drawn by his experience—he had served in the French and Indian War—and aura of command. A tall, well-constructed man, the 46-year-old father of seven seemed to be fit enough for anything—but some inner demon gave him a gauntness that was compelling; his eyes watched the road from dark circles and he was clearly worn out from a night without any rest. This inner enemy—which was, in fact, pulmonary tuberculosis—would kill him by October.

For the men, this was the second muster of the morning. The first had come just after Revere's midnight warning. As the ranking man on the spot, Parker had taken command of the few score who had turned out on Lexington Green and waited

The Great Escape

While British troops marched toward Lexington, a colorful drama unfolded in the home of the Reverend Jonas Clarke, where Samuel Adams *(above, left)* and John Hancock *(above, right)* had hidden after friends warned they faced arrest in Boston.

In the early hours of April 19, when Paul Revere brought word that the British intended to arrest them, the theatrical Hancock polished his sword and cleaned his pistol, while the more prudent Adams insisted they flee. Finally, Adams slapped Hancock on the shoulder and told him that fighting "is not our business. We belong to the Cabinet." Hancock relented, but swore, "If I had my musket, I would never turn my back on the troops." The two men slipped out for the safety of Woburn (now Burlington).

Whether Gage sought to arrest the two men is unknown. His scouts inquired about their whereabouts but—whatever Gage's intentions—had little chance to act. By the time the British reached Lexington, thanks to Paul Revere the quarry had fled.

with them in the moonlight. In typical colonial fashion, they had conferred, officers and men, and decided, as Parker put it, "not to be discovered or meddle or make with" the regular troops. They would let the soldiers pass through—and why not? Hancock and Adams had fled, some said toward Woburn, and the stores that formerly were hidden in Concord had largely been dispersed to other hiding places. Let the regulars march about all they liked.

Indeed, as the Lexington men waited they had begun to wonder whether there were really any companies coming their way at all. Parker sent out scouts to reconnoiter toward Boston, dismissing the rest of his men so that they could seek some rest and refreshment in the Buckman Tavern. As was the custom, before they entered they had fired a sporadic sort of volley to clear their loaded muskets—the sound that had frightened Major Mitchell, not a mile away. And there the militia had waited.

Then, as the eastern sky paled with dawn, one of Parker's scouts, Thaddeus Bowman, had come thundering over the hill from the direction of Cambridge. Bowman brought an alarming report: Not only were the regulars out, but they were out in strength—more than 1,000 of them, he reckoned—and not half an hour from Lexington. Parker had bid his young drummer, William Diamond, to beat a call to arms, and once again the Lexington militia had formed up smartly on the green. Muskets charged with powder and ball, a few bristling with a bayonet, the men arranged themselves in a wide double rank, perhaps to spin the illusion of being more than they were.

Parker stood in front of the militiamen and off to their left, so that he could see between the meeting house and the Buckman Tavern to the point where the road divided, with one half turning due north, directly toward his position, and the other veering off to the northwest toward Concord. He saw some of the villagers gathered in small clusters—by the tavern, by the church, and off to his right rear, where they watched from behind the granite shield of a stone fence.

The militia had not been on the green for a particularly long time when Parker saw the regulars coming. With the sun rising behind them, they made a daunting sight, their companies of flankers pounding along 100 yards on either side of the 200 men who marched on the road. Then Parker saw the remainder of the expedition, another dozen or so companies, most of them wearing the tall red-and-gold hats of British grenadiers. A cluster of mounted officers eddied in the lead column like a raft on a human sea.

Recent events had conditioned Parker to expect a certain script for this confrontation. On the regulars' previous marches into the countryside, a militia that stood firm had carried the day; the king's troops had invariably yielded rather than fight. And Parker was confident that Lexington would be no exception. The men of Lexington could stand at arms upon their own green. They might exchange some mild unpleasantries, but nothing more than that—it was not in the character of an Englishman to massacre his compatriots. The two forces would brush, and then the regulars would march past on their already-compromised expedition to Concord.

Yet even as he watched, the British ranks seemed to accelerate, and to split around the meeting house, like a river dividing around a great boulder. The first units flowed up one branch of the Y, straight at his position, the others, including the clutch of mounted officers, up the other, passing out of sight behind the meeting house and church.

Parker knew better than to fight from his exposed position on the green. He ordered his men to disband, to scatter, and

The Lexington militia marched to the tune of this drum and fife on the morning of April 19, 1775. Sixteen-year-old William Diamond played the drum; the player of the applewood fife is unknown.

"There appeared a number of the King's troops, about a thousand as I thought, at the distance of about sixty or seventy yards from us, huzzaing, and on a quick pace towards us...."

MILITIAMAN JOHN ROBBINS

some began to leave the field, although not as quickly as he would have liked. To Parker's surprise, their dispersal seemed to excite the regulars, who now began to run toward the green, the point fanning out from a narrow column of redcoats to a broad line of more than 30, moving forward with their muskets at the ready, bayonets gleaming. Ahead of them, a young officer wearing the distinctive red and blue of the Royal Marines led the skirmish with his saber raised. "Damn them," came his voice, "we will have them."

It was an infantry charge! Incredibly, Parker heard the soldiers' cry of "Huzza! Huzza!"—the traditional cheer that put fear into one's enemies and courage into one's madly beating heart. The regulars were not 200 feet away now, moving swiftly, and not quite under anyone's control. On Parker's right, the mounted officers emerged from behind the church, riding hell for leather, pistols out, sabers drawn. A major of marines seemed to be in charge, if one could consider the hurried, conflicting shouts he made as being in command of anything. "Mind your space," he yelled, and "Keep your ranks, and surround them," and "Don't fire!" Better than half a dozen other British officers were likewise shouting commands at the men, who could not hear them in any case for their own Huzzas.

"Lay down your arms, you damned rebels!" cried one of the British officers.

Parker's men continued to drift away from the formation but kept their weapons in hand; some headed for the fence of good New England granite that stood a few yards behind the green, looking for cover. Then, sharply audible even in that chaos of noise and motion came an unmistakable sound—a shot!

The shot, or shots—some heard more than one—might have come from militia firing from the cover of the stone fence, as Pitcairn later reported, or from a sniper stationed in the Buckman

Flanked by the mounted Major John Pitcairn, British regulars fire at retreating colonists at Lexington in this 1775 engraving by Amos Doolittle. A militiaman himself, Doolittle accurately rendered the scene, showing the tavern to the left of the large tree and to its right the church and its separate belfry, as well as the long shadows cast by the rising sun.

Tavern, as it seemed to others of the regulars. Major Mitchell may finally have discharged the pistol he had brandished earlier at Paul Revere, who, not far away from the action, thought the first report had been a pistol shot. It might have been the hot-blooded Lieutenant Sutherland, who was also carrying a pistol, or, although Pitcairn denied it unto death, it might have come from the major's own fancy pair of handguns. It might have been an accident, the hammer of a worn provincial musket triggered by a jolt or careless touch. Who fired that shot, or why, did not really matter—the trigger that had lain cocked and ready in Massachusetts for decades had been pulled.

Immediately, acting without orders, the British troops began to fire, at first sporadically. Then, as they formed up into ranks, the isolated shots blended into the ugly crash of a combined volley. But well drilled as they were, few of the young soldiers had seen actual combat, and like most green infantry they fired too high. The militia, who saw the British fire but did not see anyone fall, thought the troops were firing powder but no ball. That view quickly changed when the men saw lead spatter the granite wall behind them. The soldiers—trained to get off an astonishing three rounds a minute from a muzzle-loading brown Bess—reloaded swiftly and fired again, this time to better effect. Frightened spectators melted away from the edges of the fight. Lexington Green lay awash in a pallid cloud of musket smoke, broken by the anxious prancing of the officers' horses.

Pitcairn rode among his men, slashing down with his saber to signal a cease-fire, but nothing could stop them now, for the other companies, drawn by the fight, had moved up on their comrades' flanks and fanned out among the houses, shooting militia where they could. Then, their mus-

GREEN DRAGON TAVERN

When we meet to Plan the Consignment of few Shiploads of Tea
Dec 16 1773
John Johnson
Water Street
Boston Mass. 1773

A SPY IN THE HOUSE OF LIBERTY

In 1775, a troubling mystery beset the rebel leaders who met secretly at Boston's Green Dragon Tavern *(above)*, where events such as the Boston Tea Party had been planned. Details about the meetings, as well as Massachusetts Provincial Congress business, were being leaked to the British. The only people who knew of the secret meetings were congress members John Hancock, Samuel Adams, Joseph Warren, and Benjamin Church Jr.

Hancock and Adams, devoted rebels, seemed beyond suspicion. And Warren and Church, though less famous, also were highly trusted. Church, for one, gave fiery orations, satirized the British in newspapers, and ran the Continental Hospital. But in September 1775 the Boston rebels learned the truth: Church had disclosed their secrets to the British, apparently for profit. "Good God!" wrote John Adams. "What shall we say of human nature?"

Church was discovered when a coded letter he wrote to the British—and gave to a mistress for delivery—was intercepted. Faced with the evidence, Church claimed his secret letter was intended to scare the British into peace. But the rebels would not have it. The letter contained such damning statements as "make use of every precaution or I perish." After a November court martial, Church was jailed. In 1778, he passed from infamy to oblivion when a ship carrying him to exile disappeared, never to be seen again.

kets empty, they ran for the provincials, bayonets fixed. As the men of Lexington fell back in confusion, the British troops eddied wildly through the town. Behind them, on the green, lay two dead and several wounded, and others beyond the wall. Militiaman Jonathan Harrington, fatally wounded in the ranks, managed to crawl the short distance to his own doorstep and die in the arms of his family.

To Colonel Smith, who rode up from the main body of grenadiers, Lexington Green looked like the end of the world. Six companies of light infantry ran amuck, firing in all directions at everything that moved. Smith acted swiftly to restore order. Bulling his horse into the heart of the melee, he called to Sutherland, "Do you know where a drummer is?" The lieutenant quickly found one, and Smith ordered the boy to sound cease-fire. The drum brought the men around, and under the angry supervision of their officers, they reluctantly coalesced into units. "The Men were so wild," wrote John Barker, a young British lieutenant, "they cou'd hear no orders."

Then, having brought the command back under some semblance of control, Smith took his officers aside. It was time to tell them where they were going, and what they were meant to do. They were aghast at what he proposed. Continuing the march to Concord, with this slaughter on the green behind them and every man in Massachusetts risen to arms around them, would be suicide. It was time to return with all speed toward Boston. Smith was adamant. "I have my orders," he told them. "I am determined to obey them."

As the British marched away from Lexington they left in their wake seven dead from the town proper, and an eighth, a captured Woburn man, who was shot "while trying to escape." Nine other militiamen had been wounded, a serious matter in an age when any significant trauma could prove to be fatal. In the few minutes that the skirmish had taken, the life of every Lexington family had been irrevocably altered.

On the green, while neighbors eased the wounded and carried off the dead, Captain Parker re-formed his men, whose numbers had swollen now because of the arrival of fresh members of the town's militia, and considered where he would march them. It would be necessary for the regulars to return to Boston on this same road, and Parker wanted to be waiting.

Concord offered a more complicated battlefield than Lexington Green. Its municipal heart lay in a kind of meadowed bowl of land, where the Assabet and Sudbury Rivers merged into the Concord. Around the town center, the land rose suddenly into small hills and ridges, among them Punkatasset Hill, a mile north, and Arrowhead Ridge, a long, triangular formation that jutted eastward from Concord center about a mile, where it tapered to a point at a place called Meriam's Corner. The road from Lexington came down into Meriam's Corner, crossing the Mill Brook bridge, then followed the flank of Arrowhead Ridge into town. Continuing westward, the road split, one branch running toward the South bridge, across the Sudbury, the other turning straight north from Concord center for about 500 yards, where it veered sharply to the left and crossed the Concord River on the North bridge. A military force that held the two bridges could use the Sudbury and Concord as a natural moat; if they also controlled Arrowhead Ridge, they held the town.

Beyond the North bridge, the road wound generally westward, following the north bank of the Assabet River past the training field near the Buttrick farm, where Concord's two regiments—one of militia and one of Minutemen—practiced. Two miles from the town center, the road crossed Spencer Brook, where a prosperous mill was operated by one of Concord's leading citizens, James Barrett, lately better known as Colonel Barrett. A militia captain during the French and Indian War, the 65-year-old Barrett had also sat upon the General Court and as a member of the Provincial Congress.

REBEL SCISSORS

Melicent Barrett, the oldest daughter of Concord colonel James Barrett, used these scissors to fashion musket cartridges that were fired at the British on April 19, 1775. Ironically, she had been taught how to make the cartridges by a young British soldier who was amused by her patriotic fervor. Melicent Barrett's cartridges, along with those made by other Concord women, were rushed off to the militia by her brother James as the British approached the town.

Barrett was so well trusted that he had been given the command of the Middlesex militia.

Barrett and his men had been busy ever since a false report of a British approach 10 days earlier. The town's citizens had spent Tuesday transporting by wagon what they could to Acton, Stow, and Sudbury. Some of the cannon were disassembled and buried in furrows on Barrett's farm. Even so, Concord remained a considerable arsenal at 2:30 Wednesday morning, when young Dr. Prescott, completing Revere's interrupted ride, galloped into town with news that the British regulars had come out of Boston, Concord bound.

Now, several hours after sunrise, Barrett was painfully conscious of everything still hidden among a score of houses and farms, including his own. His bravely stubborn 56-year-old wife, Rebecca, had elected to remain at home. "I can't live very long anyway," she declared, "and I'd rather stay and see that they don't burn down the house and barn." Clearly, it would not be necessary for the soldiers to search for very long before finding the hidden weaponry and virtually disarming the province. If the regulars even came close, Barrett knew he would have to offer more than advice—he would have to lead his men in battle.

Since Prescott's bad news, six companies had mustered on the green outside Wright's Tavern, in the center of Concord proper. Some were from Barrett's regiment and others were from the Concord Minutemen, led by Major John Buttrick, the Minuteman regiment's third in command and their ranking officer on the field. When there was not any sign of the British troops, Barrett had dismissed them. Most of the men waited to learn what the new day would bring. The night had swirled with rumor, but there was no sign of the British regulars. At first light, Barrett sent Reuben Brown, a Concord saddlemaker, scouting down the road toward Lexington.

As the day brightened, other Minutemen and militia mustered in the town: two companies from the Concord militia, two more from the Concord Minutemen, and two companies each from Bedford and Lincoln. The Bedford men brought more than rumor with them. They had seen Josiah Nelson's saber wound and had heard of trouble at Lexington. Waiting to march early that morning, they had crowded into the tavern owned by militia sergeant Jeremiah Fitch. "Come boys," urged their captain, 41-year-old Jonathan Wilson, "we'll take a little something, and we'll have every dog of them before night." While the men from Bedford munched on cheese and rye bread, Wilson kept pumping up their courage. "We give you a cold breakfast, boys, but we'll give the British a hot supper."

Soon Reuben Brown rode back into town with further news of Lexington: The regulars had attacked Parker's boys.

"Were they firing ball?" asked an incredulous John Buttrick.

"I do not know," Brown answered, "But I think it probable."

It was a momentous answer, as Buttrick knew only too well. Powder would have frightened, but ball was intended to kill.

As the men heard about Lexington, their blood boiled for a fight. But Barrett was too old and wise to fly out against an enemy that might easily destroy him. He did not have any intention of being the first to fire, partly because that initial volley would ignite a war—but also for a reason that was purely practical. It was military dogma that the side firing first inevitably lost the skirmish against a charging line of infantry, which could return fire and be in with their bayonets before the defenders had a chance to reload.

In the meantime, Barrett's resources were improving steadily; he now had about 250 armed men behind him. He deployed Captain David Brown's Minuteman company down the road as scouts, with two Concord militia companies moving in parallel along Arrowhead Ridge. The rest of his troops he moved to a rise just north of the hill where the village burial ground was located.

They were not there long before they heard the sound of British drums, keeping brisk cadence for the marching soldiers. Soon Barrett could see the crimson line, the flanking companies beating along beside it—a terrible thing to fight.

David Brown backed his Minutemen toward the village just ahead of the advancing column as it crossed the Mill Brook bridge. Then, as he watched, the lead companies of light infantry fanned off the road to one side, moving smartly in an assault line toward the militia on the point of Arrowhead Ridge. Like Brown, the militia retreated in good order. By now the British and provincial units were so close together that both marched to the cadence beat out by the column's fifes and drums. Recalled one of Brown's Minutemen: It made "a grand Musick."

As Barrett's companies pulled back to the village, his fellow officers talked about making a stand there, but Barrett used his veto, moving them to high ground some 400 yards north of the town center, just out of musket range of the light infantry now swarming along Arrowhead Ridge. He had decided to abandon the town to the British, at least for the time being.

As the provincials looked on sick at heart, the jubilant troops cut down Concord's flagpole, then flowed down into the village in order to join the column of grenadiers who had marched up the highway. Some of Barrett's men may have wondered about their leader, who had given up Arrowhead Ridge and the town.

Under the eyes of the watching militia, the king's troops moved with smooth dispatch to secure Concord. One company of light infantry was deployed to hold the South bridge. Seven companies, about half of the column's total strength, were sent toward the North bridge, but only three of them would remain at the crossing; the other four would continue west under the command of Captain Lawrence

In Amos Doolittle's engraving, Britain's Major John Pitcairn and Lieutenant Colonel Francis Smith survey Concord from a hill in the town cemetery as their troops enter the town and search for hidden weapons.

Parsons. One of Francis Smith's most trusted young officers, Parsons was determined to locate the cannon and other supplies that Gage's spies had reported as being at Barrett's farm.

Seeing the approach of Parsons's force, Barrett moved his troops—along with a horde of women, children, old men, and dogs that had gathered to observe the proceedings—across the North bridge and out about a mile until they reached the slopes of Punkatasset Hill, where they had a clear view of the village. Leaving Major Buttrick in command, Barrett galloped off toward his farm, in hopes he could hide any matériel that re mained before the regulars arrived. Painfully conscious of the growing militia force that waited on the high ground that lay 1,000 yards to the north of him, Parsons crossed the North bridge. After some dithering, he installed one company to hold the bridge, under the command of Captain Walter Laurie. A few hundred yards farther along, Parsons set out the other two companies in order to take some knolls located between the bridge and the men who were beginning to look more and more like the enemy. Then he and his remaining four companies marched off to search the Barrett farm.

A somber Rebecca Barrett met Parsons's search party at her front door, her husband having had time for only a hasty inspection before riding out again by a back way. After cautioning the men to respect private property, she followed them through the house as they moved from room to room hunting for weapons. But everything had been plowed in a field, buried in manure, or concealed in trees. Before leaving, some of the soldiers demanded breakfast. Mrs. Barrett grimly served them brown bread and milk but refused their offer of money. When they tossed some coins to her anyway, she snapped: "This is the price of blood."

On Punkatasset Hill, meanwhile, Major Buttrick observed everything that was unfolding below him, noted the two British companies deployed not very far away, and took stock of his situation. The British had stationed barely 100 men at the North bridge; Buttrick now had 10 companies, a total of nearly 300 men, behind him. With that kind of advantage, he thought, one might safely crowd the redcoats. He ordered his men toward the field they used for training, across the lane from his own farm. To his surprise, the two light-infantry companies on the knolls fell back to the bridge, so that Buttrick was able to occupy the high ground that had they vacated. And there, for the moment, the day's action suspended in a tense waiting game. The provincials watched from a vantage point some 50 feet above the bridge and 400 yards away, looking down upon the smaller force of regulars who were nervously clustered there.

That was the scene Colonel Barrett found upon his return—that and a few hundred more men. Units had arrived from the towns of Acton, Littleton, Chelmsford, Carlisle, Westford, Groton, and Stow, along with other men who were ready to serve but not part of any unit. Then the provincials saw, above the trees, a pale column of smoke that was rising from the houses in Concord. Lieutenant Joseph Hosmer, a 39-year-old Concord artisan and Barrett's fiery acting adjutant, turned to his commander. "Will you let them burn the town down?" The militia loaded their muskets.

Since reaching the village, the British troops had gone about their searches with grim courtesy, following the edict of their general that the people of Concord and their property be treated with respect. The fire that had alarmed Joseph Hosmer was an accident. Sparks from a bonfire of cannon mounts and other equipment had ignited the roof of the nearby meeting house. Even as the militia loaded, preparing to save their town from British torches, redcoats and the citizens of Concord had begun a bucket brigade in order to rescue the building.

After forming up along the ridge, the militiamen began moving toward the North bridge and the three companies that were commanded by Captain Laurie. They came in a well-ordered column of twos, marching to a spirited rendition of

the song "The White Cockade" from young Luther Blanchard's fife. The tune was a favorite of Captain Isaac Davis, the 30-year-old gunsmith who was leading the way with his Acton Minutemen. Thanks to Davis's energy and skill as a gunsmith, the Acton men were the best-equipped provincials in Concord.

Outnumbered by about five to one, Laurie hurriedly withdrew his men to the other side of the bridge and formed them up in the road, one company behind the other. He had arranged his men for street-fighting—narrow ranks in which those in front volleyed, then ran to the rear of the formation to reload while the second rank fired, and so on. Under normal conditions of command it could provide near-continuous fire along a narrow avenue— or a bridge. But these were not normal conditions. Laurie was leading two light-infantry companies that he barely knew, and he was asking them to do something that they had never attempted before.

Filling the road from top to bottom, Isaac Davis's Minutemen halted at the bridge, facing the small

TOOLS OF DEFIANCE

Although made in England, the cutlass and battle flag seen here became tools of colonial defiance during the first days of the American Revolution. The steel naval sword, made in about 1750, belonged to Colonel James Barrett, the colonial commander at Concord. The flag, which shows a hand holding a dagger and the Latin motto "Vince aut Morire—"Conquer or Die"—was carried by the Bedford militia who fought the British at Concord. Believed to have been made in England in the late 1600s, the flag is one of the oldest to have been used in America.

force of regulars across the river. Inevitably, as tensions built, a musket discharged—Laurie thought it belonged to one of his young privates. Several other shots followed, then an uneven volley from the first rank of British troops. "God damn them," cried one of the Minutemen, "they are firing balls!"

As at Lexington, the inexperienced musketeers fired too high; still, two colonists fell dead, and several were wounded. Surprised that the whistling rounds had not done more damage, the provincials poised on the far bank, barely 50 yards from the British. Then John Buttrick turned to them. "Fire," he shouted, inventing the order as he went, "for God's sake fire!" The ensuing volley was well directed and aimed low enough to have effect. The British soldiers answered with another volley. One ball smashed into Isaac Davis's heart, flinging the lifeless body of the Minuteman captain into the air; the wound sprayed those around him with a fountain of blood. Among them was militiaman Thomas Thorp, who would later say that the memory of Davis's blood would spur him on to do his duty.

The Massachusetts men set up a withering rain of continuous shooting, striking four of the eight British officers at the bridge, as well as a sergeant and six privates, one of whom lay dead and another dying. This was all the pinned-down regulars could stand; the formation broke for Concord.

Colonel Francis Smith rode up to find his soldiers once again in disarray—this time, in headlong retreat. He watched helplessly as half the provincials swarmed across the North bridge behind the regulars and took cover on higher ground, where it looked as if they were about to fire on the British. For about 10 minutes, the two forces faced each other only 250 yards apart. But for some reason—

perhaps reverting to their old policy of not firing unless fired upon—the provincials did not fire; instead, they trooped up to the ridge overlooking Concord village and resumed their watching of the enemy. For his part, Smith reluctantly abandoned the idea of retaking the North bridge and went to await Parsons and his four companies on the vantage point of the town's burying ground.

Sending out infantry to keep the rebels off his flank on Arrowhead Ridge, Smith prepared his column for the long march back to Boston. But the fighting was not yet over. As his troops pulled out, the militia and Minutemen flowed into the vacuum. One group took control of the South bridge, and Barrett's men already held the other. While the British waited, the provincials outflanked the flankers and crept east toward Meriam's Corner. Although Smith was evidently not aware of it, they had encircled him.

Finally, the colonel saw Parsons's column in the distance, on the far side of the Concord River and beyond his help. The British companies advanced at a trot, warily eying the hundreds—it had begun to look more like thousands to Smith—of armed provincials on the slopes just above the bridge on both sides of the river. Parsons did not blink but took his troops through this gantlet, past their fallen comrades, including one whom a young Minuteman named Ammi White had whacked on the head with a hatchet. "The poor object," reported one observer of the fatally injured soldier, "languished for an hour or two before he died."

His column whole at last, Smith turned the men back toward Boston. Buggies and wagons that were commandeered in Concord served as litters for those wounded at the bridge who had been able to hobble back to their units. The spring sun stood at its noon point as the half-mile-long caravan moved out, and for a short time—barely a quarter of an hour—it must have seemed to Smith that he had escaped his fate. In fact, it waited for him down the road, at Meriam's Corner.

There, the highway descended toward Mill Brook, crossed on a narrow bridge. As the British approached this natural barrier, the flankers on the north side of the column pulled in to use the bridge rather than ford the stream, pinching the column inward and exposing its north flank to provincials,

Repelled by heavy musket fire, the British retreat over Concord's North bridge in an engraving by Amos Doolittle. In this first true engagement of the war, the well-positioned Americans held their fire until fired upon and then unleashed a volley that struck at least 11 British soldiers.

who again filled the vacuum. The militiamen following them felt a wary respect for this enemy who was so tough looking. "The British marched down the hill with very slow but steady step," recalled a Reading private, "without music or a word being spoken that could be heard. Silence reigned on both sides." But only for a moment.

Hidden behind trees and stone fences and sometimes in houses located along the road, Minutemen and militia began harassing the regulars with a withering fire of musketry. At first they tossed off their shots on the move, trotting along the column's flanks, firing at the regulars from cover. The British returned fire, but not to much effect. Instead of scaring off the provincials, one officer recalled, the British fire had an opposite effect, imparting to "the rebels more confidence, as they soon found that notwithstanding there was so much, they suffered but little from it."

As the column of British soldiers hurried across the bridge at Meriam's Corner, it came under fire from two provincial regiments that were waiting on the far slope behind rocks, trees, and stone fences. There, militia captain Jonathan Wilson paid with his life for his brave talk the night before. "He was as lively as a bird," recalled a Bedford comrade in arms, "but he never came home 'till they brought him home." And Private Thomas Ditson, a Billerica Minuteman who had been tarred and feathered a month before for attempting to buy a redcoat's brown Bess, had found a weapon after all. His skin still raw from the hot tar, he lay in ambush with the Billerica men and repaid the troops as they marched into range.

The British continued their march, as more provincial units waited to harass them with incessant fire. Marching as swiftly as possible along the road, the regulars slipped toward exhaustion, numb to everything but the need to keep moving forward, walking like zombies under the hail of musket balls. When they passed the Nelson farm, the wall of trees where Revere had been captured teemed with armed men, hiding in the shadows—

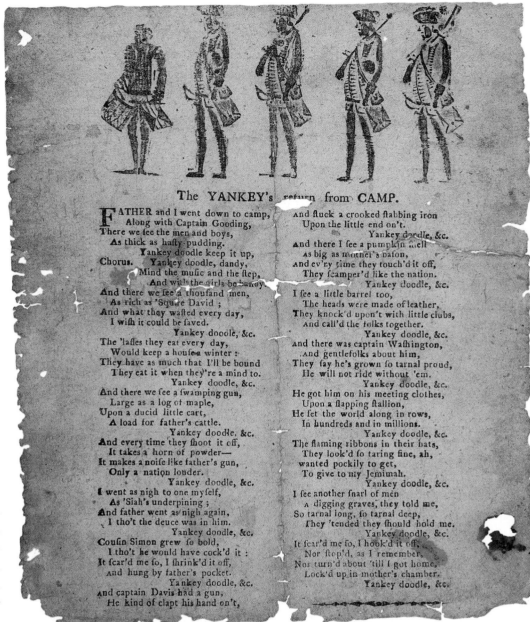

The British intended "The Yankey's Return from Camp," a variation on the song commonly known as "Yankee Doodle," as a mockery of the poorly trained colonial militia who had trouble "minding the music and the step." The tune was even played by the British reinforcements marching to Lexington on April 19. But the defiant Americans soon adopted the song as their own—and continued singing it long after the war was over.

John Parker and his Lexington volunteers, positioned to exact their revenge.

As the road brought the front of the column within point-blank range of Parker's muskets, his men loosed a volley that wounded Smith in the thigh and Parsons in the arm and struck a handful of soldiers. Major Pitcairn took command and swiftly deployed grenadiers and flankers to push the Lexington company out of their position. Parker was forced to fall back, but he had done more than cripple the column's leaders—he had delayed the head of the fast-moving train of men, who now bunched up in the road, giving other provincial companies a chance to overtake the regulars.

Major Pitcairn tried to whip the column back into shape. As the companies re-formed into a semblance of a military column, he set them marching up the long incline of Fiske Hill, where again the provincials opened up a withering fire, shooting from cover. As the volley swept the lead company, Pitcairn's horse bolted, throwing the major and galloping away from the fight. The marine's twin pistols would become cherished souvenirs for the provincial who found them on the saddle. Pitcairn was only roughed up, but the spirit of the British soldiers had now snapped, and they began a blind stampede for the distant safety of Boston.

Ensign Henry DeBerniere, who had somehow come unscathed through the hail of musket fire and now led the column, recalled, "When we arrived within a mile of Lexington, our ammunition began to fail, and the light companies were so fatigued with flanking they were scarce able to act, and a great number of wounded scarce able to get forward, made a great confusion; Col. Smith (our commanding officer) had received a wound through his leg, a number of officers were also wounded, so that we began to run rather than retreat in order—the whole behaved with amazing bravery but little order; we attempted to stop the men and form them two deep, but to no purpose, the confusion increased rather than lessened; at last, after we got through Lexington, the officers got to the front and presented their bayonets, and told the men if they advanced they should die."

At this desperate moment, facing their own officers' sharp blades, the beaten men suddenly began to cheer. Half a mile ahead of them, arranged along the rising ground beyond the village, stood more than 1,000 fresh British men at arms, drawn up

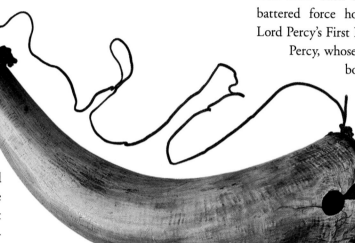

A Fatal Memento

A musket-ball hole in the powder horn of James Hayward serves as a grim reminder of his death. The 25-year-old Hayward might have been exempted from military service because of an accident with an ax that had claimed several of his toes. Yet he left his father's house on the morning of April 19 with 40 musket balls and a pound of powder. Fighting the British as they retreated from Concord, Hayward, his powder and ball nearly spent, was getting a cooling drink from a well near Fiske Hill when confronted by a British soldier who, according to local tradition, said, "You are a dead man." "And so are you," exclaimed Hayward. They fired simultaneously. The Britisher died instantly; Hayward succumbed later to the ball that passed through his powder horn, carrying bits of horn splinters into his body.

in regiments, flags flying. From the center of the neat red-and-white ranks, there came a puff of smoke and the muffled sound of an explosion; a black six-pound cannonball flew across the afternoon sky. Terrified by the artillery fire, the provincials drew back momentarily, and Smith and his battered force hobbled toward their salvation— Lord Percy's First Brigade.

Percy, whose orders to reinforce the Concord-bound regulars had been delayed by several hours, had learned of the battle at Lexington only an hour earlier, and he had received only preliminary reports of events at Concord. He had no sense of how badly things had gone there until the ruin of Smith's force, smoke-blackened, exhausted, and bloodied, stumbled into his view.

The earl soon determined that his only option was to lead the beleaguered troops back to the safety of Boston. But at 3:30, when he ordered the regulars to pull out, the provincials suddenly came alive again. They began attacking the rear guard in strength, and rebel marksmen were able to pick off more than 30 men. Out on the flanks, mounted provincials would gallop out ahead of the column, dismount, rest their musket barrel across their saddle, and fire; then, reloading, they would gallop farther down the flank, and again wait for their marching targets. Percy would later describe the day's activities as marching within "a moving circle of fire."

As the long column started down Pierce's Hill in the direction of Menotomy, it seemed as though they would survive this second ordeal by musket. The firing was sporadic and quite tolerable—nothing like what Colonel Smith's men had endured earlier. However, though they might have been able to outrun the 2,000 provincials harassing their flanks and worrying their tail, 2,000 more waited for them along the Boston road. And it would be necessary for them to pick a way through Menotomy, which bristled with rebel snipers.

One of them was 80-year-old Samuel Whittemore, a veteran Indian fighter who had spent the morning in his house on Main Street cleaning and oiling his well-worn musket. His family had urged him to flee, citing an apprehension that the regulars might kill or capture him. "They will find it hard work to do it," he growled.

When the troops passed through the town, Whittemore crouched behind a stone wall as five British soldiers approached him. Too lame and too proud to run, he challenged them. "I am 80 years old," he is reported to have said, "and I will not leave, for I shall be willing to die if I can kill one redcoat." He did better than that. Killing one with his musket, he drew a pistol and killed another, and managed to get off another shot before a British musket ball slammed into his cheekbone.

"We have killed the old rebel!" yelled one of the regulars. And just to make sure, the remaining redcoats leaped over the wall and stabbed Whittemore repeatedly with their bayonets.

Miraculously, the old rebel survived, and when fellow townsmen found him they carried him to Cooper's Tavern for treatment. Whittemore lived on to the age of 98, and when he was asked later if he regretted the bravery that had brought him such grievous wounds, he replied: "No, I should do just so again. I would run the same chance again."

In another Menotomy home, three redcoats burst into the bedroom where Mrs. Hannah Adams lay with her three-week-old baby. One of them pushed aside the fourposter's curtains and aimed his bayonet at the woman's breast. "For the Lord's sake," she cried out, "do not kill me."

"Damn you," replied one man dangerously.

Then another said, "We will not hurt the woman, if she will go out of the house, but we will surely burn it."

A soldier pulled aside the bedclothes and ordered the woman to leave the house. She got up, wrapped her baby in a blanket, and went out into the chill April night, where she huddled in the corn barn, worried to distraction by what she had left behind: Her five youngest children still hid under her bed. They watched with interest as the big infantry boots stomped back and forth across their floor-level field of view. Finally, one of them—Joel Adams, aged nine—lifted the valance to get a better look and was spotted by a soldier. "Why don't you come out here?" asked the man.

"You'll kill me if I do," said the boy.

"No we won't."

Joel wriggled out from under the bed and into plain sight, then followed the men around as they pillaged the house of its valuables. But they kept their word and did him no harm.

Joel Adams was very much the exception in Menotomy that night. By the time Percy's troops

One of Britain's finest young officers, the 32-year-old Lord Hugh Percy saved Gage's mission from complete disaster when he rescued the beleaguered soldiers retreating from Concord. "I had the happiness," Percy later wrote, "of saving them from inevitable destruction."

had fought their way through the town—looting as they went, shooting any armed provincial in sight—they had lost more than lives. Like the people of Lexington and Concord, the regulars had lost any sense of British brotherhood.

Now they had an hour less of daylight, and their ammunition was about gone. Still pushing for Boston, Percy had to hurry the men along in order to keep the rear of the column from being tied up by the pursuing militia. The troops surged past the Menotomy River (now Alewife Brook) into the more open country beyond.

Then Percy saw a regiment of militia massed off to his right front at a barricade across the road to Cambridge. He quickly brought up his two cannon to suppress that rebel force, then wheeled the formation off to his left in the direction of Charlestown. As his column moved past Prospect Hill, a prominence that was covered with companies of militia, he used his cannon again, along with

infantry, to clear the high ground. By 7 p.m. he had got his men within sight of Bunker Hill and Breed's Hill, the highest points in Charlestown—but not out of harm's way. Clamoring behind them came 3,000 provincials, who were trying to force the rear guard to stand and fight. Out in the dusk, fresh colonial regiments from other communities converged on Boston.

Eying the buildings of Charlestown in the fiery light of sunset, Percy decided not to try to reach the river through the town—not at night, not with a provincial force three times the size of his own baying at his heels. Instead he elected to move his men across the narrow way at Charlestown Neck, past the frightened civilians streaming from the town. Then, on the slope of Bunker Hill, which with the smaller Breed's Hill offered him a commanding position within the protective range of the anchored *Somerset*'s 68 cannon, Percy turned his troops to form a defensive line. They began digging

In this engraving by Amos Doolittle, fresh troops under Lord Hugh Percy *(left)* come to the rescue of the weary British expedition *(foreground)*, which had been fired upon from houses, stone walls, and trees. Upon seeing Percy's men, the demoralized soldiers began to cheer—the popular commander had saved their lives.

in. If the provincials wanted more, they would have to assault a reinforced brigade of British regulars under the guns of a man-of-war.

The ranking rebel in the field, 38-year-old William Heath, would report that when Percy turned on them, "our general," as Heath called himself in his memoir, "judged it expedient to order the militia, who were now at the common, to halt, and give over the pursuit, as any further attempt upon the enemy, in that position, would have been futile." It was as well for the regulars, who were exhausted, hungry, and down to a few rounds of ammunition; not even the *Somerset* could have saved them from a serious assault.

Percy sent a message to Gage, telling him where and how he was. Gage replied quickly: Reinforcements and fresh ammunition were on the way. Moreover, men were coming over to throw up a redoubt on the hill, to be manned by 200 soldiers. Percy turned to the reports that told the cost of the Concord expedition: Seventy-three regulars had been killed, 174 wounded, 26 were missing; 18 officers had been wounded.

Some of the British dead were buried by the colonists. Mary Hartwell of Lincoln recalled watching the burial of several red-coated soldiers in a common grave. Her thoughts, she said, "went out for the wives, parents, and children away across the Atlantic, who would never again see their loved ones."

The provincials, however, had also paid a price, although it was not so high as the one that they had exacted from the British. Nearly two dozen Massachusetts towns had contributed to the 50 dead, 39 wounded, and 5 missing; half of their casualties had fallen at Menotomy. But at the same time, they had gained considerably in the grudging esteem in which they were held by their new enemy.

"Whoever looks upon them as an irregular mob," Percy wrote a colleague the day after the action, "will

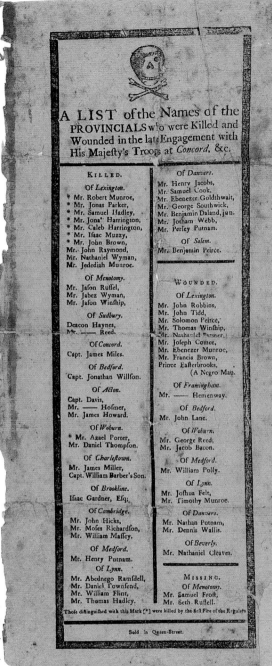

The names of 62 colonists who were killed or wounded on April 19 are listed in this Boston broadside prepared shortly after the fighting. The final figures came to 50 men dead, 39 wounded, and 5 missing. British casualties included 73 dead, 174 wounded, and 26 missing.

find himself much mistaken. They have men amongst them who know very well what they are about, having been employed as Rangers agst the Indians & Canadians, & this country being much covered with wood, and hilly, is very advantageous for their method of fighting.

"Nor are several of their men void of a spirit of enthusiasm, as we experienced yesterday, for many of them concealed themselves in houses, & advanced with 10 yds. to fire at me & other officers, tho' they were morally certain of being put to death themselves in an instant.

"You may depend upon it, that as the Rebels have now had time to prepare, they are determined to go thro' with it, nor will the insurrection here turn out so despicable as it is perhaps imagined at home. For my part, I never believed, I confess, that they would have attacked the King's troops, or have had the perseverance I found in them yesterday."

Lieutenant John Barker wrote the project's epitaph: "Thus ended the Expedition, which from beginning to end was as ill plan'd and ill executed as it was possible to be." For "a few trifling stores the Grenrs. and Lt. Infantry had a march of about 50 miles (going and returning) through the Enemy's Country, and in all human probability must every Man have been cut off if the Brigade had not fortunately come to their assistance."

Great Britain paid for the long day of Lexington-Concord with more than blood and pride. The fight curdled whatever affection might still have remained between the colonists and their king, destroying all possibility of settling differences without a war. "No man was a warmer wisher for reconciliation than myself before the fatal nineteenth of April, 1775," wrote Thomas Paine, the British-born essayist who would become America's most persuasive voice for freedom, "but the moment the event of that day was known, I rejected the hardened, sullen-tempered Pharaoh of England forever." ◆

DIARY OF A QUAKER HOUSEWIFE

On December 24, 1773, a Philadelphia Quaker named Elizabeth Drinker recorded in her voluminous diary that she had just read in a newspaper "an account from Boston, of 342 Chests of Tea, being thrown into the Sea" by colonists protesting a new British tea tax.

Elizabeth Drinker had not usually recorded events that occurred outside her circle of family and friends in Philadelphia. But news of the Boston Tea Party was important and ominous to her on at least two counts. For one, her husband, the prominent merchant Henry Drinker, had a tea ship en route from London. For another, the rebellious move by the Boston colonists must have seemed a violent act that could in time lead to even greater conflict with England—a grim prospect for a pacifist Quaker like Elizabeth Sandwith Drinker.

Born in 1735, Elizabeth began her journal in 1758, three years before marrying Henry Drinker, referred to in the diary as HD. Elizabeth's unmarried sister Mary lived with them, along with their children, servants, and boarders. The Drinkers were well-to-do and wore silk, velvet, and cashmere. But in concession to Quaker simplicity, the colors were dark. Similarly, they declined to sit for portraits, preferring simpler, less costly paper silhouettes such as the one seen above.

With the outbreak of war between Britain and the American colonies, the Drinkers kept true to their beliefs and remained neutral, but at a price. In the winter of 1777-1778, while the British occupied Philadelphia, Henry Drinker and other Quaker leaders were forced by the Americans into exile on the Virginia frontier. In April, Elizabeth and the wives of three other detainees set out for Lancaster, Pennsylvania, to plead with state authorities for the release of their husbands. Along the way they had dinner with George and Martha Washington at Valley Forge. After nearly three weeks of meetings with the governor and other officials, the women were finally reunited with the exiles and returned with them to Philadelphia.

Meticulously kept in a series of small, soft-cover booklets, the diary of Elizabeth Drinker spanned nearly half a century. Her almost-daily entries—written with the irregular grammar and spelling typical of the day—provide a matchless firsthand look at the era of the American Revolution as experienced by a Philadelphia family.

Silhouette of Elizabeth Drinker, made in about 1791

Fireing again this Morning Cannon and small arms,—an Amrican Schooner burnt in our river this morning by the English, partly opposite our house.

November 22, 1777

38 *An East Perspective View of the (*
1. *Christ Church* 3. *Academy*
2. *State House* 4. *Presbyterian Chu*
Engraved from the Original Drawing sent over from Philadelphia, in the possefsion of Carington Bowles.

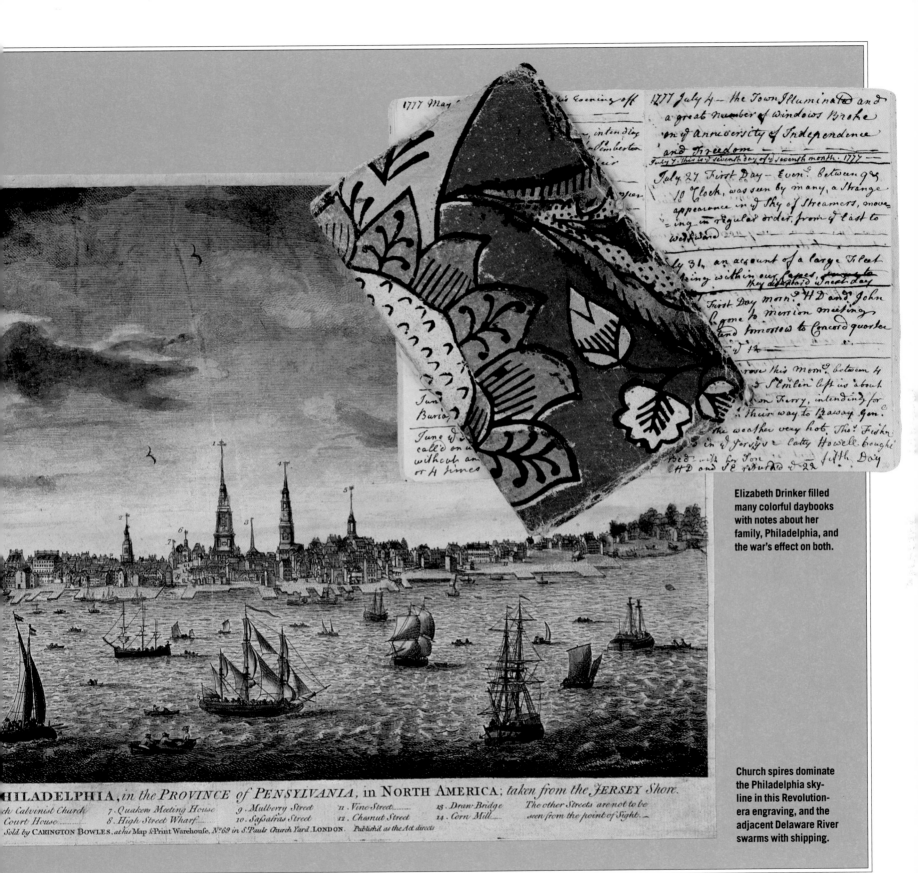

1777 July 4 — the Town Illuminated and a great number of windows broke on ÿ Anniversity of Independence and freedom

July 7. this is ÿ seventh day of ÿ seventh month. 1777 —

July 27. First Day — Even⅁ between ÿ 10 oClock, was seen by many, a strange appearance in ÿ Sky of Streamers, move = ing in regular order, from ÿ East to Westward ———

July 3ᵗ, an account of a large fleet being within our Capes, —— to they disappear'd next day

First Day morn⅁ ÿ HD and John —— gone to meeting meeting and tomorrow to Concord quarter = ÿ ——

—— rove this morn⅁ between 4 & 5 ſſmlin left us about —— on Ferry, intending for —— their way to Bassay Gon⅁. —— the weather very hot. Tho:ˢ Fisher —— in ÿ Jerseys & Catty Howell bought —— for ſon —— fifth Day HD and ſE returned d 22

1777 May —— —— evening off —— intending —— Pemberton —— ſin

—— June —— Buria —— June ÿ —— call'd on —— without an —— or 4 times

Elizabeth Drinker filled many colorful daybooks with notes about her family, Philadelphia, and the war's effect on both.

Church spires dominate the Philadelphia sky-line in this Revolution-era engraving, and the adjacent Delaware River swarms with shipping.

PHILADELPHIA, in the PROVINCE of PENSYLVANIA, in NORTH AMERICA; taken from the JERSEY Shore.

—ch Calvinist Church   7. Quaker Meeting House   9. Mulberry Street   11. Vine Street........   13. Draw Bridge   The other Streets are not to be
—Court House...........   8. High Street Wharf......   10. Saſsafras Street   12. Chesnut Street   14. Corn Mill......   seen from the point of Sight.—
Sold by CARINGTON BOWLES, at his Map & Print Warehouse, Nᵒ 69 in St Pauls Church Yard, LONDON.   Publish'd as the Act directs

REVOLUTIONARY BUSINESS

Laden with dutied British tea, Henry Drinker's ship *Charming Polly* was slated to arrive in Philadelphia in December of 1773. For months, though, a committee of revolutionaries had pressured the city's merchants not to trade in such cargos, issuing threatening broadsides such as the one at right.

Early in the month, Drinker promised not to land his tea. On December 25, the day after she learned of the Boston Tea Party, Elizabeth noted that the *Charming Polly* was at Chester, just downriver from Philadelphia. Two days later she wrote, probably with relief: "The Tea Ship, and Cargo, were sent of[f] this Morning."

In a broadside issued on November 27, 1773, the Committee for Tarring and Feathering warns the captain of the *Polly* not to unload his tea in Philadelphia. Shipowner Henry Drinker wisely agreed that Captain Ayres and his cargo should promptly return to London "without the wild Geese Feathers."

TO THE
Delaware Pilots.

WE took the Pleasure, some Days since, of kindly admonishing you *to do your Duty*; if perchance you should meet with the *(Tea,)* SHIP POLLY, CAPTAIN AYRES; a THREE DECKER which is hourly expected.

We have now to add, that Matters ripen fast here; and that *much is expected from those Lads who meet with the Tea Ship*.----There is some Talk of A HANDSOME REWARD FOR THE PILOT WHO GIVES THE FIRST GOOD ACCOUNT OF HER.----How that may be, we cannot *for certain* determine: But ALL agree, that TAR and FEATHERS will be his Portion, who pilots her into this Harbour. And we will answer for ourselves, that, whoever is committed to us, as an Offender against the Rights of *America*, will experience the utmost Exertion of our Abilities; as

THE COMMITTEE FOR TARRING AND FEATHERING.

P. S. We expect you will furnish yourselves with Copies of the foregoing and following Letter; which are printed for this Purpose, that the Pilot who meets with Captain *Ayres* may favor him with a Sight of them.

Committee of Taring and Feathering.

TO
Capt. AYRES,

Of the SHIP *POLLY*, on a Voyage from *London* to *Philadelphia*.

SIR,

WE are informed that you have, imprudently, taken Charge of a Quantity of Tea; which has been sent out by the *India* Company, *under the Auspices of the Ministry*, as a Trial of *American* Virtue and Resolution.

Now, as your Cargo, on your Arrival here, will most assuredly bring you into hot water; and as you are perhaps a Stranger *to these Parts*, we have concluded to advise you of the present Situation of Affairs in *Philadelphia*---that, taking Time by the Forelock, you may stop short in your dangerous Errand----secure your Ship against the Rafts of combustible Matter which may be set on Fire, and turned loose against her; and more than all this, that you may preserve your own Person, from the Pitch and Feathers that are prepared for you.

In the first Place, we must tell you, that the *Pennsylvanians* are, *to a Man*, passionately fond of Freedom; the Birthright of *Americans*; and at all Events are determined to enjoy it.

That they sincerely believe, no Power on the Face of the Earth has a Right to tax them without their Consent.

That in their Opinion, the Tea in your Custody is designed by the Ministry to enforce such a Tax, which they will undoubtedly oppose; and in so doing, give you every possible Obstruction.

We are nominated to a very disagreeable, but necessary Service.---- To our Care are committed all Offenders against the Rights of *America*; and hapless is he, whose evil Destiny has doomed him to suffer at our Hands.

You are sent out on a diabolical Service; and if you are so foolish and obstinate as to compleat your Voyage; by bringing your Ship to Anchor in this Port; you may run such a Gauntlet, as will induce you, in your last Moments, most heartily to curse those who have made you the Dupe of their Avarice and Ambition.

What think you Captain, of a Halter around your Neck----ten Gallons of liquid Tar decanted on your Pate----with the Feathers of a dozen wild Geese laid over that to enliven your Appearance?

Only think seriously of this----and fly to the Place from whence you came----fly without Hesitation---- without the Formality of a Protest----and above all, Captain *Ayres* let us advise you to fly without the wild Geese Feathers.

Your Friends *to serve*

Philadelphia, Nov. 27, 1773   THE COMMITTEE *as before subscribed*

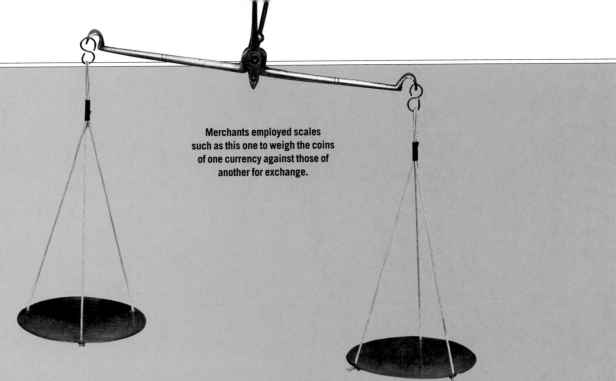

Merchants employed scales such as this one to weigh the coins of one currency against those of another for exchange.

BW. was mistaken in his account of the fire at Atsion, it was the Furnice, not the Forge, that was burnt, all the wood work, and the Bellows &c—the loss, HD. thinks, including repairs and loss of time, will amount to, one thousand pounds and more money.—October 2, 1794

Elizabeth frequently entertained her husband's associates at dinner or tea, and always took a lively interest in his business affairs—which, she claimed, occupied "ten-twelfths" of his time. Indeed, his commercial activities were many and varied. In addition to the Atsion Ironworks, located across the Delaware River in New Jersey, he and his partner, Abel James, owned merchant ships; an import-export business in tea, trade goods, and indentured servants; and various pieces of prime real estate.

After the *Charming Polly* incident, Henry stopped trading in British tea, but commerce in other goods would continue throughout the war years—although trade of any kind was complicated by rampant inflation that constantly devalued the Continental paper currency. European gold and silver coins of established weight and value had always circulated in the colonies, and during the war merchants and others sought to standardize and maintain the value of their paper money against hard coinage. Such efforts were often complicated by the fact that some states—Pennsylvania among them—issued their own money:

A Committee of Merchants, as they are call'd, lately mett, and came to a resolve, that the Continental Money, (which now passes at upwards of 100 for one) should pass at 75—and that debts &c should to paid at that rate.—they have appointed men to go round the City to the Inhabitants with a paper to sign to the above effect—those who refuse, are to be held up to the Populace as enemies to their Country—the committee are to meet weekly.
—November 23, 1780

The Continental Money has past for some time past at 200 for one; yesterday and to day it goes at 6 and 700 for one, but few will take it at that rate, the State Money at 3 and 4 for one; this fall occasions great confusion among the People Generaly.
—May 5, 1781

The Sailors getting togeather by hundreds with Clubbs, cursing the Continental Money, and declaring aginst it—state Money goes 6 to one.
—May 8, 1781

An early caddy used to hold tea leaves

39

QUAKER CHILDHOODS

Of Henry and Elizabeth Drinker's nine children, only five—shown at the bottom of the family tree at right—lived into adulthood. A doting and conscientious mother, Elizabeth kept careful note in her diary of the children's milestones. "Began this Morning to Ween my Sally," she began on March 31, 1763, just days after she had miscarried at eight weeks. "The Struggle seems now (April 2) partly over.—tho it can scarcely be call'd a Struggle she is such a good-natur'd patient Child."

Sally was one of the lucky ones. She survived the often deadly childhood diseases and accidents of the day, received a proper Quaker education, and went on to marry and raise a family of her own.

This painted rocking horse, complete with tail, was crafted around 1793.

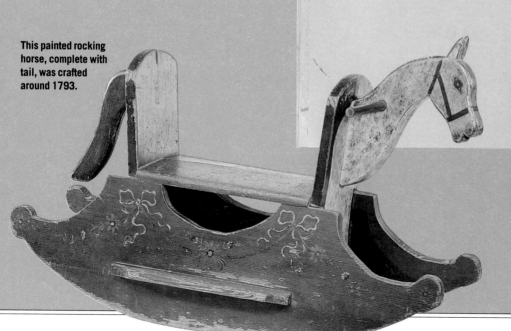

Henry Drinker and Elizabeth Sandwith Drinker's five surviving children complete this short genealogy of the Drinker and Sandwith families.

HD. self and 4 Children went this afternoon, to the Burial of little Hannah Drinker, daughter of Jos. Drinker [Henry's brother]—not 10 months old—they bury'd last week a Son and Daughter (twins) who were born the week before—Aquila and Prissila.—July 9, 1775

Our little Henry was run over by a Horse in the Street, his Knee was Brused, but not meterially hurt.—March 1777

Philadelphia Quakers created an excellent system of schools for their children. Latin; French; mathematics; and natural philosophy, or science, were among the subjects taught:

This early-18th-century wood doll wears a fashionable hoop skirt.

HD. went to Town this Morning. MS. [sister Mary] John the Child and myself went to School, which is held at the Meeting House—a Jamess, W Parr's and J. Foulk's Children go there. tis a large School—We call'd in our way home at M Foulk's—Thos. Bolsbey and Wife there, drank Tea with them; HD. came home —while we were there—the Weather is very cool and Pleasent.—August 15, 1763

In April 1778 state authorities required all schoolmasters to take an oath of allegiance to the American Revolutionary cause. Those who did not could be removed from their positions and fined 500 pounds plus costs. Some Quaker schoolmasters were imprisoned for their principled refusal to take the oath, and by 1781 the Americans, suspecting the Quakers of Loyalist sympathies, closed their schools:

Joseph Yerkes was had up yesterday before a Magistrate for keeping School; his School is stop'd, and our Son Billy is at a loss for employment, as well as many others, in consiquence of it; sad doings.—August 25, 1778

Defiant schoolmasters and students then met in various homes, including the Drinkers':

Charles Mifflin and his Pupils mett in our little Front Room; he has lately undertaking to improve a few young Girls in writeing: teaching 'em Grammar &c—Hanh. Redwood, Sally Fisher, Caty Haines and Sister, Betsy Howel, Sally and Nancy Drinker, are his scholars at present—are to take turns at the different Houses; they began at Ruban Haines, the 8th Ultimo when Sally first attended—Nancy being unwell did not go 'till the 18th.—February 1, 1781

In the 1700s, a child's potty was known as a convenience chair.

Children learned their alphabet from hornbooks—wood paddles protectively coated with translucent horn.

Ailments and Cures

Elizabeth Drinker could turn to a variety of medicines and treatments for the manifold ailments that frequently afflicted her and her family and friends. Many of her remedies were mixed from home recipes using various plants and liquids; others could be found at an apothecary shop. And some were more effective than others. The widely used Carolina pink root, for example, does indeed fight intestinal worms, and the bark will reduce fever. But the popular treatment of bloodletting, whether by incision or the application of leeches, would only further weaken a patient.

In the absence of antibiotics, even minor infections often blossomed into virulent fevers that led to death—an event that was so commonplace in the households of the era that children sometimes staged mock funerals, even placing their dolls in miniature coffins.

For centuries, the marsh mallow plant *(above)* has soothed a wide variey of complaints, among them a urinary disorder suffered by Henry Drinker.

Apothecaries dispensed medicinal leeches from ventilated containers such as this one.

42

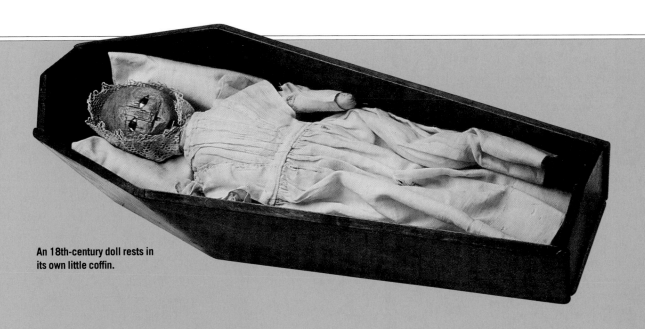

An 18th-century doll rests in its own little coffin.

Our dear little Henry [at about 7 years of age] was taken ill with a vomiting and disordred Bowels, occasion'd by eating watermellon too close to the Rine—he voided in the course of his Sickness, (which turnd out to be an inviterate Bloody and white Flux) 3 large Worms, and vomited one alive—for 12 Days he eat nothing —and is now . . . in a very poor way, reduced almost to a Skelaton with a constant fever hanging about him, tho' the disorder seems to be somewhat check'd, and he has an appetite in the Morning—he has taken 8 Clysters [enemas] and many doses of Physick— his Body comes down and he is so weak that he cannot sit up alone.—August 20 or 21, 1777

Sickness in the household could keep Elizabeth tending family members day and night. One summer, an ailment suffered by her daughter Sally kept her so busy that she did not take off her clothes for three days:

Exceeding Hott my poor Child very ill, continues sick at her Stomach, and frequently vomitts quantities of dark green Boile, which as the Weather is so warm, gives me great uneasyness, she took to day 3 Spoonfulls of Castor-Oyl— one of which she vomitted up, it work'd her twice, she is very low this evening—I have not had my cloaths of[f] since 3d. day Night, and tis now sixth day: little Henry and Billy are both unwell,—Lidia Stretch was bury'd Yesterday, she dy'd of the Flux.—July 10, 1778

This compact medicine chest held a wide variety of nostrums.

The Trouble with Servants

Like many Philadelphia householders of the time, the Drinkers kept a variety of servants to attend to such domestic chores as cooking, sewing, cleaning, and tending fireplaces and stoves. Most of these workers were indentured servants who had pledged to work for a term of years to pay for their passage from Europe to America.

Such servants could not marry without their master's permission, and they could be sold along with their contracts without their consent. At the end of their period of service they were entitled to so-called freedom dues, usually of clothing or cash.

Indentured servants were a great convenience, but as Elizabeth Drinker learned, they could also be a problem.

Slices of bread could be toasted in this cast-iron rack.

This contract for indenture was signed in 1750.

44

Nanny Oat call'd to day, to demand her freedom dues and was very impertinent and Saucy.
—September 22, 1777

Nanny Oat, also known as Ann, wanted to leave service in the Drinker home before her time was expired in order to run off with a British officer:

Our Saucy Ann came while I was at meeting desereing to know what I would take for hir time and she would bring the money in a minuit Sister told her she did not know, but that she heard me talk of puting her in the Work House, she reply'd if you talk so, you shall neither have me nor the Money, Sister then ordred her to come again at 12 o'clock, but she has not been since.
—December 2, 1777

I had a conferance with the officer who took away Ann; I stop'd him as he past the door—and after desiring him to stand still, 'till a noisey Waggon which was going by had past, (as he said he was in a hurry) I then adress'd him; if thee has no sense of Religion or Virtue, I should think that what you Soliders call Honor would have dictated to thee what was thy duty after thy behaviour some time ago in this House, who me! Yes I know thee well, I have as yet been carefull of exposeing thee, but if thee dont very soon pay me for my Servants time; as there is officers quarterd among Numbers of my acquaintance, I will tell all I meet with, he stutter'd and said I han't got your Servant, I dont care who has her, it was thee that stole her; well said he a little impudently if you'l come up to my quarters up Town, I told him If he did not bring the Mony or send it soon he should hear further from me; well, well well said he and away he went seemingly confus'd. —January 4, 1778

Elizabeth had some difficulty in finding servants whose behavior measured up to her standards:

I dismist my maid Caty Paterson this afternoon, on her return home after 2 or 3 days frolicking, our old maid Molly Hensel is to Supply her place tomorrow.
—February 10, 1780

And a servant might bring more than her services to the household:

Polly Newgent . . . has been with us a week, and appears cleaver, brought the Itch [probably scabies] with her, which I hope we have nearly cur'd.—April 27, 1781

Philadelphia's Rough Justice

Elizabeth Drinker's diary reveals that both rebels and royalists committed excesses in their struggles for victory. But the Americans seemed especially prone to use public executions to set examples and maintain control over soldiers and citizenry. On March 8, 1777, for example, Elizabeth notes that an American soldier charged with desertion and perjury was shot on the commons in "a City heretofore clear of such Business." Days later, she recorded, "a Young Man of the Name of Molsworth [convicted of seeking to hire pilots to guide the British fleet up the Delaware River] was hang'd on the Commons by order of our present ruling Gentr'y"—an unusual bit of sarcasm from Elizabeth's pen.

An unfortunate Tory, mocked by a group of rebels, swings from a liberty pole in this engraving from American poet John Trumbull's *M'Fingal*.

The Town Illuminated and a great number of Windows Broke on the Anniversary of Independence and Freedom.—July 4, 1777

Independence Day, and the days set aside to commemorate American battlefield victories, were not happy times for Philadelphia Quakers. Hewing to their principles of neutrality, Quaker shopkeepers declined to close their businesses in celebration—and were repaid by patriots who hurled rocks through their windows. Such demonstrations came to a halt during the nine-month British occupation of the city that began in late September 1777, but Elizabeth noted abuses of other kinds from the English, who "burnt houses, plunder'd and ill used" the people of Philadelphia:

We are told this evening, that, Owen Joness Family have been very ill used indeed, by an Officer who wanted to quarter himself, with many others on them, he drew his Sword, us'd very abusive language, and had the Front Door split in pieces &c.—December 19, 1777

To be sure, not all of the king's officers were so violent in their quest for lodgings, as Elizabeth had discovered not long after Henry was banished from the city by the American authorities:

An Officer call'd to Day to know if Genl. Grant could have quarters with us; I told him as my Husband was from me, and a Number of Young Children round me, I should be glad to be excus'd—he reply'd, as I desir'd it, it should be so.—October 25, 1777

After the American revolutionaries reoccupied the city in June 1778, Philadelphia returned to its normal wartime footing. Elizabeth noted that Quakers were harassed if they refused to take loyalty tests or close their schools. And the public executions continued; indeed, in separate actions, six men condemned for assisting the British were hanged in less than four months' time. But one lucky miscreant, Elizabeth later noted, managed to escape one of the era's most gruesome punishments—gibbeting, in which the executed criminal's corpse was enclosed in a metal frame and left on display until nothing remained but bones:

A poor Fellow who had been condem'd to be hang'd and Gibbeted, was this day repreav'd.—May 23, 1781

After execution, a criminal's body was sometimes encased in an iron gibbet suit, such as this one, for public display. The man for whom this suit was made in1781 received a reprieve.

47

CHAPTER 2

DIVIDE AND CONQUER

"If I were to wish the bitterest curse to an enemy on this side of the grave, I should put him in my stead with my feelings."

GENERAL GEORGE WASHINGTON, WRITING
FROM HARLEM HEIGHTS, NEW YORK, SEPTEMBER 30, 1776

The day after their victories at Lexington and Concord, the provincial forces—now grown to some 15,000 strong—entrenched themselves in Cambridge and Roxbury, bringing the two sides to a stalemate. The provincials could not hope to attack Boston by land, through the fortified neck, and they could not go against the city from the water as long as Britain commanded the sea.

By the same token, the British, although now reinforced to a strength of about 5,000 men, did not have sufficient force, Thomas Gage believed, to break out and command the countryside, which swarmed with militia. There were the odd skirmishes as regulars made sorties for hay and meat, and an occasional cannonade from rebel gun emplacements across the Charles River. But the only semblance of real action occurred 200 miles northwest of Boston, at Fort Ticonderoga on Lake Champlain. Surprised by a provincial force on May 10, 1775, the fort and its treasure of cannon fell to the rebels.

General Gage, for his part, pulled in his lines from the Charlestown side of the river in late April, abandoning the rough redoubt thrown up on Bunker Hill. For the time being, he would let the rebels have that high ground, as well as the southern heights at Dorchester, separated from Boston by an-

other narrow inlet. High ground was useless if one had no artillery to put on it, and the provincials had almost none. Then, acting to defuse a possible uprising within his fortress city, Gage offered townsfolk who wanted to leave freedom of passage to the mainland in exchange for their weapons; 1,800 muskets were turned in.

Something had curdled in the life of Thomas Gage, however. The orders from Lord Dartmouth that had persuaded him to send out the ill-fated April expedition to Concord had been accompanied by other, perhaps less welcome news. The ministers and His Majesty had decided to send over some additional help for Gage, in the form of three major generals—William Howe, Henry Clinton, and John Burgoyne. To Gage they must have seemed to be three walking reprimands.

And things were no longer the same at Province House; no one said now of the Gages that they enjoyed their former conjugal felicity. By May 13 he had decided that his wife would go back to England; only a few years later London would whisper that the impeccably married Gage had taken a young mistress. Some believed the marriage failed because Margaret Gage was Joseph Warren's secret informer. If she had betrayed Gage's Concord expedition, she had ripped a great hole in his career and reputation—one few men could forgive.

By the time Clinton, Howe, and Burgoyne arrived in Boston on May 25, Gage had begun to wonder how he could regain the offensive. On June 12 he declared martial law. Then, with his three helpers, he considered a limited effort, cut to the size of the force now in Boston. They should be able to seize Bunker Hill and Breed's Hill, the neck in Charlestown, and Dorchester. This would secure that high ground in case the rebels were able to find artillery—or somehow move to Boston the cannon captured at Ticonderoga. Unfortunately for Gage, there were still no secrets in Boston, and his confidential plan was the talk of the town two days later.

The rebel forces moved swiftly to preempt him. On the evening of June 16 a party of nearly 1,000 militia commanded by Colonel William Prescott moved across Charlestown Neck, with orders to seize and fortify Bunker Hill. Tall and lean, the 43-year-old Prescott was a farmer in civilian life but had served with distinction with the colonial troops that fought alongside British regulars during the French and Indian War. He had even been offered a commission in the Royal Army, an honor seldom proffered to Americans. But he declined and returned to his farm, where he tilled the soil and kept up his military interest by reading books on tactics.

Now, as he and his aides studied the lay of the land at Charlestown, Prescott made a fateful decision. The highest of Charlestown's three hills, Bunker Hill could have been rendered almost invulnerable to attack. But Prescott ordered his men to move on to the lower, more exposed Breed's Hill, a few hundred yards to the east, and to set up their fortifications there. It was not the best choice. Unlike Bunker Hill, Breed's Hill did not abut the

massed provincial troops and was open in the rear to an attack from the Mystic River.

Shortly before midnight Prescott's army of diggers went to work with their picks and shovels. Across the river in Boston, British sentinels could hear the clanging of steel tools against the rocks that larded the hillside. In Charlestown, Amos Farnsworth heard the men working, too, and later he would write that they "careed it on with the utmost viger all night."

As the first dim glow of sunrise exposed the rebel works to British view, Prescott's exhausted men were still at it. Then the big guns aboard the warships anchored in the Charles began firing on the unfinished redoubt. Cannonballs whistled through the brisk morning air, shattering the diggers' water barrels and leaving them only a cask of water and a few casks of rum to drink. As militiaman Asa Pollard started down the hill to bring more water, a cannonball took off his head, splattering those around him with bloody fragments. Pollard was swiftly buried, but afterward some of the men slipped off down the hill in fear. Prescott rallied the rest by drawing his sword and leaping to an exposed position. There, as cannonballs harmlessly shattered the earth around him, he paced back and forth, shouting, "It was a one in a million shot, men! See how close they come to hitting me!"

Inspired by the dash and daring of their commander, most of the men continued with their hammering and digging. By early afternoon they had completed their simple redoubt near the top of Breed's Hill and extended their left wing all the way down to the banks of the Mystic. Then they managed to put some 3,500 militia and Minutemen on the hill—as one American general would describe it later, "raw lads and old men half armed, with no practice in discipline, commanded without order, and God knows by whom."

They were just in time, for by then General Howe, under the umbrella of the artillery barrage, had moved across the river from Boston with a fleet of 28 barges bearing about 1,500 grenadiers and

A remnant of the Battle of Bunker Hill, this brass bullet mold was used by Continental soldiers to cast both musket balls and buckshot. The mold originally had wooden handles, which were used to press the halves together after they were heated over a fire. Molten lead was then poured into the troughs on either side and, once hardened, knocked out of the cavities.

BOSTON

CHARLES TO[WN]

light infantry. His plan was to take the rebel position by frontal assault, with a flanking movement toward the provincial's left wing. Lord Percy was given Boston Neck to protect, and Gage remained in Boston, ready to help; Burgoyne was detailed to the artillery battery on Copp's Hill, from which he could observe the day's proceedings.

About 3 p.m., as the tired and hungry defenders of Breed's Hill watched nervously from behind their hastily built breastworks, the resplendent British regulars began their slow ascent of the slope, marching to the music of fifes and drums. They were spread out in three lines of skirmishers, rather than in the narrower target of a column for-

Set ablaze with hot cannon shot from British warships, Charlestown burns in the background as British troops prepare to assault American positions in the Battle of Bunker Hill. According to Massachusetts corporal Amos Farnsworth, the town was "almost all laid in ashes by the barbarity and wanton cruelty of that infernal villain Thomas Gage."

mation; Howe led the right wing, and his brigadier, Robert Pigot, led the left, all under an umbrella of a cannon barrage from the ships. When Pigot's force came under fire from Charlestown, the anchored ships ignited the town with hot cannon shot. Carcasses—hollow balls filled with burning pitch—fired from Copp's Hill swept the provincial redoubt as well. Howe sent a column around to his right to flank the defenders. Massachusetts sharpshooters dug in near the Mystic River cut those troops to ribbons and left casualties, as one militiaman put it, "as thick as sheep in a fold." His flanking action thwarted, Howe ordered a frontal assault up Breed's Hill.

As the regulars neared the rebel line, recalled militiaman Peter Brown, it seemed as though they "advanced towards us to swallow us up." But the militia held fast, heeding their officers' frequent admonitions to hold their fire—advice that has entered history as the apocryphal "Don't fire till you see the whites of their eyes." Then came a well-directed volley of musket fire that mowed down red-coated soldiers by the score. Howe, marching boldly alongside his men, fell back, then tried again. This time the British prepared to storm the rebel lines with bayonets; but, as one officer reported, "an incessant stream of fire poured from the rebel lines, it seemed a continued sheet of fire for near thirty minutes." It was too much, and again the assault collapsed into a headlong retreat back down the cannon-pocked slope of Breed's Hill, littered with the shattered bodies of the dead, the knee-high grass trampled and bloody, and everywhere the sad, futile cries of the wounded.

Then, closing his ranks and adding 400 fresh troops from Boston, Howe prepared for a third attempt. "They looked too handsome to be fired at," said one young rebel. "But we had to do it." The British infantry once more ascended the slope. "As fast as the front man was shot down," reported one militiaman, "the next stepped forward into his place; but our men dropt them so fast, they were a long time coming up. It was surprising how they would step over their dead bodies, as though they had been logs of wood."

Howe's final charge faltered for a long moment; then, as the rebels ran short of ammunition and their salvos weakened, the British infantry loosed an angry roar that spectators could hear all the way to Boston and leaped across the ditch into the redoubt, slashing angrily at everyone they found there. From the right, the Royal Marines flowed into the struggle. The American defenders retreated along the stone fence, and across the gantlet of Charlestown Neck, raked by British cannon. Among the last to leave was young Peter Brown, who later wrote to his mother, "I ran a half mile, while balls flew like hailstones and cannon roared like thunder."

One of those who did not join in the retreat that day was Dr. Joseph Warren, a longtime leader of Boston's radical faction—he had once said he would like to die fighting British "in blood up to his knees." Newly named a general of the Massachusetts provincial army, but not yet officially commissioned, Warren had come to the battle to fight alongside his men as a common soldier, musket in hand. With a handful of others, he held off the regulars' final assault, enabling many more Americans to get away. Bleeding from a bayonet wound in his arm, he finally fell to a British volley that put a musket ball behind his ear.

"He died in his best cloaths," reported a British officer. "Every body remembers his fine silk-fringed waistcoat." Warren's undertaker on Breed's Hill was Captain Walter Laurie, the officer who had been driven off Concord's North bridge. Laurie wrote later that he "stuffed the scoundrel with another Rebel into one hole and there he and his seditious principles may remain." Months later, Warren's family and Paul Revere exhumed the body, which they identified by some metal dentistry Revere had performed for the doctor.

The morning after the battle, British troops burned the rest of the houses beyond Charlestown Neck and worked on their own fortifications of Bunker Hill—the high ground for which the battle has been named. The Boston stalemate had been restored, but at a heavy cost. Of about 2,000 British regulars sent to the fight, more than 1,000 were casualties, 226 of them killed. "A dear bought victory," observed General Clinton. "Another such would have ruined us." On the provincial side, 115 men were killed, another 305 wounded, and 30 taken prisoner.

Three days after Gage's account of the costly action reached London, the ministers named Howe commander of all forces south of Canada. Gage could only wait for recall, and probable disgrace.

The Americans entrenched around Boston also received a new commander, a man who had once fought for king and country against the French alongside Thomas Gage and who now faced his old comrade in arms down the barrel of a cannon. Two days before the Battle of Bunker Hill, the Second Continental Congress, then meeting in Philadelphia, elected George Washington "to command all the Continental forces raised or to be raised for the defense of American liberty." Although he was a tall, powerfully built man, the 43-year-old Virginian had accepted the call to service with tears in his eyes and had fretted over what such a job would do to his good name. "Remember, Mr. Henry," he told his fellow Virginian, Patrick Henry, "what I now tell you. From the day I enter upon the command of the American armies, I date my fall and the ruin of my reputation."

Washington had protested his "incapacity" for the post, and he half believed in it—but only half. Attending the Continental Congress as a Virginia delegate, he seemed almost to advertise his military

French at aptly named Fort Necessity; he had been criticized for a surprise attack on a party of French ambassadors; and he had been with General Braddock's startled, outgunned column in its panicked retreat from the Monongahela River. These experiences did not constitute much of a résumé, and the British officers with whom he served had not seen their way to giving Washington what he wanted most, a regular commission in the king's army. Despite such martial longings, however, Washington was a civilian at heart, his army background one of wilderness skirmishes, not set piece battles.

Washington took up his new command in Cambridge, across the Charles from Boston, on July 2. By then, such friendship as he and Gage might once have enjoyed had faded. Their contacts were mere bickering, Washington complaining in notes that

"As fast as the front man was shot down, the next stepped forward into his place; but our men dropt them so fast, they were a long time coming up. It was surprising how they would step over their dead bodies, as though they had been logs of wood."

AMERICAN MILITIAMAN AT BREED'S HILL, JUNE 1775

experience: Instead of wearing the suits that were favored by his colleagues, he appeared in the cream-and-blue uniform he had designed for his provincial militia. New England Revolutionary leader John Adams, for one, had noted Washington's "soldier-like air." And it was Adams who had helped shepherd through the congress an extraordinary, unanimous vote of faith and confidence in the new army commander. "This Congress," said the resolution, "doth now declare that they will maintain and assist and adhere to him, the said George Washington, with their lives and fortunes."

Part of Washington had yearned to command—had always yearned to command, despite his scant formal military training. He had little skill in the elaborate choreography of large-unit maneuvering, and such combat as he had seen was with British units in the French and Indian War 17 years earlier. He had blundered into a humiliating defeat by the

Gage was wrong to treat captured provincial officers and men alike, Gage arguing that as they were not members of a real army, the distinction between officers and men did not apply. Nor would he call Washington a general; it was always pointedly Mr. Washington to General Gage.

As the British garrison sank into hardships, unable to procure enough supplies from the sea to keep dietary problems and disease at bay, the provincial army likewise unraveled. "This unhappy and devoted Province has been so long in a State of Anarchy and the Yoke of Ministerial Oppression so heavily laid, that great allowances are to be made for their Troops collected under such circumstances," Washington wrote the congress on July 10. "The Defficiencies in their numbers, their Discipline and Stores can only lead to this conclusion, that their Spirit has exceeded their Strength." He added: "It requires no Military Skill to judge of the

Difficulty of introducing Discipline and Subordination into an Army while we have the Enemy in View and are in daily expectation of an attack."

Six weeks later, Washington wrote less diplomatically to his flamboyant colleague General Charles Lee, whose military experience with the armies of Britain and Russia had made him a runner-up to Washington for the post of commander in chief. "It is among the most difficult tasks I ever undertook in my life to induce these people to believe that there is, or can be, danger till the Bayonet is pushed at their Breasts; not that it proceeds from any uncommon prowess, but rather from an unaccountable kind of stupidity in the lower class of these people, which, believe me, prevails but too generally among the officers of the Massachusetts part of the army who are nearly of the same kidney with the Privates, and adds not a little to my difficulties; as there is no such thing as getting of officers of this stamp to exert themselves in carrying orders into execution—to curry favor with the men (by whom they were chosen, and on whose smiles possibly they may think they may again rely) seems to be one of the principal objects of their attention."

Clearly, the patrician side of the Virginia planter was uncomfortable with the undisciplined and ill-equipped Yankee horde that passed for a Continental army. If the present was bad, however, the future looked worse. Having come this far, Washington's men were ready to go home, and he was faced with the necessity of raising a fresh army to continue this new war with Britain. Bunker Hill had nearly exhausted his supply of ball and powder, and there was still no artillery worth the name. Washington's main weapons were his own imposing presence—he sat his horse with the quiet confidence of a centaur and seemed afraid of nothing, as his soldiers quickly perceived. "Not a king in Europe," observed one contemporary of the Virginian, "but would look like a valet de chambre by his side." Despite some

THE GENERAL'S TRAVELING COMPANION

When dining in the field, George Washington relied on the well-stocked camp kitchen purchased for him in 1776 by his adjutant general and close friend Joseph Reed from Philadelphian Benjamin Harrison. The camp kitchen, or canteen, is furnished with tin plates, platters, utensils, and a tankard, as well as nesting kettles—similar to those that are found in modern-day camping equipment—of four different sizes.

stuffiness in his manner, Washington enjoyed sharing a drink with his fellows, and among women he radiated charm.

Had Gage known of the problems that existed in the American camp, the Briton might have scored heavily against his former friend. Conversely, the British garrison had become dispirited enough that a strong thrust by Washington might have pushed them out of Boston altogether. Although itching to do something, neither man possessed the confidence or means of acting until action was impossible. In any event Gage would soon be out of the picture, leaving William Howe to deal with the problems of beleaguered Boston.

In August Margaret Gage sailed for England with widows and wounded aboard the *Charming Nancy*. On September 26, 16 months after his arrival as governor of Massachusetts, Thomas Gage was ordered back to England and sailed for home October 11, aboard HMS *Pallas*. What now seemed a century ago, he had written London: "There will be an end to these provinces as British colonies, give them then what other name you please." The barricaded city lying in the wake of *Pallas* was no longer part of England but of another country, a sovereign enemy in a war that Great Britain, Gage knew with awful certainty, would not win.

The night air was cold and still around Boston on March 2, 1776, although two weeks earlier a thaw had begun to loosen winter's grip on the frozen landscape. Abigail Adams sat at a desk in her house in Braintree, writing a letter to her husband, John, then attending a meeting of the Continental Congress in Philadelphia.

Writing by candlelight, Abigail described a growing tension in nearby Boston. American soldiers crowding the small shore settlements around the harbor were eager to provoke a fight with the British in town. "I have been kept in a continual state of anxiety and expectation ever since you left," she wrote. People were talking about a great battle that was likely to begin at any moment. "It has been said, 'tomorrow' and 'tomorrow' " for an entire month, Abigail explained, but "when the dreadful tomorrow will be, I know not." Then, as she paused, pen in hand, an explosion ripped through the night sky.

The bombardment began on the night of March 2 and continued the next evening. Its slow and measured pace was determined by the urgent need to conserve gunpowder. Only 24 shots were fired the first night. Then, following a secret plan, the pace of firing rose to a crescendo on the third night, March 4. A Massachusetts militia colonel named Webb looked into the sky and thought about his old neighbors in the town. "From my window," he wrote of the opening barrage, "have a most pleasing and yet dismal view of the fiery ministers of death flying through the air. Poor inhabitants, our friends, we pity most sincerely, but particularly the women and children." From Boston the British responded with their cannon. But the fusillade did no more real damage than did the blind shots by the Americans. Indeed, the cannonade was purely diversionary, a prelude to Washington's cashing in on a prize hauled in from the north.

By early February, Henry Knox, a portly amateur artillerist who discovered an astonishing aptitude for gunnery during the war, had transported the 59 cannon captured at Ticonderoga almost 300 arduous miles to Boston. Without a deep, prolonged freeze, the steep-banked, fast-flowing rivers of the region would have blocked any at-

Published according to Act of Parliament, Sept. 1. 1773 by Arch.d Bell,
Bookseller N.o 8 near the Saracens Head Aldgate.

Proceed, great chief, with virtue on thy side,
Thy ev'ry action let the goddess guide.
A crown, a mansion, and a throne that shine,
With gold unfading, *Washington!* be thine.

IN PRAISE OF WASHINGTON

In October 1775 Phillis Wheatley, a freed Boston slave whose likeness *(above)* appeared on the front of her collected poems published two years earlier, wrote a poem honoring George Washington on his appointment as "Generalissimo of the armies of North America." The poem, which ends with the couplets above, is one of the earliest examples of the hyperbolic praise for Washington that would reach a fevered pitch in the next century.

Born around 1753 in Africa, Phillis was purchased as a house servant by tailor John Wheatley in 1761. She learned to read both English and Latin while a slave in the Wheatley household and was schooled in classical literature. She published her first poem at age 14.

tempt to move the weapons. But low temperatures had transformed those rivers into frozen thoroughfares, down which Knox and his men had somehow hauled the cannon. Indeed, the freeze had favored them almost all the way to Boston, until, just short of their mark, a thaw bogged them down. Still, they had managed to drag the guns into Washington's scanty arsenal, altering the balance of firepower around the beleaguered city. The guns of early March were merely providing cover for the emplacement of Knox's weapons where they would do the most good.

No one was happier at the prospect of a fight than George Washington—it had galled his proud temperament to be forced into a waiting game. When he had first taken command outside Boston, Washington had hoped to defeat the British in open battle—at best, an unlikely outcome of any formal confrontation. But the aristocratic Virginian had been saved from such intentions by his army's material shortcomings. His store of weapons was weaker than he had been led to believe—a reported inventory of 308 barrels of powder turned out to be only 36. Volunteer militia were hard to keep. Discipline was poor. And the officers themselves were unruly, prone to quarreling over rank. Washington was also hobbled by the democratic model that governed military decision making in the Continental army. He led by consent and consulted often with his peers; he also cleared most major orders with the Continental Congress in Philadelphia. Thus, Washington would float aggressive strategies, only to be voted down by his generals.

In October Washington had launched a large but ill-starred raid on Canada, which failed shortly after Christmas with heavy losses. In another desperate gambit, Washington had urged a frontal assault on Boston in February, in which his troops would have had to march straight out on the ice from Lechmere's Point under the British guns. This plan was rejected unanimously by his officers; even Washington much later conceded that it might not have succeeded.

Hindered by shortages and procedures, Washington had felt at times that his was an impossible assignment. Writing to a friend, Philadelphian Joseph Reed, he lamented the burden of his responsibilities: "I have often thought how much happier I should have been, if, instead of accepting a command under such circumstances, I had taken my musket on my shoulder and entered the ranks" or, if he could have justified it, "retired to the back country, and lived in a wigwam." And he particularly resented the thought that some patriots— "chimney corner heroes," as his friend Reed called them—might have doubts about his willingness to fight. Washington was painfully sensitive as well to the cost of maintaining the army and the seeming waste of letting it stand idle. To the president of the congress, he wrote of his discomfort at having "the eyes of the whole continent fixed with anxious expectation" upon himself, awaiting news of "some great event." Yet all the while, he was "restrained in every military operation for want of the necessary means of carrying it on."

The congress eventually responded, granting extra funds to build up the army's corps of volunteers. Gradually the store of powder increased. By the third week of February, a thaw had made the ground soft enough for soldiers to dig fortifications. Finally, Washington had been able to write a fellow general, "I am determined to do everything in my power" to bring on an engagement, "and that as soon as possible."

After dark on the evening of March 4, under cover of the rumbling American guns, 3,000 men

"I ordered the commander to come forth instantly . . . at which the captain came immediately to the door with his breeches in his hand, when I ordered him to deliver to me the fort instantly, he asked me by what authority I demanded it, I answered, 'In the name of Jehovah and the Continental Congress.'"

ETHAN ALLEN, 1779

Brandishing his sword, Ethan Allen demands the surrender of Fort Ticonderoga. Absent from this late-19th-century view is Benedict Arnold, who was at Allen's side during the uncontested capture.

Benedict Arnold: Before the Fall

Mercurial, sometimes brilliant, sometimes brutally violent, stocky, five-foot-seven Benedict Arnold was 34 years old in 1775, when the American rebellion began. The son of an impecunious and alcoholic father, he had been a troubled and rebellious youth in his hometown of Norwich, Connecticut, where after brief schooling he had learned the apothecary's trade. Between 1758 and 1760 Arnold had run away from home three times to enlist in militia companies raised to fight in the French and Indian War. Impatient of the mundane soldier's duties, he soon headed for home. After his father and mother died in the early 1760s, Arnold opened a drugstore in New Haven; bought shares in a number of ships; and entered into trade with the West Indies, Central America, and Canada, often sailing as one of his own shipmasters. He had taken to smuggling to avoid British customs, and had become a hot-tempered leader of the radicals advocating resistance to British authority.

The elected captain of a Connecticut militia company, Arnold had marched his 50 men to Cambridge, Massachusetts, the day after he heard about the fighting at Lexington and Concord. Bored with the siege there, he wangled a promotion to colonel and permission to try to raise a force and capture Fort Ticonderoga, guarding the southern end of Lake Champlain. On his way, he encountered Ethan Allen and his

BENEDICT ARNOLD IN A 1776 HAND-COLORED MEZZOTINT

Green Mountain Boys from Vermont, who had embarked on the same mission.

Arnold had only a handful of men with him, but he brandished his commission from the Massachusetts Committee of Safety and demanded to be put in command of the expedition. Allen had no thought of letting anyone else command his unruly irregulars, but he let Arnold march at the head of the column on condition that he issue no orders.

They surprised the small garrison and took Ticonderoga on May 10. But to Arnold's frustration, Allen got the credit and remained in command. After a series of disputes and controversies, Arnold resigned and went home, only to find that his wife had died and the Massachusetts congress

would not reimburse his campaign's expenses, which he recovered only after taking the matter to the Continental Congress.

Encouraged by the northern successes, George Washington that summer ordered a two-pronged attack on Canada, along the lines of a proposal made by Arnold, whom Washington picked to lead one thrust of the assault. By early autumn of 1775, an army commanded by General Richard Montgomery, a former British officer who had joined the American side, was on the march from New York. Arnold's force, following the region's whitewater rivers northward, somehow endured a 46-day wilderness trek rendered nightmarish by famine and treacherous terrain, and finally reached the fortress city of Quebec.

In spite of the poor health and equipage of his troops, Montgomery seized Chambly, then St. Johns and Montreal in November. Still, by the time the two forces converged near Quebec in early December, smallpox and desertions had eroded their combined strength from more than 3,000 to fewer than 1,000 men. Perhaps the worst that befell them, however, was an American sergeant's desertion to the British, whom he alerted to the coming attack. As Arnold and Montgomery waited for bad weather to cover their assault, the British prepared a ferocious greeting of powder and ball.

On the early morning of December 31, a blinding snowstorm offered an opportunity for a badly outnumbered American force to storm the city's near-impregnable walls. Leading his wing, Montgomery was killed almost immediately in a hail of grapeshot. Soon after, Arnold went down with a musket ball through his left leg. The remaining troops, under the leadership of Daniel Morgan, persevered, but, unfamiliar with the winding streets and alleys of Quebec, they were eventually outmaneuvered and forced to surrender.

Arnold continued to command the siege from a hospital bed. "I have no thought of leaving this proud town," he wrote his sister Hannah, "until I first enter it in triumph." Then, "I am in the way of duty, and know no fear." Promoted to brigadier general, Arnold sustained the siege into May of 1776, then reluctantly moved to Montreal. But the slight American hold on Canada was already slipping. On the night of June 18, Arnold and a fellow officer, having shot their horses to keep them from the British, pushed off from the Canadian shore in a canoe—the last Americans to abandon a lost cause.

The mortally wounded General Richard Montgomery is comforted by aides in this romanticized rendering of the Battle of Quebec. Of the battle, Major General Philip Schuyler wrote George Washington: "My amiable friend, the gallant Montgomery, is no more; the brave Arnold is wounded; and we have met with a severe check in an unsuccessful attempt on Quebec."

from Washington's army marched in silent columns along a point of land called Dorchester Neck, which jutted into the harbor from the south. Beneath a moon "shining in its full luster," according to Washington, they carried picks and shovels, leading wagons filled with branches, hay bales, wooden frames, and barrels of sand and stones. Their objective was a line of hills in the middle of the point, called Dorchester Heights. They clambered up and quickly erected barricades, dug trenches, and emplaced Knox's cannon. At 3 a.m. a fresh crew of 2,400 men moved in, relieving the exhausted soldiers on the bluff. Although one British lieutenant colonel reported to his superiors that he heard trouble brewing in Dorchester, the other officers ignored this alarm. They assumed that anything the amateur American army did on shore that night could be undone later by British professionals.

Fog settled on the water during the night; when it burned off the following dawn, the morning light revealed a remarkable tableau. A new bulwark, bristling with cannon and manned by several thousand hostile Americans, had taken shape in less than 24 hours. Gazing up at this apparition, Boston's British commander, General William Howe, is said to have exclaimed, "Good God, these fellows have done more work in one night than I could have made my army do in three months." The chief British engineer, Archibald Robertson, estimated it must have taken 15,000 to 20,000 men to do the job. And another British officer joked that the Americans must have had help from the "genie belonging to Aladdin's wonderful lamp."

Washington believed the threat to Boston and the British navy would be so great that the enemy would have to flee—or, as he rather hoped, to attack the dug-in cannon at Dorchester. Should they attack, Washington expected to repeat the slaughter of redcoats at Bunker Hill. But, never a man for simple strategies, he had something more in mind. If the British did send a large contingent against the fortifications on Dorchester, a signal would be given to the 4,000 Americans under Israel Putnam encamped at

Cambridge. They would sail down the Charles River to Lechmere's Point and make a direct assault on the diminished garrison across the river in Boston.

As in many of the new commander's ideas, however, there was a crucial flaw. As Putnam's reserves committed themselves downriver, the tide would change, setting the Charles's currents against them and permitting no retreat. Like other plans Washington had proposed, this was a do-or-die proposition; the difference this time was that his generals agreed to it. Isaac Bangs, a Harvard-educated lieutenant of the Massachusetts troops, watched the barrage. In his journal he noted that, as the British guns responded, he saw "four and sometimes five" bombs come "flying in the air at a time." A shell broke about 25 yards from him, "and one of the pieces came with great rapidity about two yards above my head." For all its sound and fury, the nighttime gun battle did the Americans on Dorchester Heights little harm. After they had put fascines—bundles of branches—in place, the soldiers had cut down the orchards to obtain a clear field of fire and had begun to dig trenches and throw up earthen barricades.

While the light increased, redcoats and Boston citizens crowded into the streets and clambered on rooftops to see what the rebels had done during the night. Cannon began to appear in the town, and British gunners started lobbing shells at the threat on Dorchester Heights. Lieutenant Bangs noted in his journal that "we expected a salute immediately" from guns aboard ships in the harbor and from the town, and after some confusion, the enemy did let loose some shots. But "as their balls struck chiefly before they reached us, we could avoid them," Bangs wrote. The trajectory of the cannon was not enough to reach the hilltop. Some British gunners dug holes to lower the back ends of the guns and raise the barrels, but these attempts failed. In late morning, after about two hours of futile bombardment, the British quit.

Just before noon and immediately after the ene-

A self-taught artillery expert, Henry Knox was named the American commander of artillery in 1775. His retrieval of what Washington called the "noble train of artillery" captured at Fort Ticonderoga—and his successful transport of the heavy guns over a rugged winter terrain to Dorchester Heights—was largely responsible for the British evacuation of Boston in March 1776.

my cannon fire ceased, the Americans saw a flurry of activity in town. Men and women hurried through the streets. Soldiers began climbing aboard small transport boats, as others hurried down the wharves to load guns and ammunition. These forces converged on a small reinforced island called Castle William, in the southern end of the harbor, close to Dorchester, where Howe was focusing a counterattack. Howe had commanded Brigadier Daniel Jones to strike with 3,000 men at the Americans in their hillside trenches, while Howe himself planned to lead another group of 4,000 in an attack from the rear, directed at Roxbury. Howe's aim was to box the rebels in from two sides. The Americans waited for the attack, in which they "meant to emulate and hoped to eclipse the glories of Bunker Hill," according to Major John Trumble. As his men nerved themselves for battle, Washington reminded them that this day, March 5, was the sixth anniversary of

the Boston Massacre, and he urged them to "avenge the death of your brethren."

The Americans waited for the battle to begin throughout that day, but the enemy made no move—aside from letting fly two more cannon shots at one of the vessels off Castle William. Howe, it seemed, was planning a night assault. But as dusk gathered, temperatures began to plummet and the afternoon's rising breeze fanned into a full gale. Two ships in the harbor were ripped from their anchors and driven onto the beach. All night, as the British soldiers hunkered down in their small boats, the wind howled and the chill rain beat down, in what witnesses considered one of the worst storms in memory.

In their muddy bunkers on Dorchester Heights, the Americans had to shield themselves from the storm's fury with the branches that they had cut and carried up the night before. This caused Lieutenant Bangs to note that there was "nothing to cover us excepting apple trees."

The weather began to abate at dawn on March 6, and the rain stopped at 8 a.m.; the wind continued, though, scrubbing the sky free of clouds. Washington, who had asked his men to take special measures to keep their powder dry overnight, reflected in a letter on the "remarkable interposition of Providence" that had caused the confrontation between the armies to be stalled. Although God must have had "some wise purpose," Washington wrote, he felt let down, since the "principal design of the maneuver was to draw the enemy to an engagement under disadvantages," according to a "premeditated plan." Moreover, everything seemed to be "succeeding to my utmost wish," Washington thought, until the storm arrived.

In more comfortable quarters in Boston, Howe doubtless felt some relief that he and his army would not be marching up Dorchester's hill into enemy fire. Chief engineer Archibald Robertson was among them. He had been passing among the leaders of the British garrison arguing that it would be folly to attack the Americans in their dug-in position. He thought, as he wrote in a journal, that "the fate of this whole army and the town is at stake, not to say the fate of America." Howe held a council of war among his chief officers to debate the alternatives. The unanimous view was that the plan of attack should be dropped. Robertson, not invited to the council, observed in his diary that Howe had claimed his "own sentiments from the first" were to avoid battle in such disadvantageous conditions but that Howe had believed "the honor of the troops" was at stake and so had planned the assault. Next morning, Howe published an order saying: "The General desires that the troops may know that the intended expedition of last night was unavoidably put off by the badness of the weather."

Whether it was an act of God or no, the delay that was caused by the storm—combined with Howe's hesitation—forced a new course of action on the British: They could not stay in Boston. Howe issued orders that set many work parties chasing around the town, moving equipment. The Americans could see activity, but without spies in the city, they could only speculate about British intentions. The citizens of Boston themselves were confused. The Tories among them were now desperate to have the British army stay as long as possible, while the Whigs, though favoring the Revolution, hoped an American victory would not prompt the departing British to burn the town. A delegation of three Boston leaders, known as selectmen, met with Major General James Robertson to voice their concerns. Robertson visited Howe, then reported back to the selectmen that Howe would not destroy Boston "unless the troops under his command are molested during their embarkation or at departure."

On the next day the three selectmen persuaded a British major—Henry Bassett—to join them on a mission of peace. At about 2 p.m., this party of four walked out on Boston Neck toward the American army's position carrying a white flag of truce. There they were met by Colonel Ebenezer Learned, to whom they gave an urgent letter that they hoped he would take immediately to General Washington. Learned delivered it as requested. The letter began by stating simply that "his Excellency General

Sketched in the diary of the American artist-soldier Charles Willson Peale, this cannon—most likely confiscated from the British—is one of 13 types of artillery pieces used by the patriots and could fire an iron cannonball at a speed of roughly 1,000 feet per second.

Howe is determined to leave the town with the troops under his command." The authors, calling themselves "respectable inhabitants" of Boston, said they had received a promise from Howe that he would not burn the town if his troops were allowed to leave peacefully. However, they warned, "We have the greatest reason to expect the town will be exposed to entire destruction" if the Americans attacked. Pleading for restraint to avoid "so dreadful a calamity," the three civil leaders of the mission—Thomas and Jonathan Amory and Peter Johonnot—pledged their good faith and added their signatures, along with those of four other prominent citizens.

Always reluctant to let a disadvantaged enemy slip away, Washington reacted coolly. The letter, he grumbled, appeared to be "unauthorized and addressed to nobody." It might well be a trick to put the Americans off their guard while the British mobilized for a concerted attack on Boston, or somewhere else—New York was especially vulnerable to attack from the sea. Washington called in some nearby officers to look the letter over and advise him on a reply. The threat of torching the town was taken seriously: Already the British had burned two major shipping centers—Falmouth in the North, near today's Portland, Maine, and Norfolk, Virginia, in the South. Washington was keenly aware that his own beloved farm at Mount Vernon, Virginia, could easily go up in flames should British ships make a raid up the Potomac River. Moreover, there had recently been reliable reports of such distress in the British camp that subterfuge seemed unlikely. In the end Washington made no written response but decided to split the difference: He would not attack the departing troops, but he would keep them under steady pressure.

To that end Washington kept the soldiers on Dorchester Heights busy improving the trenches and earthworks, even erecting a new barracks to house 600 men. He dispatched others with a pair of brass mortars to Noddle's Island, close to Boston on the

The congress presented this medal to George Washington to commemorate the British evacuation of Boston on March 17, 1776. According to Selectman Timothy Newell, the British departure relieved the town "from a set of men whose unparalleled wickedness, profanity, debauchery, and cruelty is inexpressible."

northern side, to threaten any ships that might dare give the British aid. And on the night of March 9 he sent troops to Nook's Hill, located just across the channel from Boston on the southern side. Anticipating such a move, however, British gunners had already determined the range, and with a fierce volley of cannon fire quickly chased off the force, killing four. When the Americans returned a week later, they took the position with little trouble—the British had so reduced their artillery by then that their fire no longer posed a serious threat.

The ocean breeze, which for several days had been favorable for departure, suddenly shifted on March 15 and 16, penning the British ships in the harbor. On Sunday morning, March 17—a brilliant, clear day—the wind shifted back again to a favorable quarter. Suddenly, at 8 a.m., columns of redcoats sprang up in the streets, marching to the wharves. Men were climbing into transports, and these shallow boats were plying to and fro between the shore and the big warships at anchor. This was the moment of truth: The British were poised either for an all-out attack or for flight. Washington put his men in Dorchester and Roxbury on alert, while the reserve forces under General Israel Putnam at Cambridge came sailing down the Charles River.

General John Sullivan, who had been keeping an eye on the British garrison at Bunker Hill, knew that some redcoats had already marched out of the fort, but he was puzzled to see that Bunker Hill seemed still to be guarded. Moving to a closer vantage point, Sullivan watched the sentries carefully; none were moving. Through his field glass he saw that they were stuffed effigies dressed in British uniform.

Sullivan led a "strong party" up the slopes of Bunker Hill and charged into the British defenses. He later wrote: "We found no person there and bravely took a fortress defended by lifeless sentries" who had horseshoes in place of the silver-plated gorgets the men normally wore over their throats in battle. One effigy also carried a placard that bore the words "Welcome Brother Jonathan"—the wry collective nickname that was often applied to the colonists. After exploring the trenches and parapets, Sullivan observed, "We found all abandoned, but the works not injured in any part." When Washington later had an opportunity to inspect Bunker Hill, he marveled at its strength, appreciating anew how difficult it would have been to take the fort if the British had stood firm. "Twenty thousand men," he wrote, "could not have carried it against one thousand."

Around the harbor's curve to the south, General Putnam and Colonel Learned were preparing to enter the town along the causeway of Boston Neck. Putnam sought among the troops and citizens 500 men who bore the marks of smallpox. According to rumor, this dread disease was rampant in town, and Putnam wanted an immune advance party.

Colonel Learned and his select group of pox-exposed men marched off, removed the bars from the gates at the outer post, then gingerly picked their way down the road, which had been covered with sharp four-pronged twists of iron known as crow's feet. Thrown at random, these primitive antipersonnel devices always landed with a point facing up. The last departing British soldiers had scattered the metal thorns as they retreated toward the docks, hoping to prevent the Americans from

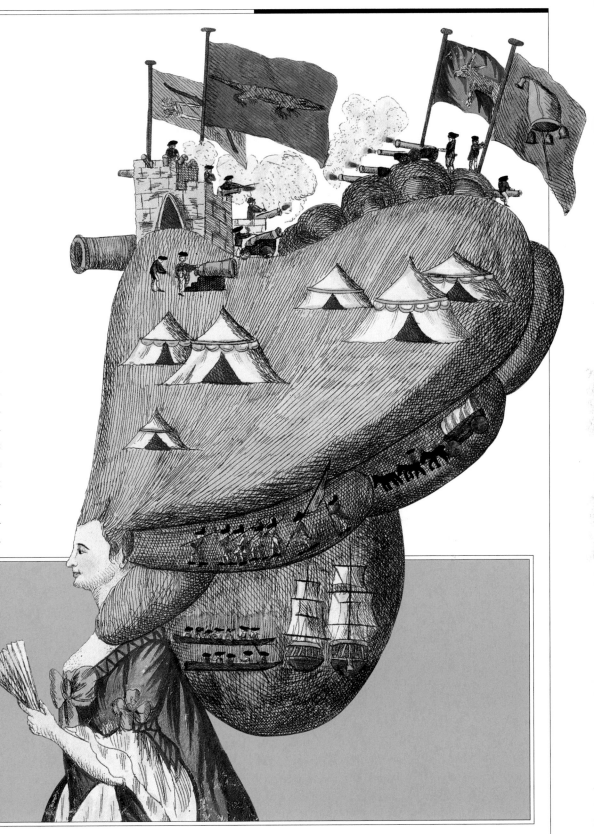

HEADING UP THE RETREAT

Like numerous other British cartoons of its era, this one is a double-barreled commentary on extravagant women's hairstyles and contemporary events—in this case the British evacuation of Boston on March 17, 1776. The top of the coiffure, an unlikely battlefield, supports smoke-belching cannon and flags bearing the images of an ass, a fool's cap, and bells. Farther down, some British regulars can be seen marching, others rowing, toward the waiting ships.

rushing en masse to the harbor and firing on the boats as they pulled away.

Once the Americans reached the town, they found that the reports of widespread smallpox were in error, although there were more than a dozen infected homes. Many of the houses had been abandoned, as more than 1,000 Loyalists decamped in fear. These desperate families had crowded themselves and as much as they could carry aboard the British vessels. Rich and poor jammed together cheek by jowl. One well-to-do Tory, Benjamin Hallowell, shared a cabin with 36 others, all camped out upon the floor. At least one man chose suicide. The British left behind a sad and threadbare, but not a plundered, town. They had ripped pews out of some churches to create indoor riding rings. They

the Israelites. On the following Monday morning, Washington made his way to Boston and inspected the scene. Men under suspicion of taking the British side flocked to the general for protection. Washington was polite, but chilly. He ordered that troops be kept out of town and that no one plunder the Tory homes. But the property of suspect families, he said, should be seized, to be disposed of by the local legislature. So scrupulously did the general enforce his own rule that he returned a beautiful horse given him by a friend, after discovering it had been taken from an abandoned Tory stable.

The British left Boston on March 17, but they did not go far. The heavily laden ships remained anchored in Nantasket road, a shipping lane in Boston's outer harbor beyond the reach of American

"We... at last have beat them, in a shameful and precipitate manner out of a place the strongest by nature on this continent."

GEORGE WASHINGTON, BOSTON, MARCH 1776

dumped salt and molasses in the streets to prevent the Americans from acquiring these valuable stores. Some buildings had been torn apart for firewood. General Howe's coach had been run off a dock and sunk in the harbor.

But much was spared. More than 40 heavy cannon had been abandoned on shore. Although their touchholes had been "spiked" against reuse, most were salvageable. Reflecting the sense of honor that prevailed in war during that era, British officers had refrained from looting the home of John Hancock—president of the Continental Congress and Britain's archenemy. Even the Hancock family portraits still hung unmolested on the walls.

Washington remained all Sunday at his headquarters in Cambridge, choosing to avoid a victor's swaggering march through Boston. He astutely let the local Massachusetts officers lead the way. Instead, Washington went to church, where he heard the Reverend Abiel Leonard give a sermon based on a passage in the Bible in which the Egyptians, mired in the muddy floor of a divided Red Sea, fled from

guns. There General Howe sat, surrounded by his magnificent fleet, for 10 days. His continuing indecision puzzled Washington. After looking over Boston's defenses, he judged the town to be "almost impregnable, every avenue fortified." As for Howe's prolonged wait in Nantasket road, Washington wrote that "it surpasses my comprehension."

Washington was not alone in questioning Howe's judgment. Some of Howe's own countrymen later challenged his handling of the war in Massachusetts. Like many of the king's officers, Howe wielded political as well as military authority. He sat in the House of Commons as a member of the Whig party, which opposed the government's stiff treatment of the colonies. In fact, this tall, elegant 46-year-old had a long and friendly involvement in American affairs, as had his two older brothers.

The eldest Howe, George Augustus, had died in an assault against the French at Fort Ticonderoga in 1758. The second brother, Richard, became an admiral, directing a British naval force sent in 1776

against the Americans. The youngest, William—the commander at Boston—joined Richard in a curious double assignment in which they were to serve simultaneously as military chiefs and agents of a peace commission. Their ambiguous assignment: to offer pardon to the rebels they were trying to destroy. Little wonder that William sometimes appeared to hesitate in battle. On more than one occasion, ready to strike a fatal blow, he had faltered, and offered terms of truce. Whatever the reasons for his puzzling behavior, William Howe would come to be known at home as the general who "lost an empire."

Howe had never intended to stay in Boston; it had always been his plan to pull out and regroup for a concentrated attack farther south. And his reasons for tarrying in the Nantasket road were born of practical necessity, not indecision. In their haste to get out from under the American guns, the British had thrown stores and equipment into their warships in a jumble, and they could not venture out upon the open sea until their cargo was secured. The troops also had to take aboard drinking water to last on the coming sea voyage. All this took time.

On the afternoon of March 27, in pleasant weather with a steady breeze coming from the north-northwest, a messenger rushed in to General Washington bearing news from Dorchester Heights. The Americans had sighted the British flagship *Fowey* giving a signal before noon, and the entire fleet had lifted canvas at 3 p.m., heading out to sea. Washington's immediate reaction, as he later wrote to his friend Joseph Reed, was that "General Howe has a grand maneuver in view or has made an inglorious retreat." It was possible, Washington feared, that Howe might be heading directly for New York, the control point for "communication between the

Seen here in a 1777 portrait, General Sir William Howe replaced General Thomas Gage as commander in chief of the British forces in America following the significant but costly British victory at the Battle of Bunker Hill in June 1775. Despite mixed feelings about the war, Howe was a force to be reckoned with: His successes included the captures of both New York and Philadelphia. But his preference for merrymaking over warmaking won out in the end, and in 1778 he resigned.

Northern and Southern Colonies." Washington believed it was "absolutely and indispensably necessary for the whole of this army" to march south as fast as possible and defend the entry to the Hudson River. He had already dispatched a brigade of foot soldiers to New York against this possibility.

Although the siege of Boston ended in victory by default, the British departure was at least a taste of triumph—of which Washington may have imbibed too deeply. In a letter to his brother Jack, he crowed that "no man perhaps since the first institution of armies ever commanded one under more difficult circumstances than I have done." Despite a lack of powder, he wrote, "We have disbanded one army and recruited another within musket shot of two and twenty regiments, the flower of the British army, when our strength have been little if any superior to theirs; and at last have beat them, in a shameful and precipitate manner, out of a place the strongest by nature on this continent."

But America's commander in chief also found the Boston victory bittersweet. He had longed for a direct contest and now regretted that his forces had not had a chance to prove themselves in open battle. He confessed to his brother that "I can scarce forbear lamenting the disappointment, unless the dispute is drawing to an accommodation, and the Sword going to be Sheathed."

The British sword was not put away on March 17, 1776, and Washington's foreboding had indeed been correct about where the war would resume: General Howe planned to strike at New York and split the colonies in two. But before this grand strategy was attempted, Howe's fleet made a detour to Halifax, Nova Scotia, where he disembarked the refugee Tory families from Boston and refitted his troops.

At this juncture the British government summoned to New York General Henry Clinton, who had unsuccessfully attacked Charleston, South Carolina. And it dispatched a naval group under Admiral Lord Howe, William's older brother Richard, to join with Clinton and General Howe in a massive invasion of New York.

While the British made these preparations, Washington hastened south from Boston with his wife and belongings—taking along a featherbed, bolster, pillows, bed curtains, camp stools, glasses, crockery, and a bookcase. On April 13, 1776, less than a month after the British evacuation, Washington was settled in his New York headquarters. General Charles Lee had already reconnoitered the city, reporting that it would be very difficult to defend. Surrounded on all sides by water, New York was particularly vulnerable to naval attack—and Britain's strength was her navy. Lee argued that New York was still worth defending, however, mainly because it could be made "a most advantageous field of battle, so advantageous, indeed, that if our people behave with common spirit, it might cost the enemy many thousands of men to get possession of it." To this end, Lee had marked out many strongpoints in the landscape that he believed should be fortified.

When he arrived, Washington inherited this strategy. Lee had departed to take charge of the army's newly created southern command. And whatever his doubts may have been, Washington realized abandoning a city as important as New York without a fight might have a catastrophic impact on the army's morale. An immediate retreat would certainly outrage the New York revolutionists and might erode the colonists' sense of common purpose. On Washington's orders the army occupied itself for weeks building Lee's designated strongholds—completing 13 within the city.

Meanwhile, Washington sought to persuade the congress that the army needed to recruit better soldiers and keep them for longer terms. He struggled against the heavily pro-Tory sentiment of the New Yorkers, even suppressing a plot against his life. And he tried to stiffen the colonists' resistance to the blandishments of the enemy. Knowing that Howe's invading force could not move without a source of fresh supplies, Washington tried to stop

the local farmers from trading with British ships. In this he was not successful.

All speculation about the defense of the city ended on June 29, 1776, for on that day the British arrived from Canada. An American rifleman named McCurtin recorded the moment in his journal: "I was upstairs in an outhouse. I spied, as I peeped out the bay, something resembling a wood of pine trees trimmed. I declare at my noticing this, I could not believe my eyes. In about ten minutes the whole bay was as full of shipping as ever it could be." General William Howe had sailed in from Halifax. Thirteen days later his brother, Admiral Howe, swept in from England with more ships and men, welcomed by a volley of gun salutes. Almost immediately, five ships broke away from the main pack—the 40-gun

After the public readings of the newly adopted Declaration of Independence in seaboard cities on July 9, 1776, many citizens celebrated by destroying reminders of the now-despised monarchy. As shown above, a jubilant but angry mob in Bowling Green, near Manhattan's tip, demonstrated popular feelings by pulling down a lead statue of King George III. Later, the statue's 4,000 pounds of lead were melted down and fashioned into 42,228 musket balls for the Continental army.

Phoenix and the 20-gun *Rose,* along with three smaller craft—and sailed up the Hudson. When they reached the city, at that time a small town at the lower tip of Manhattan Island, they fired at the houses. Cannonballs ricocheted down the streets, and families fled in terror. Washington wrote, "The shrieks and cries of these poor creatures running every way with their children was truly distressing." He was especially upset that the sight had shaken the nerves of his "young and inexperienced soldiery."

Although the five ships sailed aggressively up the river taking or sinking all vessels they met, they stopped at a wide area known as the Tappan Zee and set anchor. American militia chased through the trees on shore, discouraging the British from attempting a landing. But the Howes had not planned to make a hasty attack in any case; they were preparing for the next battle with a great deal of care, as was their custom.

After establishing a main camp on Staten Island, the Howes paused. Ever hopeful that the colonists would see the folly of their ways, the British sent a truce proposal in a letter marked for "George Washington, Esq." The letter was rejected, on the grounds that it had not been properly addressed: It failed to recognize the American general's correct rank. Compromising, the British sent a second emissary, who verbally acknowledged Washington's rank but carried a letter that did not. Washington did speak with the British envoy, however, saying that he understood the Howes had authority only to grant pardons, and objected, as he wrote later, that "those who had committed no fault wanted no pardon; that we were only defending what we deemed our indisputable right." The talks ended.

British ships continued to arrive during the hot summer months. By late August the Howe brothers had under their command more than 32,000 troops, more than 70 ships, hundreds of transport boats, and a vast hoard of supplies. At last, on August 21, the British started landing troops at the southwestern end of Long Island, at Gravesend Bay. Washington deployed his own army farther north, on a rocky bluff called Brooklyn Heights. But the Americans made one serious mistake—they left the pass at Jamaica Road, one of the key routes to Brooklyn, essentially unguarded. A large British contingent under General Clinton quickly slipped through the pass and maneuvered around the American flank, forcing Washington's men to retreat through the swamps in disarray, with heavy casualties.

Had Howe continued to press forward, according to his critics, he might have captured most of the Revolutionary army. But he paused, as he had done before, and set up camp in front of Brooklyn Heights in preparation for what might turn out to be a long siege. On the night of August 29, however, Washington orchestrated a masterful escape. Leaving campfires lit and ordering the men to

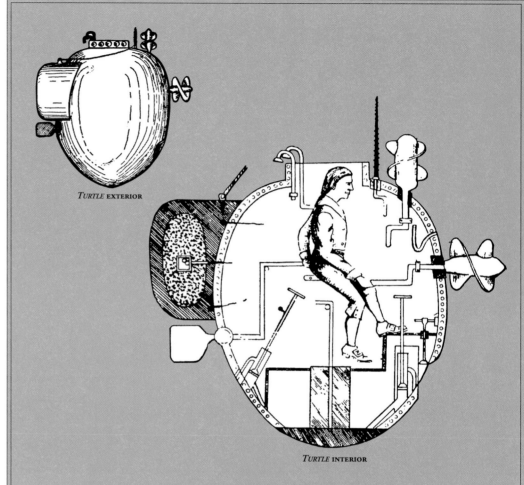

TURTLE EXTERIOR

TURTLE INTERIOR

THE WORLD'S FIRST COMBAT SUBMARINE

It was after midnight on September 6, 1776, when a rowboat towed the *Turtle,* a seven-and-one-half-foot-high submarine, into New York harbor. Its mission was to attach a bomb to HMS *Eagle,* Admiral Richard Howe's 64-gun flagship.

In order to approach the *Eagle,* the submarine's pilot, army sergeant Ezra Lee, steered with one hand and cranked a propeller with his other hand. Once Lee reached his target he submerged by the use of a foot pump that let water into the bottom of the vessel. With only the glow of phosphorescence on the compass to guide him in the inky darkness, Lee maneuvered underneath the *Eagle.* He failed on his first attempt to attach the 150-pound keg of gunpowder (located above the rudder) to the *Eagle* with an auger. As he moved to another position the *Turtle* slipped out from under the *Eagle* and, Lee reported, shot to the surface "with great velocity." Lee submerged and headed back to shore, but his activity had attracted the attention of a British patrol, which pursued him in a rowboat. Lee released the keg and activated a timing device. When the bomb exploded, the surprised British cut off their pursuit and the *Turtle* returned to safety.

maintain strict silence, he brought in small boats from along the length of the river and from as far away as New Jersey. In the dark they ferried his men across to Manhattan. When the fog lifted next morning, the British discovered that the entire enemy army had slipped away.

For Washington—his army tattered and "almost broke down," he told the congress—defending New York City had suddenly become a very risky proposition. He suggested burning it instead, a sure way to keep its riches out of British hands. "I am obliged to confess my want of confidence in the generality of the troops," Washington explained. "Til of late, I had no doubt in my own mind of defending this place, nor should I have yet, if the men would do their duty. But this I despair of." The congress declined to permit the drastic step the commander in chief recommended.

As the armies regrouped, the British once again made an offer of peace. Negotiations began at the highest level, with a delegation headed by Benjamin Franklin representing America and the two Howe brothers representing Britain. Like earlier peace talks, this meeting failed. But the two-week respite from battle gave Washington a chance to arrange his forces in what he considered the best disposition for defending Manhattan. He stationed 5,000 troops in the city itself, at the island's southern tip; another 5,000 were spread out in the broken farmland north of the city; and Washington took the remaining 9,000 north with him to a cliff at Harlem Heights at the top of the island.

For two weeks General Howe slowly tightened the noose around the Americans on Manhattan Island, waiting for the right moment to move. Then he struck. During the night of September 14 and the following morning, two groups of British warships moved northward—three sailing up the Hudson River on the island's west side, and another five gliding along the eastern shore. They moved under cover of darkness, arriving at their destinations in the predawn hours of Sunday, September 15. The

British detachment in the Hudson did not attempt a landing, which the rugged shoreline made difficult in any case. The ships stopped at the island's midpoint, beyond the reach of American guns. Their aim was to prevent the rebels from using the river to move supplies from the city at Manhattan's tip to the army in the uplands. But over on Manhattan's east side, the British were to see more action, for Howe had ordered the men under General Clinton to make an amphibious assault at an inlet known as Kip's Bay. This curve in Manhattan's eastern shore provided the sheltered area required by Howe's plan.

Washington was braced for a blow, though he had no inkling of where along Manhattan's long shoreline it would come. The first to see the British face to face, in fact, were some of the greenest soldiers in Washington's young army. The troops rested, according to one 16-year-old private, "quite unmolested" that Saturday night before the British landed. Once, as the American sentries called out their half-hourly "All is well," a British voice answered from the ships, "We will alter your tune before tomorrow night."

The night soon gave way to dawn, the air muggy and thick. As the light rose that Sunday morning, September 15, the men on shore could make out through the haze several large warships anchored bow to stern, stretching in a line 1,100 yards long, the cannon facing the Americans. There in the river just a musket shot away stood HMS *Carysfort, Orpheus, Phoenix, Roebuck,* and *Rose.* The crews on board ship were busy. As the sun climbed higher, flat-bottomed boats carrying soldiers emerged from a creek on Long Island. The British had augmented the numbers of their own redcoats with mercenaries—Hessian grenadiers in blue uniforms, and jaegers, or light infantry, in green. Watching this landing party as it formed, rank upon rank, bobbing on the tide, one soldier imagined "a large clover field in full bloom."

The British prepared all morning for the attack, marshaling the troops from dawn until 11 a.m., withholding their fire all the while. Remarkably, no officer among the Americans seems to have sent word to Washington in his headquarters on Harlem Heights, miles to the north, that a major battle was about to begin. Instead, officers at Kip's Bay under Major General Joseph Spencer were scouting out the enemy's probable landing spots, leading some men along shore to the left, others to the right, hoping to intercept the British. All told, there were three regiments of Connecticut militia and one regiment of conscripts at Kip's Bay proper, all under Colonel William Douglas. In the rear they were supported by smaller brigades of regular Connecticut Continentals and Massachusetts militia. Farther south were additional regiments of militia, and about five miles to the north, a group of reserves under Thomas Mifflin.

At 11:00, a sheet of fire ripped along the line of British frigates, which soon became engulfed in smoke. The guns roared at a deafening volume for an hour or more—"such a peal of thunder," recalled one infantryman, "that I thought my head would go with the sound." The men in the front lines were pinned down in their trenches; behind them, the support troops hung back at least a half-mile from the river to be able to stay clear of the fire zone. The redcoats and Hessians advanced across the water, hidden in the pall of smoke from the black powder and protected by the intense rain of shells and grapeshot from the ships' cannon. A British sailor aboard the *Orpheus* estimated that his crew alone expended more than 5,300 pounds of gunpowder. The Americans continued to lie low, until, seeing they would soon be overwhelmed, their officers ordered them to leave the lines.

The Connecticut militia scampered westward across an open meadow that made a green V, coming to a point at Kip's Bay. In their haste to escape they left behind their packs and equipment. But the young volunteers stopped in flight at a farmhouse long enough to ask for a bottle of rum, from which each took a drink as they headed for the main road. Behind them, at the beach of Kip's Bay, enemy boats were landing, one after another, and soldiers jostled their way along the shore to form orderly ranks for the next stage of assault. The Americans had not fired a single shot at the advancing redcoats and Hessians, who quickly overran the trenches. The British light infantry, Howe's well-trained strike force, held the center, with redcoat grenadiers advancing on the right and Hessians on the left.

Washington, in his command post on Harlem Heights, heard the rumble of "a most severe and heavy cannonade" down toward the East River, turned his horse, and galloped to the south. With his aides, he approached Kip's Bay, arriving a short distance from shore to find his troops in utter confusion. He saw that the forward lines at the bay had been abandoned, the men running in all directions along the road. Washington pulled his horse athwart their path, and his officers did likewise, in an attempt to block the frenzied retreat. But it was too late. The giddy panic that convulsed the American ranks could not be overcome. Although the British were outnumbered at the start, the inexperienced Americans were awestruck by the enemy's professional demeanor. As one soldier put it, "the demons of fear and disorder seemed to take full possession of all and everything on that day." The terror increased when some of the men saw the Hessians—who had been told by their commanders that Americans took no prisoners—bayonet some of their fellow volunteers, even as they raised their hands in surrender.

Two local American officers in charge of the support troops, Colonel John Fellows and Brigadier General Samuel Parsons, tried to corral their men into orderly positions, commanding them to face the enemy squarely. Washington, coming up among them in a deepening rage, bellowed, "Take the wall!" gesturing toward a potential line of defense. "Take the cornfield!" he shouted. The soldiers scattered in search of shelter, then watched silently as a group of 60 or 70 redcoats marched in neat ranks over a rise in the road. In a moment the Americans began to flee, scattering just as they had earlier that morning, racing along inland roads that led west and north. They simply dropped their packs, muskets, and supplies, and ran. Washington lashed at them with his riding crop as they passed.

The British continued their advance up the road, as Washington sat in his saddle, glaring at them. Seeing the lone general, defiant and unmoving in the crossroads, the British began to fear they were walking into an ambush. They slowed their pace. At this point, one of Washington's aides came rushing up, tugged at the bridle of Washington's horse, and led the commander to an unwilling retreat.

When Washington was safely back in headquarters—the former Morris mansion in Harlem—he vented his rage, calling the behavior of the men "disgraceful and dastardly." He later wrote to his brother Jack that he regretted "the dependence which the Congress has placed upon the militia." Relying on these unskilled volunteers, Washington thought, "has already greatly injured and I fear will totally ruin our cause." But a chaplain among the Connecticut men, Benjamin Trumbull, believed the failure that day should be blamed as much on the officers as on the men. Although the troops had been called cowards, he wrote in his diary, "the fault was principally in the general officers in not disposing of things so as to give the men a rational prospect of defense and a safe retreat should they engage the enemy." Nor did Trumbull think the hasty retreat had been a mistake, for it seemed "probable that many lives were saved."

Thanks to General Howe's cautious orders, the British troops under Clinton near Kip's Bay had paused for reinforcements most of the afternoon and did not immediately advance west or south to close the noose on New York City. They waited until evening. During this delay, most of the 4,000 American troops in southern Manhattan retreated northward, filtering past the British lines along the scrubby western side of the island. Some hid until dark, stealing across the Hudson River in small

Joseph Reed, close friend and trusted adviser to George Washington, was serving as president of the Second Provincial Congress of Pennsylvania when Washington asked him to be his military secretary in 1775. A year later Reed would be named Washington's adjutant general.

boats. Although they left the cannon behind, most of the men escaped.

Before dawn next morning—on Monday, September 16—Washington dispatched a small party of about 150 men under Lieutenant Colonel Thomas Knowlton of Connecticut to reconnoiter the area around the defenses on Harlem Heights. He wanted to find out how close the redcoats had crept and whether they were now on the move again. Then the general sat dutifully at his desk to write to the congress of the sad news. Explaining that his men now held the advantage of high ground, Washington wrote, "I should hope the enemy would meet with a defeat in the case of an attack," but only, he added, "if the generality of our troops would behave with tolerable resolution." He lamented that recent experience, "to my extreme affliction, has convinced me that this is rather to be wished for than expected. However, I trust that there are many who will act like men and show themselves worthy of the blessings of freedom." No sooner had the general finished writing these words than a messenger arrived with news from the scouts: They had bumped into the enemy.

Knowlton's scouts—a select group of daring rangers—had ventured out at morning's first light. They had crept south, marching down from the bluff at Harlem, crossing an open area running east-west across the island known as the Hollow Way, and entered a woods on the south side. It was some distance farther south, in the fields of a farmer named Nicholas Jones, that British sentries spotted the Americans and began to fire at them. The rebels returned the challenge and appeared to be holding their own. The infantrymen battled for approximately two hours along a major route running north and south, called the Bloomingdale road. Apprised of the skirmish, Washington climbed on his horse and rode to an American forward post. There he encountered his friend, Adjutant General Joseph Reed, returning from the front on horseback, excited and encouraged by what he had seen. He told Washington that, although the Americans had been outnumbered by the British perhaps two to one, they were fighting well and deserved help from reinforcements.

As Washington was considering Reed's request, he and Reed could see a group of Americans burst out of the wooded area at the far side of the Hollow Way, pursued by British soldiers. The redcoats paused at the crest of the hill, an area known as Claremont. The enemy bugler raised his horn and played an odd tune—more of an insult than a battle call. Washington and Reed, seasoned fox hunters, flushed with anger when they recognized the signal. It was the tune that marked the end of the hunt after the fox has run to hide in its hole. Coming after two major retreats in the face of the British army, the taunt stung Reed sharply. He later told his wife that "I never felt such a sensation before. It seemed to crown our disgrace."

Reed argued that Washington should let the army redeem its honor; he pleaded for reinforcements. Perhaps because Washington, too, felt the insult of the fox-hunting call, he agreed to send more troops into the skirmish. At his command, Knowlton's rangers were joined by three companies of Virginia riflemen under Major Andrew Leitch. Their orders were to slip along the back side of the British "fox hunters" under cover of some trees at the eastern edge of the Hollow Way, then move west toward the Hudson River, closing off the British rear and preventing the redcoats from making a retreat. Meanwhile, Washington sent another group of volunteers from Brigadier General John Nixon's brigade to make a frontal attack on the same enemy party, keeping them occupied.

The plan seemed to work well at first. Nixon's men pushed forward into the Hollow Way, and the redcoats took the bait. They clambered down the opposing bluff on Vandewater's farm and spread along the low ground behind fences and bushes. But the Americans on the flanking march under Knowlton then made a serious mistake—and broke

the fragile spell. Instead of completing the maneuver, some of the Virginia riflemen began firing on the British as soon as they realized they had the enemy at a disadvantage. In consequence, the well-trained redcoats wheeled on Knowlton's men and engaged in a general fight.

There followed a rare scene: an open field battle between American and British troops, with neither side giving way. Shortly after the exchange began, two of the American leaders fell—first Leitch, hit by three musket balls, then Knowlton, lethally wounded. These two were carried off the battlefield, but their men continued fighting. Washington committed more troops to the fight, including the men who had run dishonorably the day before at Kip's Bay, bringing the total number of Americans engaged to 1,800. This time, the Connecticut militia fought well. The British began to come under unexpected pressure and called in reinforcements of their own from the south. The redcoats gradually began to retreat from the open field to the wooded slopes, and from there they continued backing up until they came to a large buckwheat field on Vandewater's farm.

The fight continued in the buckwheat field for another hour or so, as the Americans reveled in a new experience—a British retreat. Soon, however, the battle came within range of two forces that were destined to bring it to a close: the main body of the British army and enemy guns aboard ships in the Hudson. When the action came near Stryker's Bay, not far from the spot where the skirmish had begun that morning, the British began firing randomly into the island. Although the Americans suffered little from this attack, it was an escalation they could not match, and in a short time they received orders to withdraw.

To Americans all too accustomed to defeat, the fight felt something like a victory. For the first time, they had challenged the British in a conventional skirmish, and the redcoats had been forced to yield ground to them—at least for a time. Washington

had hoped for more. The British losses, he announced to the men in his general orders, referring to the botched attempt to trap the British at Vandewater's farm, "would undoubtedly have been much greater if the orders of the Commander-in-Chief had not in some instances been contradicted by inferior officers." Washington spelled it out: His juniors "ought not to presume to direct" the battle, and no one should depart from Washington's orders without explicit counter orders from authorized deputies, whose names he then listed.

For the British officers, the battle of Harlem Heights was an embarrassment, but not much of one. Captain Frederick MacKenzie of the Royal Welsh Fusiliers dismissed it in his diary as "an unfortunate business," noting, however, that it had caused their commander "a good deal of concern." General Clinton later interpreted it as resulting from an error by the light infantry, which had rushed too far ahead of the main army's support. It was this "ungovernable impetuosity," Clinton felt, that "drew us into this scrape."

Washington, in his official report to the congress, expressed hope that the affair "will be attended with many salutary consequences, as it seems to have greatly inspirited the whole of our troops."

Illuminated by flames, New Yorkers and British soldiers scramble to rescue valuables from buildings torched by anonymous arsonists on September 20 and 21, 1776. Threats of patriot arson were rampant following the British occupation of New York, although American authorities had urged citizens not to damage their city.

Joseph Reed made the same point more enthusiastically—and perhaps reflected the mood of the men more aptly—in a letter to his wife: "You can hardly conceive the change it has made in our Army. The men have recovered their spirits and feel a confidence which before they had quite lost."

The sweet taste of victory soon soured, however. In the days following the battle of Harlem Heights, Washington's army seemed to fall apart beneath him. Members of the volunteer militia, never reliable, began to vanish from Manhattan like a mist at sunrise. One Connecticut regiment, for example, dwindled in a matter of days to just 30 fighting men, another to 14. The chronic shortage of equipment—particularly of tents, horse teams, and wagons—grew so severe that Washington dismissed his quartermaster, Stephen Moylan, and replaced him with Thomas Mifflin. The British, meanwhile, took over scores of cannon and all the stocks that had been abandoned in southern Manhattan.

Although Washington—in keeping with his instructions from the congress—refrained from destroying the warehouses, other rebels took matters into their own hands. Arsonists spread fire through the city, which raged out of control for 24 hours on September 20 and 21, burning nearly a quarter of the buildings. To maintain discipline Washington issued stern orders against looting and threatened harsh penalties for soldiers caught deserting the army. Those who remained steadfast on Harlem Heights were put to work fortifying the ramparts.

On October 9 the lull ended. Three British battleships made their way up the Hudson, avoiding injury from cannon fire along the shore, and came to rest off Tarrytown. Anchored there, they blocked any attempt to use boats to supply the American army from the north. Three days later Howe sent out a large force of 5,000 men under General Clinton aboard transport boats from Kip's Bay. Making their way in dense fog, they first came ashore at Throgs Neck, a point nine miles northeast of Harlem, linked to the mainland by a bridge. Their goal was to march around the flank of Washington's fort at Harlem Heights and cut it off from communication by land. Washington's men bought some time by burning the bridge at Throgs Neck, forcing Clinton to camp there for four days, awaiting further orders.

Now it became clear to almost all the officers that Washington's army could not hold the island of Manhattan, much less recover New York. Washington called a gloomy council of war among his generals on October 16. All but one agreed it was necessary to retreat, so they quickly began the long-postponed withdrawal. Behind them, on October 18, Clinton's force made a second landing several miles farther north at Pell's Point. Overcoming fierce resistance by a group of Massachusetts men, the British and Hessian troops established a secure beachhead. This marked the end of the American defense. Washington retreated to the north, accompanied by militia, on October 21, in one of a series of maneuvers that led the British on a chase through the hills and valleys of New York before the old fox went to ground in White Plains on October 23. Five days later the British defeated him in battle there, forcing him to resume his retreat. By December 8 he and his army had crossed the Delaware into Pennsylvania.

From there the winter of 1776-1777 looked like a long, despairing one for George Washington. Reflecting on the army's losses, Washington at this low moment in his career began to doubt whether he should even continue as commander in chief. Even before he had abandoned Harlem Heights, he had poured out his heart in a letter to his cousin Lund Washington, manager of the estate at Mount Vernon: "If I were to wish the bitterest curse to an enemy on this side of the grave, I should put him in my stead with my feelings; and yet I do not know what plan of conduct to pursue. I see the impossibility of serving with reputation, or doing any essential service to the cause by continuing in command, and yet I am told that if I quit the command, inevitable ruin will follow from the distraction that will ensue. In confidence, I tell you that I never was in such an unhappy, divided state since I was born." And worse was yet to come. ◆

DECLARING INDEPENDENCE

"When in the course of human events it becomes necessary for one people to dissolve the political bands which have connected them with another . . ."

"The revolution was in the minds of the people," according to John Adams, "and this was effected from 1760 to 1775, in the course of fifteen years, before a drop of blood was shed at Lexington." During these years Americans had increasingly challenged British authority, which they believed infringed upon their rights as British subjects—especially when it came to taxation. They based their claims on the writings of ancient and modern European thinkers, especially the philosopher John Locke, and on British constitutional law, including the doctrine that taxes could not be levied without the people's consent. "We claim nothing but the liberty and privileges of Englishmen," wrote the Virginian George Mason, "in the same degree as if we had still continued among our brethren in Great Britain."

Americans wanted reform, not independence. "There are not five men of sense in America who would accept of independence if it were offered," Mason wrote in 1770. "We know our circumstances too well; we know that our own happiness, our very being, depend upon our being connected with our Mother Country."

But the king and the Parliament did not agree with the Americans, and they continued to impose taxes. In September 1774 King George III wrote: "The dye is now cast, the Colonies must either submit or triumph . . . there is no inclination for the present to lay fresh taxes on them, but I am clear there must always be one tax to keep up the right."

The colonies did not submit but instead continued their opposition to the taxes, urged on by the turn of events and by radicals such as John Adams—while at the same time conservatives like John Dickinson tried to slow the process. "America is a great, unwieldy body," John Adams wrote. "Its progress must be slow. Like a coach and six, the swiftest horses must be slackened, and the slowest quickened, that all may keep an even pace."

The conservative and radical delegates to the First Continental Congress labored together in Philadelphia, enduring heat and flies in the summer, cold in the winter, illness and separation from their families, personal feuds, and the knowledge that they were considered traitors by the Crown. In Philadelphia and throughout the land citizens debated the process as the 13 colonies moved toward the day when the bells in Philadelphia would proclaim the United States' independence from Great Britain.

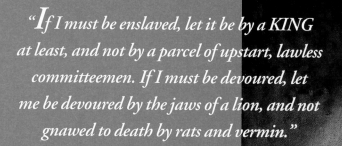

"If I must be enslaved, let it be by a KING at least, and not by a parcel of upstart, lawless committeemen. If I must be devoured, let me be devoured by the jaws of a lion, and not gnawed to death by rats and vermin."

A War of Words

Americans agreed on no taxation without representation, but actions by the congress were not unanimously accepted. One persuasive opponent, the Anglican minister Samuel Seabury, argued that it had acted irresponsibly and tyrannically, with no legal authority, and that "Virginia and Massachusetts madmen . . . have made laws for the province of *New York,* and have rendered our Assembly *useless.*" The congress, he said, had made "the breach with the parent state a thousand times more irreparable than it was before."

Conservative members, such as John Dickinson of Pennsylvania, tried to mend the breach. They backed the American cause but wanted to remain part of the British Empire. The king, they believed, could set matters right by dismissing the "Villains and Ideots"—as Dickinson put it—who were his ministers. However, after Lexington it was harder to trust the king. "Will the distinctions between the prince and his ministers," wrote Dickinson, "between the people and their representatives, wipe out the stain of blood?" Dickinson made one last attempt at reconciliation in July 1775 when he wrote the congress's final appeal to the king, which became known as the Olive Branch Petition.

FREE THOUGHTS,
ON
The PROCEEDINGS of
THE
CONTINENTAL CONGRESS,
Held at PHILADELPHIA, Sept. 5, 1774:
WHEREIN
Their ERRORS are exhibited,
THEIR
REASONINGS CONFUTED,
AND
The fatal Tendency of their NON-IMPORTATION, NON-EXPORTATION, and NON-CONSUMPTION MEASURES, are laid open to the plainest UNDERSTANDINGS;
AND
The ONLY MEANS pointed out
For Preserving and Securing
Our present HAPPY CONSTITUTION:
IN
A LETTER
TO
THE FARMERS,
AND OTHER INHABITANTS OF
NORTH AMERICA
In General,
And to those of the Province of *New-York*
In Particular.

By a FARMER.

Hear me, for I WILL speak!

PRINTED IN THE YEAR M,DCC,LXXIV.

Samuel Seabury, the first American bishop of the Protestant Episcopal Church after the war, was rector of St. Peter's Church in Westchester County, New York. Following the adjournment of the First Continental Congress he penned three popular pamphlets under the pseudonym A. W. Farmer (A Westchester Farmer). His tracts so angered Seabury's more radical neighbors that the clergyman went into hiding after the conflicts at Lexington and Concord.

In the Olive Branch Petition, which was referred to by John Adams as a "measure of imbecility," Dickinson humbly requested that the king repeal statutes that distressed the colonies in order for them to show the "devotion becoming the most dutiful subjects and the most affectionate colonists." The king rejected the petition, saying that the colonists wanted "only to amuse by vague expressions of attachment to the Parent State and the strongest protestations of loyalty to me whilst they were preparing for a General Revolt."

To the **Kings** most excellent Majesty

Most gracious Sovereign,

We your Majesty's faithful Subjects of the colonies of New-hampshire, Massachusetts-bay, Rhode-island and Providence plantations, Connecticut, New-York, New Jersey, Pennsylvania, the counties of New Castle Kent & Sussex on Delaware, Maryland, Virginia, North-Carolina and South Carolina in behalf of ourselves and the inhabitants of these colonies, who have deputed us to represent them in general Congress, entreat your Majesty's gracious attention to this our humble petition.

The union between our Mother country and these colonies, and the energy of mild and just government, produced benefits so remarkably important and afforded such an assurance of their permanency and increase, that the wonder and envy of other nations were excited, while they beheld Great Britain rising to a power the most extraordinary the world had ever known.

Her rivals observing, that there was no probability of this happy connection being broken by civil dissentions, and apprehending its future effects if left any longer undisturbed, resolved to prevent her receiving such continual and formidable accessions of wealth and strength, by checking the growth

COMMON SENSE;

ADDRESSED TO THE

INHABITANTS

OF

AMERICA,

On the following interesting

SUBJECTS.

I. Of the Origin and Design of Government in general, with concise Remarks on the English Constitution.

II. Of Monarchy and Hereditary Succession.

III. Thoughts on the present State of American Affairs.

IV. Of the present Ability of America, with some miscellaneous Reflections.

Man knows no Master save creating HEAVEN,
Or those whom choice and common good ordain.
THOMSON.

PHILADELPHIA;
Printed, and Sold, by R. BELL, in Third-Street.
MDCCLXXVI.

"*The sun never shined on a cause of greater worth. 'Tis not the affair of a city, a county, a province, or a kingdom, but of a continent. . . . 'Tis not the concern of a day, a year, or an age; posterity are virtually involved in the contest, and will be more or less affected even to the end of time by the proceedings now. Now is the seedtime of continental union, faith, and honor.*"

In his 1776 pamphlet *Common Sense*, Thomas Paine argued with such force against monarchy that many colonists loyal to the king were turned toward independence. George Washington signed his copy *(above)*, praising its "sound doctrine and unanswerable reasoning."

"Resolved That these United Colonies are, and of right ought to be, free and independent States, that they are absolved from all allegiance to the British Crown, and that all political connection between them and the State of Great Britain is, and ought to be, totally dissolved."

A member of one of Virginia's foremost families, Richard Henry Lee became a leader of the radicals in the Continental Congress, insisting that the colonies should become an independent nation.

A COMMON SENSE RESOLUTION

Long before the general population decided for independence, an obscure firebrand journalist named Thomas Paine had made up his mind. "How a race of men came into the world so exalted above the rest and distinguished like some new species, is worth enquiring into," wrote Paine in *Common Sense,* published anonymously in January 1776. Hereditary succession to kingship was "an insult and an imposition on posterity," and

to Paine, "of more worth is one honest man to society, and in the sight of God, than all the crowned ruffians that ever lived."

Common Sense was not the only stimulus for independence. Parliament had just passed the Prohibitory Bill, which, suggested John Adams, "throws thirteen colonies out of the Royal Protection." And most Americans found abhorrent the king's decision to solve the colonial issue by using force—and

hiring German mercenaries to administer it.

On June 7, 1776, Virginia's Richard Henry Lee introduced a resolution in the congress calling for American independence. The vote was deferred, but only until July 1. Several colonies, Thomas Jefferson noted, "were not yet ripe for bidding adieu to British connections." But, he added, "they were fast ripening & in a short time would join in the general voice for America."

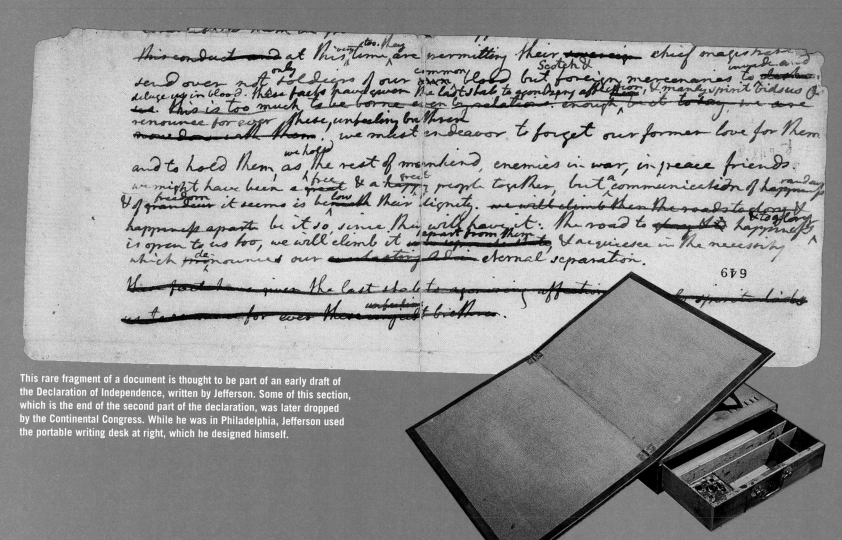

This rare fragment of a document is thought to be part of an early draft of the Declaration of Independence, written by Jefferson. Some of this section, which is the end of the second part of the declaration, was later dropped by the Continental Congress. While he was in Philadelphia, Jefferson used the portable writing desk at right, which he designed himself.

DRAFTING THE DECLARATION

On June 11, 1776, the Continental Congress, sensing that a vote for independence was inevitable, appointed a five-man committee to draw up a declaration. Thomas Jefferson, who had a reputation as an effective writer, was chosen to draft the document. The other members of the committee were John Adams, Benjamin Franklin, Robert Livingston, and Roger Sherman.

Jefferson wrote three parts to the declaration. The first part, the preamble, stated the principles upon which Americans believed their liberties were based. Echoing George Mason's recently completed *Virginia Declaration of Rights,* Jefferson boldly avowed that "all men are created equal, that they are endowed by their Creator with certain unalienable rights, that among those are life, liberty, and the pursuit of happiness."

In the declaration's second section Jefferson adapted his own *A Summary View of the Rights of British America* by listing 28 grievances against the king. "In every stage of these oppressions," he wrote, "we have petitioned for redress in the most humble terms." Jefferson concluded that like the rest of mankind, the British would be "enemies in war, in peace friends."

The concluding section of the Declaration of Independence renounced allegiance to the king, dissolved all political connections with Parliament, and declared the colonies to be free and independent states.

"*Reason first—You are a Virginian, and a Virginian ought to appear at the head of this business. Reason second—I am obnoxious, suspected, and unpopular. You are very much otherwise. Reason third—you can write ten times better than I can.*"

JOHN ADAMS TO THOMAS JEFFERSON

Jefferson sat at the swivel chair at right, which he adapted from a standard Windsor chair, when he wrote the declaration—completing his draft in less than 17 days.

*"**I** am well aware of the toil, and blood, and treasure, that it will cost us to maintain this declaration, and support and defend these States. Yet . . . I can see the rays of ravishing light and glory. I can see that the end is more than worth all the means, and that posterity will triumph in that day's transaction."*

THE VOTE FOR INDEPENDENCE

During early sessions of the congress, John Adams of Massachusetts, a fervent believer in independence, tried to appear restrained, lest he alarm his more moderate colleagues. But during the debate on Lee's resolution, which began on July 1, Adams earned the title Atlas of American Independence.

By the end of the day, South Carolina and Pennsylvania still opposed voting for independence. Delaware was split, and New York had not received authority to vote for the resolution. The vote was put off until the next day, at which time John Dickinson and Robert Morris absented themselves in order to allow Pennsylvania to vote for the resolution. South Carolina joined in for the sake of unanimity, and Caesar Rodney, who favored independence, rode through the night in a pouring rain and arrived in time to break Delaware's tie. (New York's delegates would not receive authority to vote for the resolution until July 15.) And so on July 2, 12 states approved the resolution declaring independence from Britain.

"He was the pillar of its support on the floor of Congress," wrote Thomas Jefferson of his friend and colleague John Adams *(above)*, "its ablest advocate and defender against the multifarious assaults it encountered."

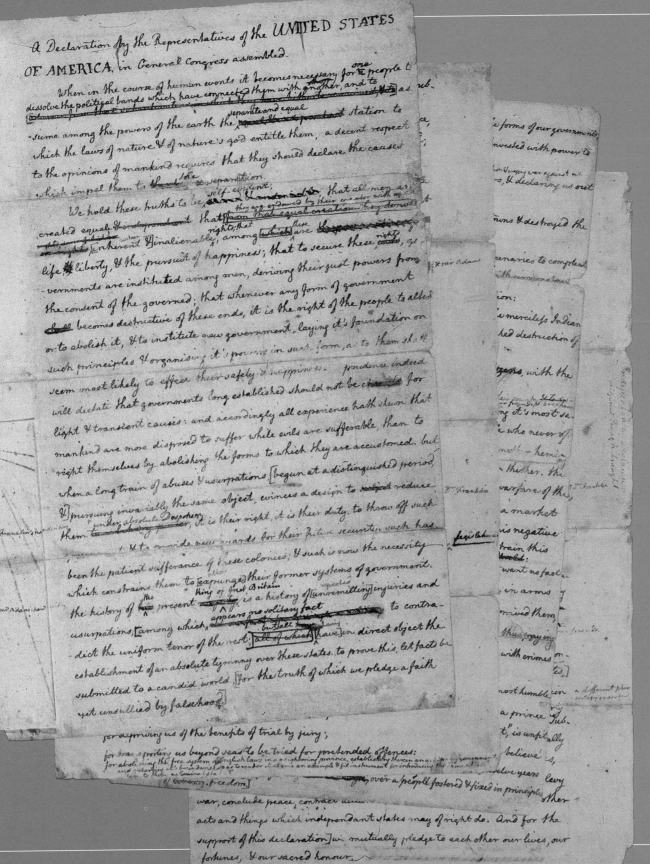

Bearing minor changes by John Adams and Benjamin Franklin, Thomas Jefferson's rough draft of the Declaration of Independence had been submitted to the congress on June 28. Since the vote for independence had not yet taken place, the declaration was temporarily set aside.

> *"It was intended to be an expression of the American mind, and to give to that expression the proper tone and spirit called for by the occasion."*
>
> THOMAS JEFFERSON TO
> RICHARD HENRY LEE, MAY 8, 1825

A UNANIMOUS DECLARATION

After the congress had voted for independence, deciding on what John Adams called "the greatest question . . . which ever was debated in America," it turned its attention to the declaration. Jefferson, who was not a public speaker, listened uneasily to the proceedings while Franklin tried to console him with droll stories. In deference to Georgia and South Carolina, and to New England's slave traders, the congress dropped Jefferson's charge that the king violated the human rights of Africans by "captivating & carrying them into slavery in another hemisphere, or to incur miserable death in their transportation thither." Congress also shortened several passages, dropped a reference to Scottish mercenaries, and incorporated Richard Henry Lee's resolution for independence.

And then, on a mild summer day—Jefferson had noted the temperature was 76 degrees at one o'clock—after two and one-half days of deliberation, the Declaration of Independence was adopted on July 4, 1776.

On July 2, 1776, with committee members Roger Sherman and Robert Livingston behind, Adams, Jefferson, and Franklin present the declaration to the president of the congress, John Hancock, and the secretary, Charles Thomson. John Adams assumed that the anniversary of independence would be celebrated on this day rather than on July 4, the day the declaration was approved.

INDEPENDENCE IS PROCLAIMED

"Time has been given for the whole people maturely to consider the great question of independence," wrote John Adams, "and to ripen their judgement, dissipate their fears, and allure their hopes, by discussing it in newspapers and pamphlets, by debating it in assemblies, conventions, committees of safety and inspection, in town and country meetings, as well as in private conversations, so that the whole people, in every colony of the thirteen, have now adopted it as their own act." The first public reading of the Declaration of Independence occurred on July 8, in Philadelphia. One critic noted that there were "very few respectable people" present, but John Adams was impressed by the parading military units and by the spontaneous joy displayed by the cheering crowd. On the following evening, George Washington, awaiting General William Howe's attack on New York, gathered his troops for a reading of the declaration.

Now the soldiers in the field, and the families at home, had an eloquent statement of what they were sacrificing and fighting for—for independence from Great Britain and for freedom of the individual and for the United States of America.

By August 2, a formal copy of the declaration *(opposite)* was ready to be signed. Using this silver inkstand, John Hancock, seen above in a painting by John Singleton Copley, wrote his name large enough that King George could read it without spectacles—so large, in fact, that "John Hancock" became slang for "signature."

"And for the support of this declaration, with a firm reliance on the protection of Divine Providence, we mutually pledge to each other our lives, our fortunes and our sacred honor."

CHAPTER 3

DEFEAT INTO VICTORY

"Come on, boys! If the day is long enough we'll have them all in hell before night."

MAJOR GENERAL BENEDICT ARNOLD, NEAR SARATOGA, NEW YORK, OCTOBER 1777

The sight of the American army scrabbling up the west bank of the Delaware River into Pennsylvania, early in December of 1776, was for one of their number—the once and future painter from Philadelphia, Charles Willson Peale— "the most hellish scene I ever beheld."

Peale was especially appalled by one soldier who waded through the mud toward him. The poor wretch "had lost all his clothes. He was in an old, dirty blanket jacket, his beard long, and his face so full of sores he could not clean it." But when the man called his name, Peale recognized the apparition's voice—it was his brother's.

Four months earlier this shattered force had been soundly defeated in the first pitched battle of the Revolutionary War, on Long Island. It had been beaten on Manhattan Island in September and hounded across New Jersey ever since by a confident, numerically superior British army.

At least one observer, however, discerned a kind of nobility in the American soldiers' agony, a 40-year-old journalist and recent enlistee named Thomas Paine. Earlier, his pamphlet *The Crisis,* a plain-spoken exposition of the American cause, had entered the scripture of the Revolution. "These are the times that try men's souls," Paine had written while the army was still at Newark. "The summer soldier and the sunshine patriot will, in this crisis, shrink from the service of his country; but he that stands it now, deserves the love and thanks of man and woman. What we obtain too cheap, we esteem too lightly; 'tis dearness only that gives every thing its value."

Another who watched, from the broad back of his white horse, remote and grim, was the army's commanding general. George Washington would write to his brother Jack that "the game is pretty near up," and would tell John Hancock, then president of the congress, to expect the loss of Philadelphia. "We were obliged to cross the Delaware," he wrote, "with less than 3,000 men fit for duty owing to the dissolution of our force by short enlistments, the enemy's numbers, from the best accounts, exceeding 10,000 and by some 12,000 men."

Yet it was neither the number nor the suffering of his men that seemed to bother him most, but their abysmal performance in battle. Nearly half his men were members of state militias, poorly trained, and disinclined to fight. When they had broken at the first roar of battle on Long Island, Washington's famous temper had exploded. "Good God!" he raged. "Are these the men with whom I am to defend America?" In addition to all his other difficul-

In this romanticized painting by John Trumbull, George Washington gestures toward the mortally wounded Colonel Johann Rall, commander of the Hessian troops at the Battle of Trenton. The Hessians scoffed at the Continental army and made scant effort to fortify Trenton against attack, thus helping Washington to achieve his first decisive victory of the war.

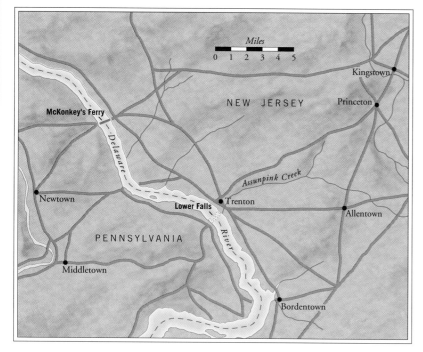

On Christmas Day in 1776, Washington's forces crossed the Delaware River at McKonkey's Ferry and marched on Trenton, where they defeated the Hessian mercenaries occupying the town. On January 3, 1777, the Continentals won a second victory at Princeton before moving into Pennsylvania. Its supply lines threatened, the British army withdrew into New York and eastern New Jersey.

ties, he was under a stern time limit. Congress had created the Continental army for a term of one year, and now fully half of the men were eagerly looking forward to December 31, just a few weeks away. On that terrible day, Washington believed, the triumphant British army would find the road wide open to Philadelphia—and to victory. America was about to lose its war of independence.

General Sir William Howe, the Englishman who had brought the rebels so low, was well known to Washington through American officers who had served the king in the French and Indian War. Howe was an experienced courtier with powerful friends in London. Built on a large frame, dark of complexion, he was introverted and suspicious. Howe had believed from the beginning that a strong show of English imperial force would quickly bring the American rebels to the negotiating table. But he was evidently in no hurry to strike the fatal blow.

Running ahead of the British force, Washington had commandeered every boat for 70 miles along the Delaware River. When Howe reached the river on December 8 and found the American army on the other side, he behaved predictably. Leaving the New Jersey troops under the command of Major General James Grant, he returned to his lavish winter quarters—and ardent mistress—in New York.

If Howe could afford to wait through the winter, Washington could not. He desperately needed to change the appearance of British invincibility and American collapse. But to do so successfully he had to have more men, especially the 5,000 who were still guarding the Hudson River highlands in New York. In fact, Washington had been trying to get those men to join him for a month, but their commander, General Charles Lee, did not consider himself to be under Washington's command.

Lee was a mercurial, aristocratic, and eccentric officer who had served the British army in the French and Indian War and in Europe. He stood second in seniority in the army but saw himself as the obvious candidate to replace the faltering Washington. Thus Lee chose to view Washington's urgent command not as an order but as a "recommendation."

Lee had expressed his views of Washington to the commander in chief's adjutant general and trusted friend, Joseph Reed. "I received your most obliging, flattering letter," Lee had written Reed about their commander, "[and] lament with you that fatal indecision of mind which in war is a much greater disqualification than stupidity, or even want of personal courage." When the letter had arrived at headquarters, Reed had been away, and Washington, anxious for news of Lee's whereabouts, had opened and read it.

Stunned, Washington had merely pressed his lips more firmly together and had sent the letter along to Reed, with a note apologizing for having opened and read it. Mortified, Reed had resigned, then retracted the resignation and, no doubt with considerable foreboding, returned to work. Neither then, nor for years to come, did Washington mention the betrayal.

Washington was equally polite, and as frosty, in ordering that Lee bring his men to New Jersey. Lee reluctantly complied, inching his men southward at a rate of about a mile a day. Then, on the night of December 12, Lee had wandered away from his camp at Morristown to spend a more comfortable night in a tavern three miles to the southwest. In the morning, a troop of English cavalry, sent to find Lee's army, found him instead, took him prisoner, and detained him at the command headquarters in Brunswick.

While the days ran implacably down to December 31 and the dissolution of the Continentals, and while Washington cast about with increasing desperation for a plan, his army began to grow. Some militia units arrived from Pennsylvania, and another 1,200 men came in from Albany. By December 20, Washington had 6,000 men, with more en route from Philadelphia and General John Sullivan hurrying Lee's men from Morristown.

Howe had left the Delaware's eastern bank in the hands of Hessians—German mercenaries from the state of Hesse. They occupied a 10-mile stretch of the Delaware shore from Trenton southeast to Bordentown and then around the 90-degree bend of the river southwest to Burlington, less than 20 miles northeast of Philadelphia. Colonel Johann Gottlieb Rall commanded the three infantry regiments—numbering, with artillery and dragoon detachments, about 1,400 men in all—quartered in the Trenton area. Rall was pugnacious, a heavy drinker, cruel in battle, and contemptuous of his enemies.

Trenton was a prosperous and well-established town, boasting not only 100 houses but a stone barracks, built during the French and Indian War, which was big enough for 450 men. Trenton's size was a consequence of its location—at the falls, or head of navigation, of the Delaware River, and at the junction of three roads from the north and one leading south across a bridge over Assunpink Creek. Although Rall enjoyed the town's abundant quarters, he paid little attention to its defenses, such was his contempt for American military

An Immigrant General

General Charles Lee, an experienced soldier and a liberal thinker, emigrated in 1773. Later joining the Continental army as the second-highest-ranking officer, he angled to replace Washington as commander in chief. This contemporary caricature barely exaggerates Lee's eccentric appearance: a lank, spidery frame and a beak-nosed face, always in the company of "a troop of dogs."

prowess. He built no entrenchments, paid little attention to placing his pickets, and spent his time carousing and listening to command performances by his regimental band.

Inevitably, such omissions had attracted the attention of General Washington. The westward point of the triangle of land he occupied was opposite Bordentown. The main force—comprising the Continental army brigades of Generals Stirling, Stephen, and Mercer, joined in the third week of December by Sullivan with Lee's men—was deployed along the river from McKonkey's Ferry toward Trenton. Opposite Trenton, to Bordentown, Brigadier General James Ewing had his Pennsylvania and New Jersey militia. Camped from there to the riverbank opposite Burlington were Colonel John Cadwalader's fresh Pennsylvania militia and veteran New Englanders. Studying this disposition of forces, Washington decided he might be able to give the Hessians a Christmas surprise.

On Christmas Eve it began to snow again as Washington and his generals gathered for supper and a final council of war at the headquarters of General Nathanael Greene, the Rhode Islander who had become Washington's confidant and friend. Washington ordered a coordinated attack by three separate columns. With the main force of Continentals, he would cross the Delaware at McKonkey's Ferry and attack Trenton from the northwest. Ewing was to cross the river below Trenton and take control of the main road where it crossed Assunpink Creek, thus preventing the enemy from either escaping to, or getting reinforcements from, the south. Cadwalader's assignment was to attack the Bordentown garrison, to prevent it from participating in the battle for Trenton. It was a dangerously complex plan, in which any failure could produce disaster.

On Christmas morning, while the weak sun raised the temperature to a level that was just above freezing, Washington assembled 2,400 troops back of McKonkey's Ferry. About 2 p.m., the march to the river commenced. Major James Wilkinson remembered for the rest of his life that along their route the snow was "tinged with blood from the feet of the men who wore broken shoes." As the first contingents of men were poled across the water in the boats, the wind rose and the temperature dropped. "It was as severe a night as I ever saw," remembered Thomas Rodney, a captain in the Delaware militia. "The frost was sharp, the current difficult to stem, the ice increasing, the wind high, and at eleven it began to snow. It was only with the greatest care and labor that the horses and artillery could be ferried over the river."

Washington crossed around 8 p.m., sat down on an empty wooden beehive, wrapped himself in his cloak, and glumly watched as the army fell further and further behind schedule. He needed everyone across, men and guns, by midnight in order to complete the nine-mile march to the attack position by dawn. But because of the ice it was 3 a.m. before the artillery was over and, he reported later, "near four before the troops took up their line of march."

At that, the terrible weather took a turn for the worse. For several hours, sleet driven on a vicious northeast wind pounded the miserable troops. Washington rode up and down the lines, his horse slipping frequently on the ice, urging the men onward: "Press on, press on boys."

About four miles from Trenton, General Greene, accompanied by Washington, led his division away to the left of the route of march, to take the Scotch and Pennington roads into the northern extremity of the town. As General Sullivan took the lead of the advance down the River road, he sent back a dismaying report: Every man he had asked to check had found his priming powder wet.

Responded Washington: "Use the bayonet. I am resolved to take Trenton."

Leaning on a captured British cannon amid grounded British battle flags, General George Washington stood for this painting by Charles Willson Peale celebrating the victories of Trenton and Princeton in 1777. Peale, who had served as an officer in both of the battles, included such eyewitness details as the American troops in the background guarding British captives within sight of Princeton's Nassau Hall.

Just after dawn, Washington rode along his column one more time, telling the men, "For God's sake, keep by your officers!" Then, with Trenton about a mile away and the first enemy outpost 800 yards ahead, the men broke into a trot. The first house to be seen was a cooper's shop being used as an advance outpost by the Hessians. The morning patrol had just come in, reporting no activity in the area, when the lieutenant commanding the guard stepped to the doorway and saw the van of the American army emerge from the woods. His men tumbled out of the house and opened fire.

Exactly "three minutes later," Washington recalled, firing erupted on the River road. Sullivan's division had encountered Hessian pickets. Both parties of Hessian sentries, seeing that they were overwhelmingly outnumbered by the advancing Americans, headed for the rear. While those in front of Sullivan ran though the lower end of the town and kept going toward the Assunpink bridge, those in front of Washington and Greene fell back on their main body, which was now assembling in the middle of town.

On the high ground at the northeast end of Trenton, Colonel Henry Knox unlimbered his guns. As the Hessians tried to form up in King and Queen Streets, Knox's cannon opened fire with grapeshot. When the Hessians dodged into the cross streets, they found themselves under flanking fire from Mercer's brigade, coming in from the west.

Hessian gunners tried to bring their guns into action but had great difficulty just getting the horses hitched and the guns into position on the icy streets. By the time they were ready to open, they were already under devastating fire— grapeshot from the front and mus- ketry from the flank—and within minutes half the Hessian gunners and most of the horses were down.

Colonel Rall sat his horse in an al- ley, sword in hand, saying over and over, "Lord, Lord, what is it, what is it?" Then, shaken into action, he began to move his men to the east,

"You have done all I asked you to do, and more than could be reasonably expected, but your country is at stake, your wives, your houses, and all that you hold dear. You have worn yourselves out with fatigues and hardships, but we know not how to spare you...."

GEORGE WASHINGTON TO
HIS SOLDIERS DECEMBER 30, 1776

Washington used this brass-fitted portable writing case, containing compartments for paper, pens, and sealing wax, throughout the war.

where open fields and an apple orchard offered room to maneuver, and the Princeton road offered an escape route.

"Perceiving their intention," Washington wrote later, "I threw a body of troops in their way which immediately checked them." Rall, wounded and losing blood, tried to wheel his men back toward the town, but one of his units misunderstood and marched off instead toward the Assunpink bridge.

Now Rall decided to try to regain the apple orchard, but before he had time to act on the deci- sion he was hit by two more bullets and went down. His men made it to the orchard, looked out through the snow and rain at the closing circle of Americans, and surrendered.

The regiment that had mistakenly headed for the Assunpink bridge was still fighting, although the bridge was firmly in the hands of Sullivan's Ameri- cans after their drive through the lower town. The Hessians decided to try to cross the creek above the bridge, but their cannon mired down in swampy ground, and they were pressed in more firmly on every side by arriving Americans, until they, as well, had no choice but surrender. Nearly 1,000 men laid down their arms.

Wilkinson located Washington on King Street and told him about the surrender. The general smiled at Wilkinson, gripped the younger man's hand, and said, "Major Wilkinson, this is a glorious day for our country."

Washington called a conference of his officers and posed the question: Should they press on to Princeton, 10 miles to the north? Knox and Greene had their blood up and were all for it, but cooler heads prevailed. Although only four Ameri- cans had been wounded in the fight, all the men were badly worn down by their travail. The enemy they would face at Princeton were British regulars, and there would be no advantage of surprise. More- over, there was no sign that either Ewing or Cadwalader had made it across the river downstream, and if they had not, the Hessians at Bordentown would still be a serious threat.

There remained besides the work of recrossing the river with their guns and prisoners, daunting enough for men who had been marching and fighting for nearly 24 hours. Mainly, there was their precious victory, the first American battlefield triumph of the Revolution, which must not be squandered. Washington ordered the men formed up for the return to Pennsylvania.

"We did not get to our tents until next morning," a young captain recorded; "two nights and a day in as violent a storm as ever I felt." But now they had the mantle of victory for warmth. They had taken 918 prisoners, 15 regimental flags, and 6 guns, and in addition they had managed to inflict more than 100 casualties.

As for the generals who had failed to get their columns across the river, Washington simply observed that "I should have been able, with their assistance, to have driven the enemy from all their posts below Trenton." He longed to replicate his success, but it was necessary for the army to be rested and fed, and on December 31 the enlistments of all but a handful of Pennsylvania and Virginia troops would expire.

Yet on December 30, Washington led his men across the Delaware again, this time with the snow deeper, the ice thicker, and the wind colder than it had been during their first crossing. He marched them south through Trenton and across the bridge over the frozen Assunpink. There he formed them in lines abreast, rode out in front of them, and did what he hated most to do— what he had mostly avoided doing during his service in the Virginia House of Burgesses and the Continental Congress. He made a speech. They had done

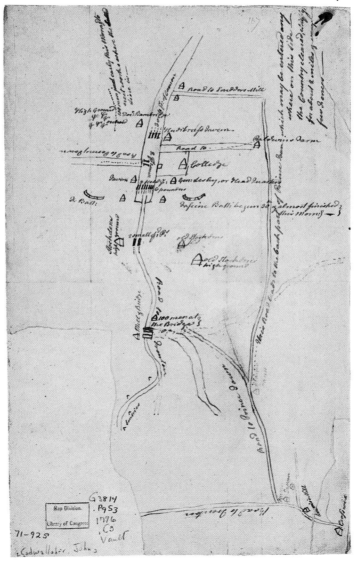

With the Delaware River to his back and General Cornwallis marching a force of 5,000 troops toward him, Washington once again outwitted the enemy. Skirting Trenton at night along a back road—shown on this map drawn by an American spy as the "Road to Prince Town"—he eluded the British in a daring maneuver and attacked Princeton.

well at Trenton, he said, but their country still needed them. If they would stay with the army for just six more weeks, he would get them a $10 bounty in addition to their pay. That was all. He rode back to the side of the line and watched while the regimental officers told those who would accept the bounty, and reenlist, to step forward. The drummers played a long roll. No one moved.

In the cold and the silence, Washington saw the end of everything—and rejected it. He wheeled his horse to the front again to address the men, and this time he spoke from the heart. "You have done all I asked you to do, and more than could be reasonably expected," one sergeant remembered him saying, "but your country is at stake, your wives, your houses, and all that you hold dear. You have worn yourselves out with fatigues and hardships, but we know not how to spare you. If you will consent to stay only one month longer, you will render that service to the cause of liberty, and to your country, which you probably never can do under any other circumstance."

There was no more to say. He rode off to the side again and waited through a long, embarrassed silence. Finally, a grizzled veteran, saying he could not go home while the army needed him, stepped forward. More followed, and more, until in the end 1,200 Continentals, not quite half the army that had made the first crossing of the Delaware, agreed to stay. In addition to these seasoned, if exhausted, troops, Washington had 3,400 fresh, relatively well equipped but utterly inexperienced militia. He gathered his men at Trenton and considered his options, such as they were.

As Washington was keenly aware, the enemy was once more on the prowl. General James Grant had concentrated a force of 6,000 men in Princeton, just

10 miles to the north, and was about to march them south toward Trenton. And on the evening of January 1, Grant was joined by 2,000 more crack British regulars under Charles, Lord Cornwallis, a general of daunting reputation. News of the disaster at Trenton had reached New York just as Cornwallis had been preparing to board ship for home. Under Howe's urgent orders to return to duty and "bag the fox," Cornwallis had made a 50-mile march on New Year's Day. Then he ordered men and guns to be ready to march before daylight the next morning.

The fox decided there was nowhere to run, and dug into his position south of Assunpink Creek, primarily because he did not have enough time to seek another one. Washington's men threw up rudimentary earthworks along a three-mile length of the creek's south bank, with their left on the Delaware River and their right in the air—that is to say, unprotected by earthworks or natural terrain. "It appeared to me then," wrote a soldier named Stephen Olney, "that our army was in the most desperate situation I had ever known it."

But the northeastern winter had more than enough hard times to go around. Cornwallis marched from Princeton on schedule in the early morning of January 2, but not nearly as rapidly as he had intended. The weather had turned unseasonably warm, and it had rained all of New Year's Day and through the night. The wheels of his 28 guns sank into the softened red clay, while men and horses struggled in ankle-deep mud. Nevertheless, by midmorning he reached Maidenhead, nearly halfway to Trenton, where he posted a brigade and struggled onward through the mud with the rest of his army, about 5,500 men.

Washington sent out a force to delay the British advance as long as possible. At 10 a.m., from the south bank of Five Mile Run, Colonel Edward Hand's Pennsylvania riflemen fired their first shots at the skirmishers of the British vanguard. The British skirmishers fell back, the main body halted, the troops of the advance deployed into line of battle, brought up their artillery, and advanced—only to

THE BRIGHT FLAGS OF BATTLE

At the start of the Revolution, militias had their own regimental colors, and each state prescribed a sequence of colors to be used as new units were formed. When Washington reorganized the Continental army in 1776, he called for each regiment to carry a small standard that bore "some kind of similitude to the uniform of the regiment to which they belong."

The Philadelphia Light-Horse Troop carried the regimental flag shown here at the Battles of Trenton, Princeton, Brandywine, and Germantown. Washington valued the tactical versatility of cavalry and in early 1777 persuaded the congress to authorize a force of 3,000 light horse.

find the Americans gone. This proved to be a time-consuming procedure, so the Americans did it again and again—stinging the British advance, then falling back while the enemy army lumbered into attack formation and swung at the air.

Thus harried, Cornwallis, who had marched 50 miles the previous day, took all day to cover the 10 miles from Princeton to Trenton. It was 4 p.m. before his troops saw the village's streets, and they were still facing stiff resistance from the stubborn Pennsylvanians. Washington was with the riflemen now, and Knox's artillery had opened fire on the enemy.

In the last of the twilight, with the British advance force of 1,500 men closing in, Colonel Hand and his men trotted across the Assunpink bridge into the American lines. Washington sat his big white horse at the far end of the bridge, calmly watching the advancing red-coated columns. "We let them

The mortally wounded General Hugh Mercer and his fallen horse lie at the center of this depiction of the Battle of Princeton—painted sometime after 1786 by William Mercer, the son of General Mercer. In the foreground Washington, sword in hand, addresses two officers thought to be Generals Greene and Cadwalader, while Cadwalader's cannon fires on British troops taking cover behind a fence.

come on some ways," recalled a sergeant of artillery, Joseph White, "then by a signal given, we all fired together." The enemy recoiled, re-formed, and advanced again, to take another punishing blast from the guns. They tried it a third time, and now the American gunners fired canister. A third of the British force was down. "The bridge looked red as blood," wrote White, "with their killed and wounded, and their red coats."

It was dark when Cornwallis rode into Trenton. Aggressive as he was, he did not like the idea of a frontal assault against an entrenched enemy of unknown strength, with men who had worn themselves out in the mud all day. Besides, Washington had no place to go. "We've got the old fox safe now," Cornwallis told his officers at a council of war. "We'll go over and bag him in the morning."

But Cornwallis's quartermaster general, Sir William Erskine, did not agree: "If Washington is the general I take him to be, his army will not be found there in the morning."

It was not. During the night, Washington decided that the way out of his dilemma was to attack Princeton. The gunners wrapped their wheels in cloth to deaden the noise and formed up. Regimental commanders issued orders in whispers, and soon the entire army was in column, except for a detachment ordered to keep the campfires burning and the enemy deceived with sounds of digging and patrolling.

At 2 a.m. the main force marched away to the northeast. In the moonless night, men and horses slipped and stumbled, colliding with one another, frequently halting in confusion. The ammunition wagons labored over frozen clods of mud and fetched up against tree stumps. The exhausted men fell asleep on their feet when the army halted, and one of them was seen to doze off frequently while marching, each time falling heavily to the ground. Still, hour after hour, they groped through the night, swinging gradually toward the north until they were converging on the Princeton road—behind Cornwallis's main force. But at dawn, the time Washington had intended to attack, they were still two miles from their objective.

As the Americans approached Princeton from the southeast, two of the three British regiments posted in the town, under the command of Lieutenant Colonel Charles Mawhood, were marching south on the main Princeton road, under orders to join Cornwallis. At about 8 a.m. the two forces spied each other across a half-mile of rolling, wooded country. Mawhood assumed he had caught sight of a raiding party, and moved confidently to attack.

Halfway between the roads, Mawhood ran into a detachment of 350 men under General Hugh Mercer, whom Washington had sent to destroy a bridge on the Princeton road. A force of 50 British cavalrymen caught Mercer's troops in an apple orchard and held them there until the British infantry could form a line of battle and launch a bayonet charge. After a brief, vicious, hand-to-hand fight among the apple trees, Mercer's men broke and ran, leaving their dying commander behind.

The response of the main American body to this emergency was awkward. Sullivan's Continentals were almost into Princeton, while Cadwalader's green militia, as usual having difficulty with their marching, had lagged 1,000 yards behind. When at last they were in formation, they crested the hill, to confront a horrifying scene: A British line of battle was forming to attack them, a battery of four cannon thundered in their faces, and British troops were chasing down and killing the survivors of Mercer's detachment on a field littered with American bodies. The militia turned and ran.

One small detachment of artillery—about 20 men with two guns—held firm and blazed away. Under their fire, unsure what had happened to the large American force he had glimpsed on the hill, Mawhood paused. It was a brief hesitation, but it provided enough time for Washington to arrive on the hillside at the gallop, followed closely by his hardiest veterans. "There is but a handful of the enemy," he shouted to the demoralized militiamen, "and we will have them directly!"

In minutes Washington had cobbled together a line of battle and led it forward personally, hat clutched in his hand, his horse prancing. He told his men not to fire until his command, and took them to within 30 yards of the waiting British line before he gave the order. The answering volley from the British line was instantaneous. When the tremendous cloud of smoke cleared, Washington sat his horse untouched, waving his men forward.

For endless minutes the two small armies stood virtually toe to toe, firing muskets and cannon as fast as they could be reloaded. Then Colonel Daniel Hitchcock's New Englanders charged the British left flank. The highly disciplined British saw they were being overwhelmed and tried to maintain an orderly retreat, but then they, too, broke and ran pell-mell for safety. Washington, who had never before in his life seen an enemy in full flight, galloped after them, yelling, "It's a fine fox chase, boys!"

With a third of the British force at Princeton destroyed, the Americans could turn their attention to the remainder, drawn up in line on a crest in front of the town. From their vantage points the British troops had seen the destruction of Mawhood's force, and the sight had unnerved them. At the first probe, the British ran.

One of the best units in the British army in America, the Fourth Brigade, had been effectively destroyed, with 300 of its men killed or wounded and another 300 captured. It had happened in less than an hour, with only 44 Americans killed. The happy Americans spent the next two hours eating the breakfasts that had been prepared for the British; confiscating British supplies of food, blankets, and clothing; and—in the soldierly tradition of the day—looting the town. Then pickets came in from the south to report that Cornwallis was approaching.

Once again Washington formed up the weary men and marched away, to the north. At a fork in the road, with one arm leading east to Brunswick and its enormous British supply depot, Washington and his generals sat their horses for a time, gazing wistfully down the path not taken. The men had been marching and fighting for 48 hours and could not be asked to fight again. Regretfully, Washington headed the army north toward Morristown, where at last they stopped and rested. They had earned this respite, and much more. By standing bravely against British and German professionals, America's citizen-soldiers had done more than interrupt the enemy's string of victories—they had restored an infant nation's faith in its army. After the battles at Princeton and Trenton, neither side could take anything for granted; suddenly, America had a chance of winning its war of independence, and both Howe and Washington now knew it.

With the winter weather worsening, the British decided not to try to root Washington out of his natural fortress. Since the American army was within easy reach of the British supply line from New York to Trenton, Howe decided to pull all his troops back into New York and eastern New Jersey. Having thus accommodated each other, in the manner of two grumpy bears settling down in a large cave, the armies went into winter quarters.

While the hibernating armies were beginning to stir once again, in March of 1777, two generals departed from their capitals—one from London, the other from Philadelphia—on journeys that would bring them face to face as enemies, three decades after they had become comrades in arms. In 1745, young lieutenants eager to make their mark, they had been mustered together into a regiment of the British army. They had shared much—questionable parentage, burning ambition, extraordinary ability, and touchy vanity—but they

In the aristocratic and fashionable world of the glittering French capital city, Benjamin Franklin quickly realized that he was admired for his uniquely simple way of dress—including at times a fur cap that he wore to conceal a persistent rash. Franklin, who thought of chess as a model of diplomacy, often played while in Paris, traveling with the portable set seen at far right. "Several very valuable qualities of the mind," he wrote in *Morals of Chess*, "are to be aquired or strengthened" by playing the game.

BENJAMIN FRANKLIN IN PARIS

Desperately short of supplies and money, the Continental Congress in the fall of 1776 dispatched Benjamin Franklin to serve as an envoy to the court of the French king Louis XVI. His instructions were "to press for the immediate and explicit declaration of France in our Favor."

In pursuit of that goal, Franklin threw himself wholeheartedly into the social whirl of the French capital. Indeed, the somewhat prudish John Adams, who arrived in France in 1778, would later complain that Franklin's life in Paris was "a Scene of continual dissipation."

Perhaps so, but his behavior only endeared him to the French. Even the critical Adams conceded that Franklin's name was "familiar to government and people, to kings, courtiers, nobility, and philosophers, as well as plebeians." One friend reported that "Women, especially, flocked to see him, to speak to him hours on end." Despite his hectic social life, Franklin pushed hard for the American cause. And in 1778 the French government signed an alliance with the newly independent United States of America.

At the same time Franklin was serving as a diplomat for his country, his son, William, who had been the royal governor

*"And lastly, we learn by chess the habit
of not being discouraged by present appearances in the state
of our affairs, the habit of hoping for a favorable change,
and that of persevering in the search of resources."*

BENJAMIN FRANKLIN, *MORALS OF CHESS*

"Somebody gave it out that I lov'd Ladies," wrote Franklin, "and then every body presented me their Ladies (or the Ladies presented themselves) to be embrac'd, that is to have their Necks kissed." At the gathering depicted here, the prettiest of 300 ladies was chosen to crown Franklin with laurel and kiss him on both cheeks.

"Nothing has ever hurt me so much and affected me with such keen Sensations, as to find myself deserted in my old Age by my only Son; and, not only deserted, but to find him taking up Arms against me, in a Cause, wherein my good Fame, Fortune, and Life were all at Stake."

BENJAMIN FRANKLIN TO HIS SON, WILLIAM, AUGUST 16, 1784

WILLIAM FRANKLIN

of New Jersey, was serving a term in prison. Despite his father's efforts to lure him to the American side, William Franklin had remained a staunch Loyalist. In 1776 the Continental Congress, of which his father was an influential member, had accused William of being "an enemy of the liberties of this country" and ordered him imprisoned in Connecticut. Although they had once been close, Benjamin Franklin did nothing to help his son and

little to help William's wife, who died while he was in prison.

Father and son met only once after William's imprisonment. Benjamin arranged to meet William in England on his journey home from France in July 1785. Even then their meeting was chilly, dealing only with legal matters. Although Benjamin Franklin negotiated the peace treaty with the British, he never came to terms with his only son.

were also very different: One of them had been raised in society, whereas the other had emerged from grim commoner's poverty.

John Burgoyne, the elder of the two, had been born in London on February 4, 1723, according to persistent rumor the illegitimate son of Lord Bingley of Yorkshire. Burgoyne's nominal father was an impecunious army captain who, because he was the second son of a baronet, lived on the fringes of aristocracy. An annuity left by Lord Bingley allowed Burgoyne to get his schooling at prestigious Westminster, where he became friends with Lord James Strange and thereafter enjoyed the patronage of Strange and his father, the earl of Derby. Choosing an army career, Burgoyne was also able to buy an officer's commission in 1737.

Horatio Gates, born in 1727, was thought to be the illegitimate issue of the duke of Leeds, for whom Gates's mother was a housekeeper. Gates had no claim to social station—his legal father was a waterman—and went to a school for commoners. But he, too, came under influential patronage when the duke of Bolton, who hired Gates's mother after the death of Leeds, took a liking to her son. In 1745, Bolton raised a new regiment for service in putting down the Highlands rising of "Bonnie" Prince Charles and the House of Stuart. As the regiment was new, commissions did not have to be bought, and Lieutenant Horatio Gates was number 15 on the regimental roster. Number 16 was another young lieutenant: John Burgoyne.

Burgoyne developed a reputation as an avid, and not always prudent, gambler. In two years he moved on to a captaincy in another regiment, presumably purchased with his winnings, and two years after that sold his commission, probably to settle his losses. He got back into the army in 1744, in time for King George's War, and in 1751 eloped with the sister of his friend Lord Strange. After serving creditably in France early in the Seven Years' War, he was given his own regiment in 1759. His talents in recruiting, leading men humanely, and organizing quickly produced a model regiment, which performed valiantly in Spain, bringing Burgoyne by 1762 the rank of colonel and a seat in Parliament. Promoted to major general in 1772, Burgoyne was still serving both careers without particular distinction in 1774, when the simmering colonial resistance to British taxes started to boil. "I look upon America as our child," he told the Parliament, "which we have already spoilt by too much indulgence." Still, he "wished America convinced by persuasion rather than by the sword."

Gates, meanwhile, had found the key to success in mastering army regulations and procedures, making him invaluable to superior officers who had no training in military affairs. He won high regard as an administrator, but his regiment was disbanded in 1749, and the only employment he could find was with an expedition to establish a naval base in Nova Scotia. Five years later he married the daughter of a major, bought a captaincy in a regiment serving in Maryland, and went to fight the French and Indian War. There he became acquainted with the young George Washington before being wounded at Braddock's retreat from the Monongahela River in 1755.

Finding himself without any prospects for advancement in the postwar army, Gates sold his commission and in 1772 established a comfortable estate in Virginia's Shenandoah Valley, where he became so "mad an enthusiast" for independence from Britain that he frightened more moderate people "out of their wits." Immediately on hearing about the fighting at Lexington in 1775, he had galloped to Mount Vernon to talk revolution with his friend and distant neighbor, George Washington.

The same year, Burgoyne entered the gathering storm in America. Sent with Generals Howe and Clinton to assist Thomas Gage in dealing with the rebellion, Burgoyne soon modified his contempt for the colonists' military prowess. "Every private man," he wrote, "will in action be his own general." He took this new appraisal with him back to En-gland, late in 1775, to attend to pressing personal problems. His wife, Charlotte, was gravely ill, and he required surgery. Certain that his wife lay on her deathbed, Burgoyne managed despite his grief to involve himself in discussions of colonial policy with Lord George Germain, the new secretary of state for the colonies, who firmly rejected the conciliatory policy of his predecessor. Germain declared he would use "the utmost force of this kingdom to finish the rebellion in one campaign." That campaign, Burgoyne advised Germain, should be a northern strategy, in which the two principal British forces pushed south from Canada and northward from New York to meet near Albany, thus sealing off New England from the other colonies. He endorsed Germain's desire to use the Iroquois as fighting allies, something the present commander of the northern army, Sir Guy Carleton, had refused to do—he regarded the Iroquois as a weapon of terror.

Germain responded warmly to Burgoyne's support by promoting him to lieutenant general, designating him second in command of Carleton's army in Canada, and making Burgoyne his personal agent in charge of pursuing the northern strategy. Germain even allowed Burgoyne to delay his departure in order to stay with his wife, who within two weeks learned of the death of her father and mother as well

Both American and British soldiers used portable iron braziers like the one here for cooking and for heating a hut or room. The supports on top were designed to support heavy pots and pans.

as the terminal illness of her favorite sister. To leave her now, Burgoyne wrote Germain, would be to "convey her to the family grave before it is closed." Germain arranged as long a delay as was possible, but on March 30 Burgoyne had to take his leave, knowing he would not see her again. Three months later he got word of her death, and declared that "interest, ambition, the animation of life is over."

Burgoyne was with Carleton's army through much of 1776, just long enough to find much to be desired in the Canadian commander's military conduct. Although the British forces managed to raise the siege of Quebec and push southward to Lake Champlain, Carleton had unaccountably decided to abandon the campaign for the winter. Disgusted, Burgoyne asked to return to England.

There, through the winter, Burgoyne convinced King George that Carleton was, as the king later phrased it, "too cold, or not so active as may be wished," and that the next attempt to split the American colonies should have "a more enterprising commander"—namely, John Burgoyne. He sailed in late March of 1777, with orders from Lord Germain to lead his army south, take Ticonderoga, secure Lake Champlain, and then "proceed with all expedition to Albany to put himself under the command of Sir William Howe."

Horatio Gates, meanwhile, had found a warm welcome at Mount Vernon. Recognizing that he was one of the few men in America who had experience both in high-level staff operations and in large-scale battle, Washington was delighted that the congress commissioned Gates a brigadier general and appointed him adjutant general of the army. Gates also exerted a moderating influence on Washington. Unlike the commander in chief, Gates liked the militia and, with his open and engaging ways standing in stark contrast to those of the icy Washington, found ways to motivate his men and work with them.

But Gates had no intention of serving out the war as a staff officer. Quietly but resolutely, and against his commander's wishes, he campaigned for

"During our progress occasions may occur, in which nor difficulty nor labour nor life are to be regarded. THIS ARMY MUST NOT RETREAT."

GENERAL JOHN BURGOYNE'S ORDER
OF THE DAY, JUNE 30, 1777

a field command, which he won from the congress even as it rejected Washington's plan for a standing army. Gates had his field command, but he had lost Washington's confidence.

As that relationship cooled, however, another ignited. In June of 1776 Gates was assigned to command the American army in Canada, then commanded by Philip Schuyler, who had been given the post after the conquest of Ticonderoga by Ethan Allen and Benedict Arnold. Schuyler was a wealthy landholder from the Saratoga area, the scion of the leading family of Albany. Courteous to a fault among peers, Schuyler was often overbearing to those he considered his inferiors. His military experience was slight—he had served as a supply officer during the Seven Years' War. By the time Gates arrived in July, the New Yorker had acquired a reputation for emotional frailty and a paralyzing caution.

The new general joined his devastated and demoralized command at Crown Point, north of Ticonderoga, and quickly demonstrated that his grasp of logistics, concern for the well-being of his men, affable manner, and stern discipline could work wonders with an army. Maintaining a truce with the touchy Schuyler—while campaigning through intermediaries at the congress for supremacy over him—Gates prepared for Carleton's siege of Ticonderoga. When that never came, and Carleton and Burgoyne returned to Canada, Gates began looking for a way to get out from under Schuyler. In December he won permission to take eight regiments of militia whose enlistments were about to expire to join Washington in southern New Jersey.

Gates did not like any of the posts that Washington offered him, so he went to lobby the congress, then meeting in Baltimore, for a

better deal. It took him all winter to fight off attempts to reappoint him adjutant general of the army and to persuade a congressional committee already impatient with Schuyler's complaining that he was the remedy. In March of 1777, as Burgoyne prepared his return to Canada, the congress ordered Gates "immediately to repair to Ticonderoga, and take command of the army there." The stage was set for the two former regimental comrades to meet—this time in bloody battle.

They still had much in common. Each was fighting both the enemy and an immediate superior. The order placing Gates at the head of the northern army did not remove Schuyler from the department; he rushed to Philadelphia and in May had his preeminence restored, whereupon Gates took horse for the capital and was there, maneuvering for advantage, when the campaign began in June.

Burgoyne had similar problems. He, Lord Germain, and the king were all in basic agreement on the strategy of the campaign: to unite the armies from Montreal and New York at Albany, whence, having split the confederacy of rebellious colonies, they could strike in any direction and snuff out the insurrection one ember at a time. But they were hampered by the great distance between them and by the fact that Howe, who still had ultimate authority for British forces in America, was not interested in Albany. He wanted the rebel capital, Philadelphia, and his American counterpart, George Washington, with a fervor that approached obsession.

"I propose to invade Pennsylvania by sea," Howe wrote to Germain in a letter that reached London in the middle of May. Deeply worried but not willing to challenge the influential Howe directly, Germain gave official approval, "trusting, however, that whatever you may meditate it will be executed in time for you to cooperate with the army ordered to proceed from Canada."

Burgoyne marched south from Montreal on June 13, 1777, with 7,000 infantrymen, half of them British regulars and half German mercenaries, an enormous artillery train of 138 guns attended by 600 artillerymen, plus about 1,000 Indians and Canadian militiamen. On June 20, the army set sail from St. Johns, at the head of Lake Champlain, on the armada of transports and warships left there by Carleton the previous year.

The British commander did not believe that leading an army in the field should deprive him of the finer things of life. He dressed impeccably, traveled amid pomp and circumstance, and surrounded himself with considerable luxury, taking his meals on silver plate and fine linen. He permitted his officers to bring along their wives or mistresses and hosted elaborate dinner parties. In the words of Baroness Frederika Charlotte Louise von Riedesel, the wife of one of his commanders, when work was done the general would spend "half the night singing and drinking and amusing himself in the company of the wife of a commissary, who was his mistress, and, like himself, liked champagne."

For all his keen observations of the enemy's military tactics, "Gentleman Johnny" Burgoyne was oblivious to the population through which his army now moved. As he took ship on Lake Champlain, he announced to the citizens of New York and New England that he was on a crusade to restore the "blessings of legal government" in place of "the completest system of tyranny that ever God in his displeasure suffered for a time to be exercised over a forward and stubborn generation." Having insulted that generation, Burgoyne warned that if they did not support him in his "glorious task," he would unleash his Indian allies to visit upon them "devastation, famine, and every concomitant horror." He intended nothing of the kind. Indeed, as he had written Howe, he meant to "keep up their terror and avoid their cruelty," and much to the amusement of experienced frontiersmen, he had given his Iroquois a stern warning to avoid bloodshed unless opposed by arms; to spare the aged, women, children, and prisoners; and—no scalps. Whatever Burgoyne's intentions, his proclamations ignited the patriotism of his audience, who rallied to the American army.

While Burgoyne sailed south on Lake Champlain, another force of nearly 1,000 regulars and militiamen with another 1,000 Iroquois, who were commanded by Lieutenant Colonel Barry St. Leger, headed west to Oswego on Lake Ontario; from there they would march eastward along the Mohawk River toward Albany.

Burgoyne's advance reached Crown Point on June 25, finding that it was abandoned by the Americans, who had retired to Ticonderoga. Although Burgoyne did not yet know it, the garrison there consisted of a mere 2,200 men under Major General Arthur St. Clair, reflecting the belief of both Washington and Schuyler that Burgoyne's army was not invading from Canada but would travel by sea to join Howe in the Chesapeake Bay. As a consequence, there were not enough soldiers in the fort to man its fortifications, and no one occupied Sugar Loaf Hill, which overlooked the fort less than a mile to the southwest—well within cannon shot. Although Gates had taken note of the danger the previous year and had warned St. Clair about it, neither St. Clair nor his officers believed that guns could be hauled up the steep slopes to the crest. But in the opinion of Burgoyne's second in command and chief artillerist, Major General William Phillips, "Where a goat can go a man can go, and where a man can go he can drag a gun."

Phillips made that observation on July 4, after the British main force had taken up a position across the throat of the peninsula on which Ticonderoga was located. Phillips put a detachment of 400 men to work clearing a road up the side of Sugar Loaf Hill, and on the morning of July 5 had two guns in place on the crest, overlooking the fort. Dismayed by the size of the British force and the presence of the guns, St. Clair and his men escaped under cover of darkness that night, sending their wounded, guns, and supplies down the lake by boat while most of the men crossed a boat bridge to the east side of the lake and marched away.

As soon as he knew what had happened, Burgoyne gave chase. Some of his infantry made a

With cartridge boxes and canisters in short supply, American infantry carried loose powder and ball. Powder horns, obtained from slaughtered cattle, were sealed with a plug at the wide end and fitted with a stopper at the tip. This one from about 1770 is decorated with a map of the Mohawk and Hudson Rivers, the royal arms, and a depiction of New York.

forced march of 24 miles to the east, in the July heat, and actually caught up and skirmished with St. Clair's men at Hubbardton on July 7. Meanwhile Burgoyne's fleet pursued the American flotilla southward to the tip of Lake Champlain, where he destroyed three ships and captured two, and then chased the crews overland to Skenesboro. There he stopped, to wait for his guns and his supply trains. In the wake of his easy victory at Ticonderoga, Burgoyne forgot his earlier respect for his enemies.

Burgoyne now had 70 miles to go to Albany. It might have been easier for him to return to Ticonderoga, portage his boats into Lake George, and make about one-third of that journey by water. But that would involve a retrograde movement, which Burgoyne thought could have an ill effect on "the capricious workings of the tempers of men." The boats could bring the supplies by water, while the army made what appeared to be an easy, 25-mile march south along Wood Creek to Fort Edward on the Hudson River. It took the efforts of General Phillips, most of the army's horses, and three precious weeks to get the boats and supplies into Lake George, and then one day to sail them south and occupy Fort George at its southern end, which the Americans abandoned on July 21, 1777, a week before the British arrived. As soon as Burgoyne knew that Fort George was his, he began his march.

They arrived at Fort Ann, about 15 miles north of Fort Edward, on July 26 and discovered a horror waiting for them: The fort lay in ruins, dense with the smell of the decomposing rebel dead, killed by Burgoyne's Indian raiding parties and left unburied in the haste of the American withdrawal. Then, to the further dismay of the British, an Indian party proudly presented two fresh scalps, one of them taken from a woman with long black hair. A Loyalist officer immediately recognized the hair as that of Jane McCrea, his fiancée, who had been visiting friends in the area. During a running engagement with some Americans, the Indians had taken cover in the home, and in the heat of battle ended up killing and disfiguring the three adults and six children they found in the house. An anguished Burgoyne summoned his Indian chiefs to a council and demanded that they turn over the murderers for execution. When told that if he persisted the Indians would simply desert him, he backed off, insisting only that a British officer accompany all future raids. So much for separating cruelty from terror.

The route to Fort Edward led away from Wood Creek, and all supplies had to be transferred from bateaux to two-wheeled carts, which frequently broke down. Horses to draw the carts and guns were in short supply. Plagued by black flies and mosquitoes in the intense July heat, the soldiers struggled to clear the endless succession of trees felled across their path by retreating rebels. Burgoyne's force could make no more than a mile a day. It took them until late July to reach Fort Edward, and there they had to wait for weeks for artillery and supplies.

It was at Fort Edward that Burgoyne received a disheartening communication from General Howe, dated in mid-July, announcing yet again that "my intention is for Pennsylvania, where I expect to meet Washington." In fact, Howe had sailed with most of his army from Manhattan on July 19, leaving a perplexed Sir Henry Clinton in command there with a mere 7,000 men. Clinton had spent three weeks arguing heatedly against the Philadelphia excursion as insignificant compared with the need to cooperate with Burgoyne. After Burgoyne's army crossed the Hudson, he would no longer be able to get supplies from Canada, and a supply line to New York could not be opened unless the American forces were driven from the highlands of the Hudson River between Manhattan and Albany. But Howe remained intent

In mid-1777 the British launched a campaign to isolate New England from the rest of the colonies. While Burgoyne marched due south from Montreal, St. Leger moved east along the Mohawk River valley from Oswego. Their plan was to converge on Albany, but everything went awry: St. Leger's troops mutinied at Fort Stanwix and returned to Canada, and Burgoyne got bogged down moving overland below Lake George, only to be stopped by American troops in mid-September.

on the American capital, and as he embarked he left behind vague instructions. Clinton was to make some sort of diversion to help out Burgoyne. To the latter, Howe wrote: "After your arrival at Albany, the movements of the enemy will guide yours." John Burgoyne was on his own.

Not yet despairing of Howe's help—the general had hinted that he might be inclined to pursue George Washington northward, after all—Burgoyne pressed on another seven difficult miles to Fort Miller, at the confluence of the Batten Kill and the Hudson. The route was exceedingly arduous. Supplies and boats had to be hauled overland to Fort Edward, where the supplies were loaded into the boats for the six-mile trip to Fort Miller, which was interrupted by a quarter-mile portage. With horses in short supply and up to 12 oxen required to drag a single bateau, progress was agonizing. Burgoyne had to wait until this trickle of supplies—on some days only one day's provisions were delivered—accumulated enough to tide the army over for whatever it faced between Fort Miller and Albany. As a further hedge, Burgoyne dispatched a force of about 1,000 German dragoons and Loyalists to sweep to the southwest, gathering cattle, grain, and horses from the countryside for delivery to the army when it reached Albany.

As the Americans retreated, they picked up strength. The New England and New York militias began to rally to the army as the British approached. Washington sent 600 Continentals along with two well-known and effective officers: Major General Benjamin Lincoln, who commenced an effective harassment of Burgoyne's line of communications with

Canada, and Major General Benedict Arnold, who was always on the lookout for a fight.

Arnold had been selected to command one of two armies sent north to invade Canada late in 1775 but had been disabled by a leg wound during the abortive attack on Quebec. After recovering, he returned to the northern theater, where he supervised the building of a makeshift fleet on Lake Champlain, with which he bravely confronted Carleton's superior British armada threatening Ticonderoga. Although his fleet was quickly overwhelmed and destroyed, Arnold had helped Carleton decide to defer his southward march until the following spring. Still, the hot-headed American hero had been viciously criticized for the loss of the only American vessels on Lake Champlain.

In the shadow of that and many other controversies, Arnold had been passed over while five officers junior to him were promoted to major general. When he went to Philadelphia to protest, he found many congressmen "wearied to death with the wrangles between military officers," as John Adams wrote, "scrambling for rank and pay like apes for nuts."

It was finally agreed that Arnold should be promoted but his seniority was not restored, and Arnold angrily resigned. On the day he wrote the letter, Washington asked him to help Schuyler meet the British advance from Ticonderoga, and Arnold, ever eager for action, had requested a suspension of his resignation and rushed north to fight.

Burgoyne's long pause to gather in supplies gave Schuyler time to give attention to the threat of St. Leger's British force to his west. On August 3, having marched more than 60 miles east from Oswego, St. Leger's 2,000-man force laid siege to Fort Stanwix at the headwaters of the Mohawk River.

When Schuyler announced a plan to send a

Taking command of the American forces in September 1777, General Horatio Gates led a force of about 7,500 against Burgoyne at Saratoga. Gates worked well with independent militia units, putting the particular strengths of each to good use in battle; one of his most effective forces at Saratoga was a band of 98 Virginia sharpshooters led by Daniel Morgan.

part of his army west to relieve Fort Stanwix, his New England troops objected to a point just short of mutiny, one of the men claiming that Schuyler was deliberately weakening the army in the face of Burgoyne's massive threat. No officer would respond to Schuyler's call for a commander for the expedition, until General Arnold stepped forward. On August 15, he headed west with fewer than 1,000 troops.

Hopelessly outnumbered by a foe that was entrenched, Arnold resorted to psychological warfare. He sent two men, one a condemned prisoner and the other an Oneida—one of the only Iroquois tribes friendly to the Americans—into St. Leger's camp to claim that 2,000 Americans under the famed Benedict Arnold were about to fall on them. The Mohawks and Iroquois with the British were already restive—they did not like long periods of inactivity without the rewards of combat and plunder. Nor did they like defensive battles, especially when outnumbered. They had wanted for some time to abandon the siege, and the false rumors of Arnold's strength were all they needed to confirm their desire. When St. Leger tried to dissuade them, they broke out of control, with the result that the entire force was demoralized and fled the scene, heading for Canada.

Meanwhile, at Bennington, Vermont, beyond the American army's eastern flank, New Hampshire militia under Brigadier General John Stark came upon the contingent of German troops rounding up pack-horses and provisions for the British army. Stark attacked and routed the Germans on August 16.

Seemingly all of a sudden, Burgoyne's fortunes had plunged. There would be no help from St. Leger, no supplies from the German dragoons, and, he finally realized, no help from New York—by now, Howe and his army would be in the Chesapeake. "I little foresaw that I was to be left to pursue my way through such a tract of country and hosts of foes without any cooperation from New York," Burgoyne would write. He also had a re-

Left to command the New York City garrison after Howe's ill-advised departure for Pennsylvania, Sir Henry Clinton worried that Washington might attack the city. Meanwhile, Burgoyne sent an urgent message seeking reinforcements, but the fretful Clinton, worried about an attack to his flanks, offered only to "make a push" with a small force at Fort Montgomery, just a few miles north of New York City.

newed and growing respect for his foes, military and civilian: "The great bulk of the country is undoubtedly with the Congress in principle and in zeal, and their measures are executed with secrecy and dispatch not to be equaled." Nevertheless, Burgoyne saw no alternative but to press on; his orders were to get to Albany.

While he waited, the man who was to have met him at Albany was sweeping to victory in Pennsylvania. In a counterpoint that must have been intolerable to Burgoyne, Howe's forces defeated the 11,000-man force Washington had strung across their line of advance between Wilmington and Philadelphia at a place called Brandywine Creek.

On September 13, two days after Howe's Brandywine victory, Burgoyne marched his army across the Hudson River from Fort Miller, dismantling the boat bridge behind them. As he severed his only line of communications with Canada, he pronounced gravely: "Britons never retreat."

Gates, for his part, urged his laboring engineers to finish their fortifications, sent out a general call for reinforcements, prepared his men for battle, and exhorted them to "live victorious or die free." He had arrived at the confluence of the Mohawk and Hudson Rivers on August 19 to take command of the American army, which badly needed a new leader. Schuyler's relationship with the New England troops had sunk to new lows. On one occasion, while Schuyler was trying to address a formation, a bullet fired by one of his own men whistled past his head.

With both flanks of the American army now secure and its men rejuvenated by the successes, General Gates took firm administrative hold of his command. First he looked to their needs. Wagons began to roll into camp with more and better food, clothing, and equipment. Then he saw to their discipline by holding daily drills and inspections and by requiring better order and cleanliness in the camp.

By September 7 Gates's army had increased in size to about 7,500 men. Among the newcomers was Daniel Morgan's new corps of rangers. Morgan was

THE KEY TO THE CIPHER: CLINTON'S ILL-TIMED LETTER

When Clinton finally wrote to Burgoyne on August 10, 1777, in order to inform him of Howe's departure for Philadelphia, he used a simple encryption device in the event that the letter fell into enemy hands. Embedded within the text of an apparently trivial dispatch was a message whose meaning could only be understood when a separate sheet with an hour-glass shape cut out of it was placed on top, masking all but the crucial text. Clinton seems to prattle on for 20 lines with a mixture of military small talk and misinformation *(below, left)*. But when Burgoyne superimposed the sheet with the prearranged cutout *(below, right)* on top, he had second thoughts about his decision to attack Albany:

Sir W. Howe is gone to the Chesapeak bay with the greatest part of the Army. I hear he is landed but am not certain—I am left to command here with too small a force to make any effectual diversion in your favor. I shall try something at any rate—It may be of use to you. I own to you I think Sir W's move just at this time the worst he could take.

Several copies of the letter were sent by separate messengers to ensure its safe delivery. But when one of them finally made it through successfully, Burgoyne had lost his copy of the mask and had to make another from memory.

a massive six-footer who bore on his back the scars of several hundred lashes received as punishment for striking a British officer during the French and Indian War, in which Morgan had served as a civilian teamster. He was fond of telling his men that he had received 499 of a prescribed 500 lashes; that final stroke he kept back, to use upon the British at every opportunity.

Forty years old when the Revolutionary War began, Morgan was expert in the Indian manner of wilderness survival and fighting. He and his men wore thigh-length, Indian-style hunting shirts and carried tomahawks and skinning knives. They were especially proficient with the deadly Pennsylvania rifle. This slender musket had been designed by German gunsmiths to be accurate at 200 yards, more than twice the range of the British brown Bess musket, and was popular with frontier hunters and fighters who needed to make every shot count.

Morgan adapted his frontiersman's tactics to organized warfare by fighting his men in loose skirmish lines, in which they could easily dodge or take advantage of the features of rough terrain. They flitted from tree to rock, finding rests for their rifles and taking a bead on individual enemy soldiers—especially officers. Not only was this practice disconcerting to the British, but it was offensive to officers schooled in the traditional practice of firing impersonal volleys at masses of opposing troops.

Captain Morgan had commanded all the riflemen with Benedict Arnold's 1775 invasion of Canada and had taken command of the army when Arnold had been wounded. Captured when the attack failed, Morgan had been paroled in August of 1776. The following year, Washington had promoted him to colonel and had given him command of a select force of 500 Continentals officially designated rangers but widely known as Morgan's riflemen.

Not long after Morgan joined the increasingly confident army facing Burgoyne, the Americans were further energized by Gates's decision to advance toward the British. Gates had received intelligence that Burgoyne was about to cross the Hudson and march south from Fort Edward, and on September 8 he headed his army north. With Benedict Arnold in command of the left wing and Gates handling the right, they reached the town of Stillwater, about 25 miles north of Albany, the next day.

Gates did not plan to attack but to mount a more secure defense, and he did not like Stillwater. The bottom land between the river on his right and the heights on his left was too broad to defend. People in the town told him that three miles north, a 200-foot-high ridge called Bemis Heights crowded against the river, leaving a narrow defile through which passed the only road leading south. General Arnold and the Polish engineer Tadeusz Kosciuszko surveyed and fortified a line from the river across the road to a tavern owned by Jotham Bemis, and then up the flank of the ridge and along its rough, densely wooded crest.

Gates planned to wait there for the inevitable British attack, whereas Arnold wanted to use the heights as a base for an attack on the approaching army. Relations between the hard-charging Arnold and the mild-mannered Gates had been deteriorating steadily ever since Arnold's return from Fort Stanwix. Aware of the long-running contest for supremacy between Schuyler and Gates, Arnold had evidently hoped to remain neutral, retaining Schuyler's high regard without offending Gates, who had taken Arnold's side against charges of misuse of funds during the 1775 Canadian campaign. In the end, Arnold's refusal to break with Schuyler had been perceived as disloyalty by Gates, and the former friends settled into enmity. Arnold had rubbed salt in Gates's wound by taking onto his staff two close aides to Schuyler, and had wrangled with the commanding general over details of his command.

Nevertheless, Gates allowed Arnold to advance his left wing, on the afternoon of September 18, to threaten Burgoyne from the west and see if the British would attack him, in which case Gates would advance from the south. But Arnold was forbidden to attack, and Burgoyne refused the invitation to battle. Arnold returned to his lines.

Burgoyne saw no hope in an assault down the River road, with the Americans on the heights to the west; his army would be jammed into a bottleneck, vulnerable to fire and attack along its length. He also realized he could not maneuver in the thick woods as a single formation, so he divided his army into three attack elements, each with a different mission.

About 3,000 men, including German troops from Brunswick and Hessians under Baron Frederich Adolph von Riedesel, were to advance along the river against the American right flank. Most of the army, meanwhile, would first move west onto the heights, then attack southward in two columns. While about 1,700 men under General James Hamilton, accompanied by Burgoyne, struck the American left, Brigadier General Simon Fraser would take 3,000 men on a wide sweep around the American left, hoping to crush that flank and force the Americans out of their entrenchments. It was a difficult battle plan, with three widely separated columns moving through dense woods in an operation whose success depended on precise timing.

On the morning of September 19, after a thick fog lifted at about 9 a.m., Burgoyne's three columns began the march to their attack positions. Informed by scouts of the threat to his left, Gates ordered Daniel Morgan's rangers out to find and harass the enemy there. Arnold pleaded for permission to take his infantry forward and engage the enemy before they could bring their guns to bear on the American entrenchments, but Gates was for the moment more worried about what was coming at him down the River road. He not only ignored Arnold's suggestion but took under his personal control most of the units in Arnold's left wing.

Morgan's rangers moved out in two loose skirmish lines, one behind the other. They descended the wooded slope to the headwaters of Mill Creek, then approached a 12-acre clearing called Freeman's farm, a mile and a half north of the American lines. At about 12:30 they reached the edge of the farm, just as 100 Canadian and Indian pickets, the advance of the British center column, emerged from the woods on the other side of the farm. Morgan's riflemen opened a deadly fire, killing or wounding every enemy officer but one within minutes, and when the pickets fell back the riflemen gave chase.

That was a mistake. They ran into several companies of British regulars. By the time they realized they were in contact with the main British army, it was they who were falling back, outnumbered and under a punishing fire. At the sight of his men being overrun, Morgan became distraught. "I am ruined, by God!" he shouted, and frantically sounded recall, not with drum or bugle, but with his famous turkey call. At the sound of the shrill gobble, his remaining men reassembled.

Gates still thought that this action was a probe, and although he sent more infantry forward he indicated his lack of interest by allowing Arnold to take command of the engagement. Arnold did so, one of his captains remembered, "riding in front of the lines, his eyes flashing, pointing with his sword to the advancing foe, with a voice that rung clear as a trumpet and electrified the line." In short order it was the British who were outnumbered and fighting for their lives.

By 2 p.m., Burgoyne's center column was fully engaged with Arnold's forces at Freeman's farm. The Americans had brought no cannon forward, but their musket fire, recalled one soldier, was "one continual blaze." Whenever the Americans gained enough advantage to advance onto the cleared ground of the farm, they were met with a ferocious British bayonet charge. When the British advanced, the American riflemen cut them down.

A British sergeant remembered that throughout the fighting, General Burgoyne "shunned no dan-

Given up by the British after their defeat at the Battle of Saratoga, this ornate bronze cannon bears the early-19th-century inscription: "Surrendered by the Convention of Saratoga, Oct. 17, 1777." Other, older markings include the royal seal of King George III. Such heavy artillery pieces could fire a solid, 12-pound ball accurately for a range of up to 500 yards but were so cumbersome—this one weighed 2,408 pounds—that they were more a liability than an asset.

ger; his presence and conduct animated the troops (for they greatly loved the general); he delivered his orders with precision and coolness."

By late afternoon, half the troops in the British center column were down, dead or wounded, and their cannon were silent, having run out of ammunition. Burgoyne had to call his German troops away from their attack along the river, to reinforce Hamilton, which they did just in time to avoid a rout.

Meanwhile Fraser's sweep around the American flank became hopelessly entangled in deep woods and was therefore unable to engage effectively. Arnold insisted to Gates that total victory was at hand if he could but have reinforcements. Gates sent a brigade over to the left but refused to let Arnold command it, with the result that it thrashed into battle in the wrong place, against Fraser. When Arnold learned what was happening, he exclaimed, "By God, I will soon put an end to it," and rushed forward to straighten things out. Gates thought this rash and ordered him back. Darkness fell with the British, although badly mauled, still in possession of the field. Leaving nearly 600 casualties, men he had no way of replacing, Burgoyne withdrew. The Americans had lost slightly more than 300 men.

The battlefield had hardly grown quiet when Arnold and Gates went into combat with each other. Gates dispatched a report of the battle to the congress that made no mention of Arnold's command of a division or of his actions in the battle, referring only to a "detachment from the army." Then Gates ordered Morgan's regiment to report to him instead of to Arnold. At this, Arnold stormed into Gates's tent and blew up. There was an exchange, as

Marching toward Albany from Fort Ticonderoga, Burgoyne encountered Gates's army near Saratoga. As shown in this anonymous painting made in the early 19th century, the Americans adjusted their tactics to suit the terrain; concealed in a tree *(upper left)* a sharpshooter mortally wounds British general Simon Fraser, who is shown being carried from the battlefield in the lower right.

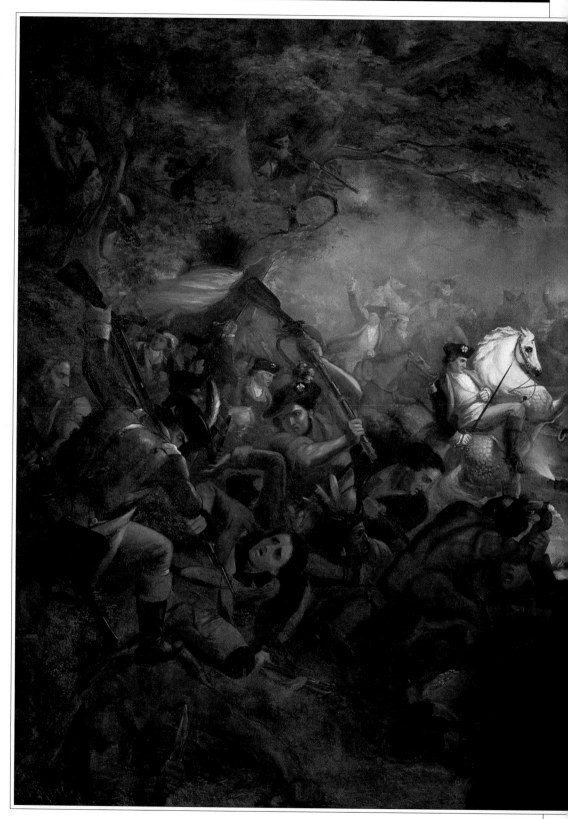

an aide to Gates recalled, of "high words and gross language." Gates belittled Arnold's ability and vowed to relieve him of command. Arnold hotly requested a pass to leave the army and join General Washington, which Gates just as hotly approved.

But Arnold's men and officers pleaded with him to stay, and with another battle undoubtedly in the offing, he agreed to do so. Gates picked another fight with him about a $50 reward given a soldier, and Arnold offended the commanding general by telling him that if he did not follow up the victory at Freeman's farm with an immediate attack, the militia would go home.

Gates reorganized his army, leaving Arnold unsure of whether he had any command at all. Both men simmered in this stew of discord, Arnold raging at Gates's "spirit of jealousy" and Gates writing plaintively to his wife that "the fatigue of body and mind which I continually undergo is too much for my age and constitution. This campaign must end my military labors."

Meanwhile, Burgoyne entrenched his disheartened army as well as he could and waited, encouraged by a tentative offer from Clinton to send a small diversionary force north from Manhattan, hoping that the Americans would come out of their entrenchments and attack him. But Gates understood that time was on his side. He was well supplied, and more militia units were coming to his side every day. American detachments captured Fort George and Skenesboro, further constricting Burgoyne's shaky supply line to Canada. As the days passed, Burgoyne had to put his men on half rations, and his top commanders began to urge him to give up and return to Canada.

Burgoyne decided that the critical date was October 12. If he was not going to get any help from Clinton, he would have to begin his retreat on that day in order to get back to Canada before the worst of the winter weather—which he especially dreaded—set in. With rising desperation, Burgoyne begged that Clinton, on behalf of the absent Howe, give "an answer conveying the plainest and most positive meaning" to the question of whether he should proceed to Albany or return to Canada.

Clinton dispatched an icy reply saying that he "cannot presume to give any orders to General Burgoyne," and that Burgoyne "could not suppose that Sir H. Clinton had an idea of penetrating to Albany with the small force he mentioned in his last letter." Burgoyne never got the message, although three messengers were dispatched with copies. Two of them turned back and the third was captured. He had swallowed the message encased in a silver ball; his captors dosed him with an emetic "calculated to operate either way," retrieved the message, and hanged the messenger.

There was another bit of news that failed to reach Burgoyne. On September 25, Howe had occupied Philadelphia with his troops, forcing the American government to flee to the village of York. Just over a week later, Howe had again defeated Washington, this time at Germantown. Victory seemed to be the British order of the day in the south. But in the chilling rains of the northern autumn, the prevailing mood among the king's men was a brave variant of despair.

With the passage of time Gates's army swelled to comprise more than 13,000 men, half of them Continentals, whereas Burgoyne's force was reduced to fewer than 7,000, with 800 men ill or injured. The British were harassed constantly by increasingly confident American patrols, and the daily food ration had to be cut to a pound of meat and a pound of bread per man. Gates understood Burgoyne and his predicament as well as anyone: Bur-

goyne was an "old gamester," in Gates's shrewd assessment, whose "despair may dictate him to risk all upon one throw."

The American was not quite right. Burgoyne was a seasoned enough gamester to spread his bets. On October 7, he assembled a force of fewer than 2,000 men and 10 guns for what he called a reconnaissance in force, which would try to get around the American left flank. The rest of the army would stay in its entrenchments and guard the river crossing, joining the attack only if the reconnaissance force gained the rear of the American lines. At noon Burgoyne marched his detachment well to the west of Freeman's farm, then south toward the westernmost extremity of the American line. When they were within three-quarters of a mile of the Americans, Burgoyne formed a 1,000-yard line of attack.

Gates's patrols reported the British movement immediately, and he was content to await the attack. At the noon mess that day, Arnold recommended that the Americans go out to meet Burgoyne, arguing that the attacker "had the advantage; for he can always take his own time, and choose the point of attack; and, if repulsed, he has only to retreat behind his own lines, and form again." But Gates worried that once undisciplined militia started to retreat they could not be stopped, even behind fortified lines. The two generals were still arguing when they heard the sound of pickets firing.

"Shall I go out and see what is the matter?" asked Arnold.

Gates did not answer, and Arnold pressed him. At length the commanding general sighed and said, "I am afraid to trust you, Arnold."

BATTLEFIELD BARONESS

Married to Frederich Adolph von Riedesel, commander of the Brunswick mercenaries under Burgoyne, Frederika Charlotte Louise von Riedesel and their three children left Germany in 1776 in order to join her husband in America. From her departure until 1783 she kept a detailed record that was published later as the *Journal and Correspondence of a Tour of Duty.*

For her comfort during the Battle of Saratoga, a log cabin was hastily erected, but within days it became a makeshift hospital. Among the casualties who sought refuge there was the fatally wounded British general Simon Fraser, carried in exclaiming, "Oh, fatal ambition! Poor General Burgoyne! Poor Mrs. Fraser!"

Arnold promised to be careful, and not to start an engagement, and Gates reluctantly let him go out to reconnoiter the lines. A half-hour later Arnold returned to say the firing, down near the river, had been inconsequential, but that a large force was advancing against the left. Gates ordered Morgan's riflemen and a regiment of light infantry out to meet the attack. "That is nothing," Arnold snapped. "You must send a strong force."

"General Arnold," replied Gates, now at the end of his patience, "I have nothing for you to do. You have no business here."

But Gates did send out more men. He ordered Ebenezer Learned's brigade to move against the center, Enoch Poor's brigade to attack the enemy left. At about 3 p.m., General Poor drove in the left in vicious fighting, during which one cannon

waistcoat. General Fraser tried to organize a defensive line behind the Germans, and was making progress despite the chaos when Morgan directed the attention of one of his snipers to the "devilish brave fellow" on the white horse. Moments later, Fraser went down. Burgoyne ordered his men back into their entrenchments.

Arnold, in a frenzy, led the entire American force forward to assault the fortifications before the fleeing British had an opportunity to reorganize themselves behind them. He rode from flank to flank—galloping in *front* of his lines, exposing himself to fire from both armies—to urge the Americans forward. They had approached to within 45 yards of a westward-facing breastwork, called the Breymann Redoubt for its commanding officer, Lieutenant Colonel Heinrich Breymann, when

"When we marched on I had a large calash readied, with room for myself and the three children and my two maids; this I followed the army right in the midst of the soldiers, who sang and were jolly, burning with the desire for victory." BARONESS VON RIEDESEL, FROM HER *JOURNAL*

changed hands five times before ending up in American hands. Arnold fretted, with nothing to do, until at length he downed a dipper of rum, borrowed a horse, and cantered to the head of Learned's brigade as it prepared to attack the Germans at the British center. Gates immediately sent an aide to bring him back—which proved to be a hopeless assignment. "Come on, boys!" Arnold shouted to one regiment. "If the day is long enough, we'll have them all in hell before night." Brigadier Learned, who had no taste for battle, was happy to allow Arnold to lead, authorized or not. Arnold rode into the fight "more like a madman than a cool and discreet officer," one sergeant recalled, and waved his sword with such abandon that he struck down an American officer on his way.

The Germans, badly shaken, began to fall back. Burgoyne tried to lead a force forward to their right, but it met a withering fire from Morgan's men. Burgoyne's horse was hit, as were his hat and

200 fresh Germans delivered a tremendous volley.

The American line continued its charge. Arnold spurred his horse through a sally port, demanded that the defenders surrender, and was shot down by their second volley. His horse fell dead, and Arnold took a bullet in the leg. "Rush on, rush on!" he implored the Americans, and stopped a soldier from bayoneting the German who had shot him: "Don't hurt him, he did but his duty."

At last, with daylight almost gone, the Germans broke and began to run. Incensed by their cowardice, Colonel Breymann killed four of his own men with his saber as they ran, before a fifth turned and killed him. Darkness now brought an end to the fighting—and narrowly prevented the destruction of Burgoyne's entire army.

Four men fashioned a litter for the suffering Arnold. "Where are you hit?" asked a fellow officer. "In the same leg," Arnold gritted out, referring to the wound he had received at Quebec. And then, no doubt thinking he was a cripple, he added, "I wish it had been my heart."

With the enemy in possession of the breastworks to his right rear, Burgoyne had no choice but retreat, leaving on the field another 700 casualties. He found some high, open ground to the north and dug in to receive another attack. But his position was untenable, so on the night of October 8 he marched north toward Saratoga. Gates let him go, for the moment. He was receiving a steady stream of reinforcements, the people of the countryside were with him, and "he felt assured," as one of his officers put it, that "there were other and less expensive means of reducing his foe than by blood and carnage."

It rained heavily for two days while Burgoyne struggled north to Saratoga, thinking he would go on from there to Fort Edward, ford the Hudson, and make his way back to Fort Ticonderoga. Gates

campaign." With more than 17,000 men at his disposal, however, Gates still did not attack. Instead, he began to envelop the British force, sending militia units around to Burgoyne's rear to cut the British communications and prevent their retreat toward Ticonderoga. For several days and nights, the Americans "swarmed around the little adverse army like birds of prey," as a sergeant recalled, firing ceaselessly on the encircled redcoats, slaughtering men and animals who could find no protection.

On October 12 Burgoyne decided to withdraw, only to find that he could not. He learned that Clinton was at last on his way from New York to try to help, but he knew that the relieving force had too few men and would be too late. The next day Burgoyne began negotiating a surrender.

The stately process began with a request to Gates to receive a British officer. At that meeting,

"General, the caprice of war has made me your prisoner."

GENERAL BURGOYNE, NEAR SARATOGA, NEW YORK, OCTOBER 17, 1777

waited until the rain stopped, and then on October 10 followed a British trail littered with discarded supplies, broken wagons, and dead horses. By 4 p.m. the Americans were again confronting Burgoyne's shattered force, camped just north of Saratoga across Fish Creek, which flowed from Saratoga Lake into the Hudson.

When his scouts told him of some British activity upstream along the Hudson, Gates jumped to the conclusion that the enemy was retreating, with only a rear guard left in place on the heights. The next morning he ordered an attack, and his brigades, led by Morgan's riflemen, began crossing the creek. Burgoyne let them come, seeing his chance to draw them in, then crush them against the creek. But two British deserters told the Americans they were approaching the entire British army, and at the last minute the doomed attack was halted, much to Burgoyne's frustration. It was, he said later, "one of the most adverse strokes of fortune in the whole

which took place on October 14, the officer suggested obliquely that they attempt to find a way to "spare the lives of brave men upon honorable terms." Gates bluntly demanded unconditional surrender. Negotiations commenced, with Burgoyne's next message proposing that his army be granted free passage to Britain "upon condition of not serving again in North America during the present contest" and that the Canadian contingent be allowed to go home.

The positions were so far apart that Burgoyne was startled, and more than a little suspicious, when on the morning of October 15 Gates suddenly accepted his terms with one condition: He stipulated that the army must surrender that afternoon and

In this view of the British surrender at Saratoga, Burgoyne offers his sword to Gates, who respectfully declines it. To the right stand important American heroes of the battle, among them Daniel Morgan, conspicuous in a white hunting frock, and, to his right, General Philip Schuyler in plain brown civilian dress.

move out for Boston the next morning. Indeed, Gates had learned of Clinton's maneuvers farther down the Hudson and believed that he might be running out of time.

Sensing opportunity, the cagey Burgoyne dragged his feet for another two days—insisting, for example, that the document be termed a "convention" rather than a "capitulation"—and he even considered breaking off negotiations when a spy came into his camp with what turned out to be an unfounded report that Clinton had arrived at Albany. Finally, on the afternoon of October 16, Gates lost all patience and sent a colonel into Burgoyne's camp to announce that the American army would attack in 10 minutes unless the surrender were signed. Burgoyne signed.

On the morning of October 17, the first clear day after nine days of rain, John Burgoyne, resplendent in a fresh, blood-red regimental uniform, rode up to Horatio Gates, who wore a plain blue coat. It had been 32 years since the two old comrades in arms had stood face to face.

"I am glad to see you," said Gates, peering at his former comrade through his spectacles.

"I am not glad to see you," snapped the ramrod Burgoyne in return. "It is my fortune, sir, and not my fault that I am here."

Gates genially agreed, and then Burgoyne returned to his army in order to conduct its formal march into captivity. Just under 6,000 men surrendered, half British, half German. The army had suffered 1,700 casualties.

On seeing the enemy army at close range, Burgoyne professed to being amazed. "The standing corps which I have seen are disciplined," he marveled in a letter to London. "I do not hazard the term, but apply it to the great fundamental points of military institution, sobriety, subordination, regularity and courage. My conjectures were very different after the affair of Ticonderoga; they were delusive, and it is a duty to the state to confess it." Having done so, he eventually returned to England, never to serve in America again.

Others were equally impressed by the American army and what it had done at Saratoga. When the American delegation to Paris reported the victory on December 4, the French foreign minister exclaimed that "to bring an army, raised within a year, to this, promised anything." Indeed, it promised a robust American ally in a fight against a perennial British enemy. Perpetually eager to go to war with England, France had held back from entanglement. Now that sharply changed. On December 5, French officials proposed opening discussions of a treaty of alliance, and two weeks later the French king recognized American independence.

In America, Horatio Gates wanted desperately to follow up his victory with an invasion of Canada, but while advocating his plan he got into a disastrous disagreement with Washington, who became convinced that Gates was plotting to take over supreme command. Washington would prevail after two years of acrimonious exchanges among Gates, Washington, and the congress.

Although Sir William Howe had won every engagement he personally led in America, his successes were not enough to save him from censure. Critics carped about his lifestyle and a perceived reluctance to take large risks with his army, and he was widely faulted for failing Burgoyne at Saratoga. Some people maintained that Howe had no stomach for a war against former British subjects. Angry and disenchanted, the general submitted his resignation as soon as he learned of Saratoga; in May of 1778, his resignation finally accepted, he would return to England, leaving America and its war to Sir Henry Clinton, who swiftly abandoned Philadelphia for garrison New York and began to brood over a southern strategy.

On the American side of the conflict, the intimations of a final victory that were glimpsed after Washington's victories at Trenton and Princeton now began to acquire a more definite form. A new nation could almost be discerned, rising from the blood and ashes of Saratoga. ◆

The Iroquois in the American Revolution

*"We are unwilling to join on either side of such a contest, for we love you
both—old England and new. Should the great King of England apply to us for our aid—
we shall deny him—and should the Colonies apply—we shall refuse."*

The Oneida tribe to the governor of Connecticut, March 1775

The American Revolution produced a new nation, but in the process a nation of American Indians was destroyed. About 200 years before the Revolution, five tribes of warring Iroquois united under the Great League of Peace to form the Five Nations confederacy. They lived in harmony along the Hudson and Mohawk Rivers west to the Finger Lakes and the Genesee River in what is now New York State. In the east dwelled the Mohawk; west of them lived the Oneida, the Onondaga, and the Cayuga, and in the far west the Seneca. Later the Tuscarora would move up from North Carolina and join the league, which then became known as the Six Nations.

In the early 1600s the eastern Iroquois, especially the Mohawk, developed ties to the English through the fur trade. The trading partners also forged political ties, and Mohawks fought alongside the British in the French and Indian War. By the time of the Revolutionary War the Iroquois had a long history of covenants with the Crown, and loyal Iroquois were rewarded with medals such as the silver one above, showing King George III on one side and an Iroquois and an Englishman sharing a pipe on the reverse.

The eastern Iroquois also established strong bonds with Anglican and Puritan missionaries who worked among them, and these ties would prove to be stronger than the ties between the tribes. As tensions began to build between Great Britain and her colonies in the late 1760s, most Anglicans, including the Mohawk, remained loyal to the king, while the Puritan Oneida and Tuscarora tended to side with the Americans.

Both the British and the Americans understood the value of the ferocious Iroquois warriors. However, the Iroquois were expensive allies, and their loyalty required a steady supply of goods. The British used their rich treasury to entice the Iroquois warriors into joining them; the Americans, short of supplies themselves, could only urge the Indian leaders to stay neutral.

The sachems, or peace chiefs, of the Six Nations sought vainly to restrain their warriors. Lamented one would-be peacekeeper, "Times are altered for us Indians. Formerly the warriors were governed by the wisdom of their uncles the Sachems but now they take their own way and dispose of themselves without consulting the Sachems. While we wish for peace and they are for war." Finally, the warriors joined the fight, shattering the Great Peace forever.

A FAMILY TRADITION OF LOYALTY

In the tug of war that was waged for the allegiance of the Iroquois, the British relied on the Indians' attachment to Sir William Johnson and his family. Johnson had lived among the Mohawk for more than 40 years and served as the British superintendent of the Six Iroquois Nations for 20 years. He had close personal ties to the Iroquois community through his Mohawk common-law wife, Molly Brant, who was a strong supporter of the Crown.

Johnson acted as a buffer between the Iroquois and land-hungry colonists. The Mohawk complained that "the very ground

To reward Iroquois for loyalty to the royal cause, Sir William Johnson bestowed these certificates for "Attachment to his Britannic Majesty's Interests, and Zeal for his Service."

under their feet" was being claimed by colonists. By the late 1760s he was also concerned about the rebellious colonists in Boston and their influence on Samuel Kirkland, a Puritan missionary to the Oneida and Tuscarora he at one time supported.

When William Johnson died suddenly in 1774, his duties were assumed by his nephew, Guy Johnson, who continued to cultivate Iroquois loyalty.

The stately Johnson Hall, built in 1755 by Indian superintendent Sir William Johnson near present-day Johnstown, New York, was the site of many councils with the leaders of the Iroquois tribes.

Wearing a combination of Iroquois and European clothing, Guy Johnson sat for this painting by Benjamin West; behind him stands a warrior who symbolizes the Johnson family ties to the Iroquois. When Guy Johnson became Indian superintendent the Iroquois gave him the name Rays of the Sun Enlightening the Earth.

"*Missionaries have it often in their power to lead the minds of the people wrong, therefore by all means do what you can to get the Indians to drive such Incendiarys from amongst them . . . the Indians well know that in all their landed disputes the Crown has always been their friend.*"

GENERAL THOMAS GAGE TO GUY JOHNSON,
FEBRUARY 5, 1775

"*I am sorry to tell you, that the face of things among the western tribes of the confederacy begins to change, and to appear different from what our expectations promised at the last treaty held in Albany. It is very evident their minds are poisoned by some enemy to the liberties of the colonies.*"

SAMUEL KIRKLAND TO GENERAL PHILIP
SCHUYLER, MARCH 12, 1776

The missionary Samuel Kirkland spent
most of his adult life ministering to the
Oneida and Tuscarora. He once confided
to a friend: "I have from my youth up had
a peculiar affection for Indians."

THE STRUGGLE FOR NEUTRALITY

When Samuel Kirkland began his missionary work among the Oneida and Tuscarora in 1766 he converted several of the warriors who would remain loyal to him even under pressure from the Johnsons. "Numbers of them," Kirkland wrote, "said they would go with me to prison or death—where I followed Christ, they would follow me." Kirkland and the Indian commissioner, General Philip Schuyler, tried to persuade the Six Nations that the Americans, not the British

General Philip Schuyler *(right)* **was appointed commissioner to the Six Nations in June 1775, when the Continental Congress recognized the role the Iroquois could play in the growing war.**

were the rightful heirs of the covenants with the Iroquois. "This is a family quarrel between us and Old England," they told them. "You Indians are not concerned in it. . . . We desire you to remain at home, and not join on either side."

In August 1775 leaders of the Six Nations met in Albany with the Americans and pledged their neutrality. The peace was sometimes uneasy, but when the Iroquois renewed the treaty a year later an observer noted, "The Indians returned to their homes well pleased that they could live on neutral ground, surrounded by the din of war, without being engaged in it."

This 18th-century sketch depicts a white settlement, typical of those found in the Mohawk Valley, at the confluence of the Mohawk and Hudson Rivers. Colonists settled first on the rich land that lay along the Mohawk River, and this densely populated area was the hardest hit by the wartime raids.

THE PEACE IS BROKEN

*"When I joined the English in the beginning of the war, it was purely on account of my
forefathers' engagements with the King. I always looked upon these engagements, or covenants
between the King and the Indian nation, as a sacred thing."*

JOSEPH BRANT, 1783

Joseph Brant, Molly Brant's brother, was sent by Sir William Johnson to a missionary school, where he studied with Samuel Kirkland. Later Brant tried to undercut his old schoolmate's influence among the Iroquois. Even so, in early 1775 Brant rescued Kirkland from Loyalist Iroquois. "He thinks he does his duty toward his country," Brant told them. "Let him then be considered as our enemy, but do not kill him."

In the summer of 1776, Brant returned from a visit to London convinced more than ever that the Iroquois' interest lay with the British and renewed his exertions on their behalf. These efforts finally paid off in July 1777, when, with the help

of gifts and rum, British agents persuaded the Seneca, Cayuga, and Mohawk to break the treaty of neutrality and join the British. The Oneida and Tuscarora, meanwhile, had secretly informed Kirkland that "if the others joined the King's party they would die with the Americans in the contest."

In late July Seneca and Mohawk warriors—among them Joseph Brant—joined an expedition led by Lieutenant Colonel Barry St. Leger, who planned to take Fort Stanwix

in central New York and then reinforce General John Burgoyne on his march to Albany. Finding Fort Stanwix heavily armed, St. Leger decided to lay a siege. On August 5 Molly Brant sent him a message that 800 militiamen, including Oneida warriors, had been sent to relieve the fort. This force blindly marched into an ambush set by Brant and his allies along Oriskany Creek. The Americans suffered heavy casualties; one report mourned that the "Flower of our Militia are either killed or wounded." The Seneca and Mohawk also suffered severe losses, and in revenge torched an Oneida village; the Oneida retaliated by burning Molly Brant's village. After 200 years the Great Iroquois Peace was shattered.

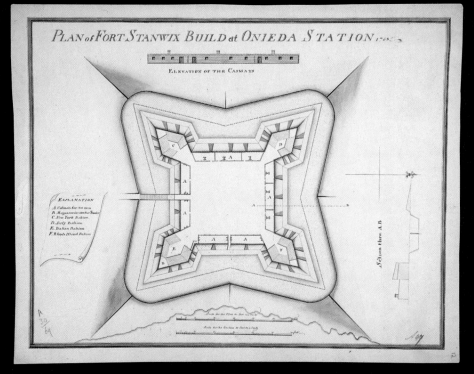

Two weeks after beginning his siege of Fort Stanwix—shown in a 1750 British plan—St. Leger was forced to withdraw because his troops panicked at a rumor that a large American detachment commanded by General Benedict Arnold was on its way to relieve the fort. St. Leger abandoned his plans to join Burgoyne and moved his troops back into Canada.

Thayeadanegea,
Joseph Brant
the Mohawk Chief.

Proudly wearing a metal gorget, Joseph Brant was vividly portrayed by painter George Romney in 1776, when 33-year-old Brant visited London to meet with British officials about disputed Mohawk lands—and to learn more about the conflict between England and its American colonies. The gorget shown above is emblazoned with the royal arms and was presented to Brant by the authorities in London.

The Frontier in Flames

*"What gives me the sincerest satisfaction is that I can with great truth
assure you that in the destruction of this settlement not a single person has been hurt of the
Inhabitants, but such as were in arms, to those indeed the Indians gave no Quarter."*

Major John Butler, leader of the Loyalists, July 8, 1778

In late June 1778 the Seneca war chief Cornplanter led his forces, who were joined by Tories and Cayuga warriors, into the Wyoming Valley of northeastern Pennsylvania. Over the next few days they burned eight forts and 1,000 houses, drove away 1,000 head of cattle, and killed 300 militiamen from Forty Fort. The Iroquois and Tories lost only a handful of men.

Throughout the summer, and fall raiders struck along the Mohawk Valley and into northern Pennsylvania. Americans and their Oneida and Tuscarora allies struck back where and when they could. In November the Tories and Iroquois launched one final raid on Cherry Valley, west of Albany. The

Tories lost control of the warriors, who massacred 33 noncombatants—including whole families—and even some Tories. Sixteen American soldiers died and more than 30 people were captured. Although survivors credited Brant with saving several families, he was condemned for the slaughter. Even Tories decried "such acts of wanton cruelty committed by the bloodthirsty savages as humanity would shudder to mention."

Wielding muskets, knives, and tomahawks, Tories and their Indian allies attack Pennsylvania militiamen in the brutal 1778 encounter known as the Wyoming Valley massacre, in which 300 Americans were slaughtered.

Seneca chief Cornplanter *(left)* was opposed to breaking the treaty of neutrality made with the Americans in 1775. But when the Seneca decided two years later to join the British, Cornplanter was chosen as one of the two leading war chiefs of the Iroquois. Shown below is a traditional wooden Iroquois war club.

"I flatter myself, that the orders with which I was entrusted are fully executed, as we have not left a single settlement or field of corn . . . or is there even the appearance of an Indian on this side of Niagara."

MAJOR GENERAL JOHN SULLIVAN,
SEPTEMBER 30, 1779

Major General John Sullivan, who led almost one-third of the Continental army through the Iroquois heartland in 1779, received this order from General Washington: "The immediate objects are the total destruction and devastation of their settlements . . . not to be merely overrun but destroyed."

THE AMERICANS STRIKE BACK

"When your army entered the country of the Six Nations, we called you Town Destroyer; and to this day when that name is heard our women look behind them and turn pale, and our children cling close to the necks of their mothers."

CORNPLANTER TO GEORGE WASHINGTON, 1790

The raids in 1777 and 1778 by Tories and Iroquois warriors disrupted the northern frontier. Militiamen left the army to defend their homes, and the turmoil reduced supplies of food for citizens and soldiers alike; New York could not meet its quota of provisions for the Continental army. Hoping to prevent further raids, Major General John Sullivan led an expedition through the western Iroquois homeland in the summer of 1779. He was joined by troops under General James Clinton, making a combined army of 4,000 men. On August 29 this force fought a fierce battle with Joseph Brant, Cornplanter, and 600 Indians and Tories near Newtown, New York. But, as an American reported, the Iroquois and their allies "left the field ... with precipitation & in great confusion." The battle so overwhelmed the Iroquois that they avoided the Americans for the rest of the campaign.

The Americans burned crops and more than 40 Cayuga and Seneca villages. Devastated by the destruction, the Iroquois flocked to British forts for food and shelter during the unusually bitter winter that followed. But American hopes that the raids would stop did not materialize. As one American officer put it: "The nests are destroyed, but the birds are still on the wing." The Iroquois and Tories struck back with a vengeance in 1780 and 1781. Oneida and Tuscarora villages, as well as Samuel Kirkland's church, felt their combined wrath.

Peace was finally imposed on the Iroquois in the summer of 1782. They paid a terrible price for the mixed loyalties that they maintained to the British and the Americans: The tribes were divided and scattered, many had died from battle or disease, and all but two of their villages had been ravaged. Abandoned by their allies at the peace conference, the Six Nations began a fight for their survival that took place not on the battlefield this time, but at the negotiating table with the new United States of America.

President Washington presented this engraved silver peace medal to Iroquois leaders as a postwar gesture of conciliation. He was given the Iroquois name Town Destroyer, eventually the Iroquois word for "president."

CHAPTER 4

ON TO YORKTOWN

*"I have been obliged to effect that by finesse which
I dare not attempt by force."*

MAJOR GENERAL NATHANAEL GREENE TO THOMAS JEFFERSON, 1781

Calling these 2,000 or so ragged, starving men an army would have seemed a cruel joke to any European military man. Camped out in makeshift wigwams made of fence rails and poles thatched with brush and cornstalks, atop a rust-colored sea of semifrozen North Carolina clay, they resembled a mob of armed beggars more than they did a fighting force. Few of them wore anything that could be called a uniform, and some wore almost nothing at all. Many had no shoes; their feet, wrapped in rags, sometimes seeped a deeper red into the ugly ground. Shivering, sick, and demoralized, barely two-thirds of the men were fit for military duty. But even in adversity, this remnant of the Southern Department of the Continental Army of the United States of America could muster to greet a new commander.

As Major General Nathanael Greene gazed back at them on this second day of December in 1780, he may have flinched internally, seeing this melancholy parody of military disorder, but he radiated only a reassuring calm. At five feet ten, the 38-year-old general was tall for his day, and an imposing presence. His wise, handsome face framed penetrating steel-blue eyes; Greene exuded a tranquil—indeed, almost a nonchalant—confidence. But he did not cut a very

military figure. He was given to corpulence, his right eye had a slight cast (the result of a smallpox vaccination), he walked with a mild limp, and he possessed little of the born leader's natural fire. And Greene was not a gentleman. A fifth-generation American, he was the son of a wealthy Rhode Island foundry owner; while his more aristocratic contemporaries attended school, Greene had helped hammer out iron anchors and chains for sailing ships. A hired schoolmaster tutored him in Latin and mathematics. But everything he knew about military science, history, and philosophy had been self-taught, and his meticulous sense of organization had been honed as an overseer of his father's business, one of Rhode Island's biggest by the time young Greene and his brothers inherited it.

As for his seeming aloofness, some attributed it to Greene's longtime membership in the Society of Friends, or Quakers, whose pacifist beliefs precluded violence. In fact, Greene had turned away from their doctrine in 1773 by attending his first militia meeting in Plainfield, Connecticut. A year later, he had helped form the Kentish Guards, a hometown militia unit in East Greenwich. His fellow guardsmen had passed him over as an officer candidate because his limp, in their view, was incompatible with

"What I have been dreading has come to pass," Major General Nathanael Greene wrote his wife, Catherine, in October 1780. He had just been ordered to take command of the demoralized American southern army; instead of a quiet winter with his family, he now faced a grueling campaign against the British general Cornwallis.

a true military bearing; Greene was stung by the slight but remained as a private. By 1774 he had become a Rhode Island state legislator with a keen interest in the coming fight for freedom. When his colony raised its first 1,500-man Army of Observation, Greene was its brigadier general. The neatly organized, well-supplied Rhode Islanders stood out against the chaos and confusion of the ragtag Americans besieging English Boston, and their leader soon caught the keen eye of General Washington, who noted that the Rhode Island troops "are under much better government than any around Boston."

Greene was, in fact, the last of the 14 generals to be appointed by the Continental Congress, but he was soon regarded by many as first among equals—the man who should take command of the Continental army if anything happened to George Washington. The Rhode Islander was, Washington declared soon after Bunker Hill, an object of his confidence, and before long the great man had dubbed Greene his "privy councillor."

Greene had been offered the plum command of the key fortress at West Point in October of 1780. The previous holder of that position—Benedict Arnold—had been exposed as a traitor and had defected to the British side.

Then, with the West Point assignment barely savored, Washington had asked Greene to take another, less desirable job: the command of America's beaten army in the South. To Greene, who had never even crossed the Potomac River, this domain was as remote as Patagonia. It meant he might not see his wife, Kitty, or his children for at least another year; and it held almost no chance of success. But he was a soldier, and when his friend and commander in chief gave an order, he obeyed.

In just two years, the Continental army of the South had gone through three commanders; Greene was the fourth. It had proved an unlucky assignment for his predecessors. Most of the Carolina and Virginia regulars formerly in this command had been among the 5,500 troops trapped and forced to surrender to British troops seven months earlier at

Charleston. Since that defeat, this ruined army had marched through brackish, fever-laden swamps and loblolly pine barrens where food was as sparse as support for their cause. They had been attacked by hordes of mosquitoes and tiny gnats that settled on their eyes to suck up the oil at the base of their lashes. They had breathed in the miasma that, according to the medical lore of the time, brought on yellow fever, malaria, and dysentery. Finally, in August, they had suffered a shocking defeat at Camden, South Carolina, by Britain's southern commander, Charles, Lord Cornwallis, and his ruthless bull mastiff of a commander, Lieutenant Colonel Banastre Tarleton, whose legion was known as the Green Dragoons after the color of their tunics. One British admirer remarked that Tarleton, the Oxford-educated son of a Liverpool merchant family, had murdered more men and ravished more women than anyone else in the British army.

Camden had been an accident. The congress, which controlled all of the top military appointments, had given the southern command to Major General Horatio Gates, the portly, avuncular hero of Saratoga. Some 4,100 American regulars and militia—with just over 3,000 of them fit for duty—had taken the field against some 2,200 British regulars, volunteer Loyalists, and cavalry commanded by Cornwallis. Gates, however, puffed up with bravado and blissfully ignorant of the territory he was now fighting on, apparently believed he commanded 7,000 men. Indeed, the Saratoga hero's judgment seemed to fail at every juncture. Rather than take a roundabout route through fertile, rebel-friendly territory, Gates had taken two weeks to push 120 miles across sucking swamp and drab pineland, through territory unrelentingly hostile to the Revolutionaries, exhausting and sickening his troops, whose stomachs griped on a diet of little more than green corn and unripened peaches. Near Camden in the predawn of August 16, a detachment of dragoons at the head of Gates's column had bumped into advance elements of Tarleton's legion marching in the opposite direc-

ENEMY IN DISGUISE

Oars muffled by sheepskin, a small boat slipped through the dark waters of the Hudson around 2 a.m. on September 22, 1780, passing quietly by American defenses near West Point. In its stern sat John André, British adjutant general and chief of intelligence. Ambition and a love of drama impelled the young major to risk himself, instead of a trained agent, this night. Awaiting him on the western bank was an American hero-turned-traitor—Benedict Arnold.

Arnold's laming at Saratoga in 1777, and the congress's failure to reward him properly then—and at other times—had embittered him. Rage deepened in April 1780 when he received a public reprimand from Washington for misconduct while military governor of Philadelphia. At the same time, Arnold was living way beyond his means. Seeking retribution and money, he persuaded Washington to name him commander of West Point. West Point's protection of the Hudson kept the British from splitting the northern and southern colonies. For £20,000, Arnold would surrender the fortress to the enemy and deliver a death blow to the rebellion.

As dawn overtook the conspirators on the Hudson, a horrified André watched as American cannon fire drove off his waiting ship, the *Vulture*. Trapped, he reluctantly agreed to don civilian garb and try for the British lines on horseback. Secreted in his stockings were papers on West Point's defenses.

With a pass signed by Arnold for "John Anderson," André rode nervously through American territory. By 9 a.m. on September 23 he was certain he had passed the last American outpost and felt his spirits rising. But as he slowed to cross a bridge near Tarrytown, three roughly clad men with muskets jumped from the bushes.

Startled, André unwisely said: "Gentlemen, I hope you belong to our party." When the leader asked which one, André replied "lower," or the king's. The man nodded, and a relieved André declared himself a British officer. New York militiamen John Paulding, David Williams, and Isaac Van Wart, who had been lying in wait to rob British sympathizers, had heard enough. They ordered André to dismount, dismissing his belated offering of Arnold's pass, and searched him for valuables. The secret papers were found. Paulding, reading them, cried out, "This is a spy!"

The captive, his pass, and his documents, written in Arnold's distinctive hand, bewildered Lieutenant Colonel John Jameson at the American post in North Castle. Wisely, he dispatched the

BRIGADIER GEN.^L ARNOLD.

This 1781 English etching of Benedict Arnold is based on a French portrait that was executed three years earlier, honoring him as a great American war hero.

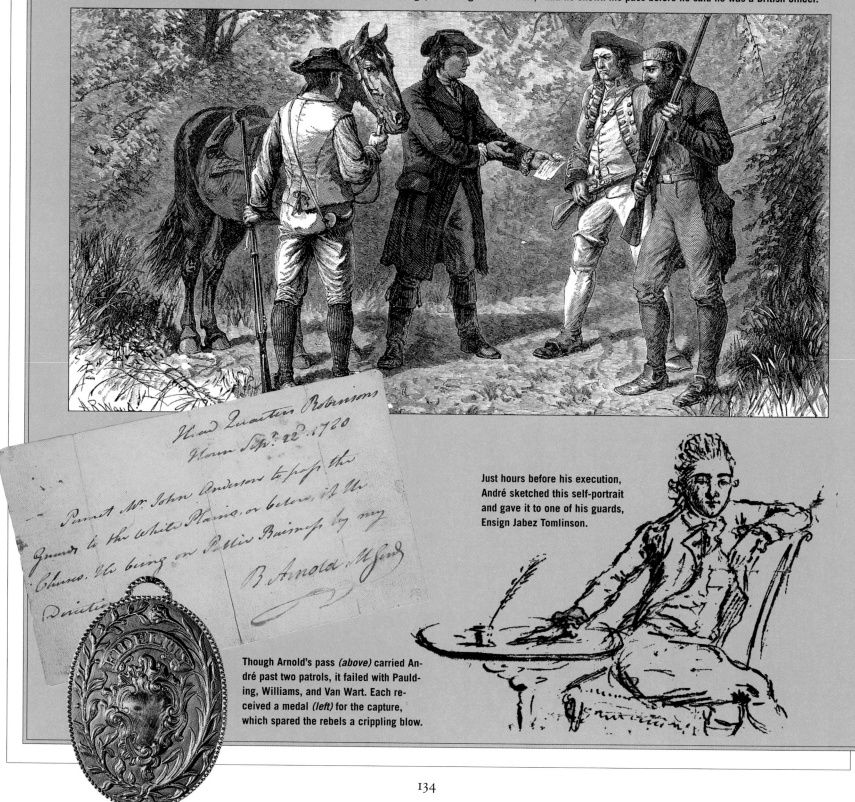

Stopped by New York militiamen John Paulding, David Williams, and Isaac Van Wart, Major John André tries without success to win his release by offering General Arnold's pass in this 19th-century illustration by Alfred R. Waud. "I would have let him go," Paulding testified later, "had he shown his pass before he said he was a British officer."

Just hours before his execution, André sketched this self-portrait and gave it to one of his guards, Ensign Jabez Tomlinson.

Though Arnold's pass (above) carried André past two patrols, it failed with Paulding, Williams, and Van Wart. Each received a medal (left) for the capture, which spared the rebels a crippling blow.

papers to Washington, even then headed to West Point for an inspection. However, he also sent word to his immediate superior, Benedict Arnold.

Arnold received Jameson's letter 30 minutes before Washington's arrival. He fled to his nearby barge and commanded the soldiers to row him to the *Vulture,* which had returned for André. Once aboard, he had the oarsmen imprisoned. Back at Arnold's house, Washington received his own dispatch. Stricken, he asked, "Whom can we trust now?"

The American traitor was safe but the English patriot was not. In a letter to Washington, André revealed his identity. He had come ashore in uniform, wrote the major, never meaning to become "an enemy in disguise." But once André shed his scarlet coat, he became a spy, condemned to death if captured.

André's final request—to be shot as a soldier, not hanged as a spy—was denied. On October 2, 1780, 30-year-old John André, dressed in the regimentals he had sent for, walked to the gallows and placed the noose around his own neck. To the American officers who accompanied him, and had come to respect him, he said simply, "I would have you gentlemen bear me witness that I die like a brave man."

"I could not think an attempt to put an end to a civil war, and to stop the effusion of human blood, a crime."

JOHN ANDRÉ, OCTOBER 1, 1780

John André's body hangs from the gallows in this picture from a 1783 book entitled *History of England.* George III, touched by the tragedy of André's death, built a monument in Westminster Abbey to the young major, who "fell a Sacrifice to his Zeal for his King and Country."

tion down the Charlotte road; the rebels were easily pushed back into Gates's main force.

Cornwallis had attacked early that morning. His disciplined troops smashed through the Virginia militia and sent them running in panic down the road. Within minutes, what had seemed to be a battle in the making had become a rout—and none had withdrawn faster than Gates, who did not end his retreat until he reached Hillsborough, 180 miles from the disaster, three days later.

Greene knew that the broken men before him had been victims of something worse than bad luck—they had been badly led by the crestfallen general who today greeted him as his successor. Greene took an appraising look at Horatio Gates and could not help but pity him. The new commander had been ordered by the congress to convene a military court of inquiry into Gates's conduct at Camden. Characteristically, he gave no sign of this other mandate, but greeted his disgraced rival with respect and sympathy, which deepened as he learned that Gates had recently been informed of the death of his only son. Greene performed a quick head count and decided there were not enough senior officers left in the command to make up the court; he would ignore the order. It was the merest detail, given their desperate situation.

Cornwallis was still in the field at Winnsboro, South Carolina, only about 75 miles southwest of where Greene stood. The Briton's powerful force of about 2,400 men awaited reinforcements under the command of Major General Alexander Leslie, whose troops were scheduled to land at Charleston in December and then march toward Winnsboro. Virtually all of South Carolina and Georgia now appeared to have come within the British grasp. One more major defeat, and the war in the South would be lost. Then Cornwallis would be free to strike north through the Carolinas into Virginia, the rich heartland of southern support for the rebellion, and bring the five-year-old Revolution to a speedy end.

Those were black clouds indeed to see on the first day of a new command, but there seemed little else on the Americans' tactical horizon—indeed, the revolutionaries had by now become somewhat accustomed to defeat. Yet, although he did not know it, Nathanael Greene was about to embark on a daring, brilliantly unconventional campaign that would prove decisive.

The Continental army could have sent no better man than Nathanael Greene to return the lethal favors of Cornwallis and Tarleton, although during the early days of his new command he would have felt little enthusiasm for the daunting task at hand. He had all of 90 cavalrymen, 60 artillerymen, and about 1,500 foot soldiers fit for duty—if one stretched the standards a bit. As far as supplies were concerned, barely three days' rations remained. Greene asked Colonel William R. Davie, a tall, elegant Princeton man turned tough cavalry officer—his troops were known to Loyalists as "the Bloody Corps"—to be the new commissary general. When Davie protested that he knew nothing of money or accounts, Greene reportedly replied: "Don't concern yourself. There is no money and hence no accounts."

They were also short on order. With food nearly gone, the soldiers had taken to disappearing for days at a time to forage for anything to break their hunger. Soon after his arrival, Greene had one such forager hanged in full view of the troops. That put an end to wandering. He then turned to making life in the miserable camp a little more tolerable by ordering his redoubtable Polish engineer, Colonel Tadeusz Kosciuszko, to build decent huts for the miserable men. He also sent a number of the nearly naked Virginians home, as they were in no condition to serve.

Beyond the sad state of his army lay a strange and hostile world that Greene found to be vastly different from anything in his northern experience. There was no prosperous base of industry or agri-

Before the war, Charles, Lord Cornwallis sympathized with the American colonies, voting against the Stamp Act and the Declaratory Act, a 1766 bill asserting Britain's right to legislate for the colonies in all cases. Loyalty to king and country reigned supreme, however, and Cornwallis, British commander in the South, rigorously fought the challenge to royal authority.

"The rebel forces being at present dispersed, the internal commotions and insurrections in this province will now subside. But I shall ... inflict exemplary punishment ... to deter others ... from sporting with allegiance and oaths."

LORD CORNWALLIS, CAMDEN
AUGUST 21, 1780

culture to draw on. Furthermore, he could not count on the loyalty of a large part of the population.

Yet even before his arrival in Charlotte, Greene had detected faint glimmerings of opportunity in the unyielding harshness of the countryside and its fractionated population—the very qualities that seemed most to preclude an American success might be turned with equal effect against the British. One need not fight set piece battles in such a place; one could fight as partisans, striking with small, highly mobile forces at the clumsy British giant. If he could lure Cornwallis into fighting on his terms and terrain, Greene believed, he could win not with major victories but by avoiding catastrophic defeats. The stronger contestant's own great weight could be used to destroy it.

Just two months earlier an American force of frontier riflemen had provided a case in point. They had trapped the left wing of Cornwallis's army—about 1,000 Loyalist troops—atop a long ridge known as Kings Mountain, just inside the South Carolina border west of Charlotte, with more than 300 casualties and 700 captured. The rebels suffered only 90 casualties.

With the riflemen's victory in mind, Greene had used his southern journey to prepare a new style of combat. He had written to Washington about the need to equip a "flying army of about 800 horse and 1,000 infantry." Washington had replied with a fine parting gift: the legion of Lieutenant Colonel Henry Lee, a young Virginian who was one of the commander in chief's favorite officers. When he arrived in January, Light-Horse Harry Lee would bring with him 140 horsemen and an equal number of fleet foot soldiers, the cream of Washington's mobile forces and the Revolution's answer to the harrying squadrons of Banastre Tarleton.

The new commander and Washington had also discussed the importance of using the myriad waterways of the region, which could be both highway and barrier to land armies. More than half a dozen major streams—the Dan and Roanoke, the Haw, the Pee Dee and Yadkin, the Catawba and Santee, the Broad—drained southeastward from the eastern foothills of the Blue Ridge Mountains to the sea. On his way to Charlotte, scavenging supplies as he traveled, Greene had stopped in Richmond and met Lieutenant Colonel Edward Carrington, who had surveyed the Roanoke River for Horatio Gates. Greene asked him to do the same for the Dan, a Roanoke tributary that meandered off to the west across the back country.

At Hillsborough, Greene met Colonel Kosciuszko and asked him to make a survey of the Catawba. A third survey party under Brigadier General Edward Stevens was sent to explore the Yadkin. In effect, even as he proceeded southward, Greene had begun to acquire a meticulous knowledge of his strategic rear. Although he had never before seen the Catawba, he would soon know it as well as men who had grown up along the river.

No matter how detailed Greene's geographic intelligence or how novel his strategy, his campaign would sink or swim on the abilities of its leaders—especially one tall, burly former teamster. Daniel Morgan had arrived in the Carolinas in September, carrying a reputation that stretched across all 13 colonies. At age 44 Morgan had been a fighter for more than half his life, first as a teamster with the Braddock expedition, then during the French and Indian War, then against the British. Tough, profane, and crafty, Morgan combined a commander's tactical sense with

CAMPAIGN FURNITURE

According to its brass plaque, this 18th-century field table was presented to a Colonel William F. Fitzhugh by Lord Cornwallis, in November 1781, as a token of the general's "deep regard and sincere appreciation." Little is known of the circumstances surrounding this event, but commanders commonly spread their maps on such tables when plotting the movement of their troops during a campaign. Like most camp furniture carried by English and American officers, the table collapses to facilitate transport. Its top is edged in rosewood and the legs are thought to be padouk, a Burmese wood then valued by the English military for strength and durability.

a frontiersman's knack for using every creek and tree bole to advantage.

Until recently, the famous partisan had brooded at his Virginia farmstead, racked by bouts of rheumatism, sciatica, and official neglect. Morgan had been passed over by the congress for promotion to brigadier general, although he received the support of General Washington. The rifleman had protested the slight by going home. After the Camden disaster Gates had entreated him to change his mind, and Morgan had finally consented.

Assured of Morgan's help, Greene reached out to the other great wilderness warriors of the Revolution, the elusive partisan commanders who had learned how to play hit-and-run war in the waterlogged fastnesses of the region—what would come to be called guerrilla warfare in modern times. Chief among them was Francis Marion, who had picked up his craft in the Cherokee expedition of 1761 and who was famous as the Swamp Fox—a nickname bestowed by Tarleton himself. A lieutenant colonel commanding the Second South Carolina Continental Regiment, Marion had eluded capture during the siege of Charleston at the cost of a broken ankle and had been ordered by Gates to organize patriotic resistance in the region between the Pee Dee and Santee Rivers.

By the time Greene arrived at Charlotte, the dark, wiry Swamp Fox had already fought from horseback for half a year against the British without any logistical support, intimidating Loyalists and sniping at Cornwallis's supply lines. He had been known to travel 50 miles in a single night to stage a sudden attack, then melt back into the watery underbrush. When chased, he would retreat, ambush his pursuers, then retreat again. "I have not the honor of your acquaintance," Greene wrote Marion from his camp near Charlotte, "but I am no stranger to your character and merit."

Another name that Greene was conjuring with was that of Colonel Andrew Pick-

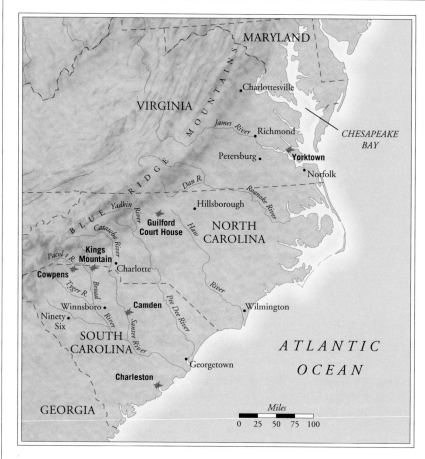

MARYLAND

•Charlottesville

VIRGINIA

James River •Richmond

CHESAPEAKE BAY

Petersburg• **Yorktown**

•Norfolk

Dan R.

Roanoke River

•Hillsborough

Yadkin River

Guilford Court House

NORTH CAROLINA

Catawba River

Haw River

Kings Mountain

Pacolet R.

•Charlotte

Cowpens

Broad River

Tiger R.

River

Winnsboro•

Camden

Pee Dee River

•Wilmington

Ninety Six

Santee River

SOUTH CAROLINA

ATLANTIC OCEAN

•Georgetown

Charleston

GEORGIA

Miles

0   25   50   75   100

The many rivers of the Carolinas impeded and aided American and Englishman alike as their armies crossed and recrossed the waterways during the southern campaign. The American and English forces clashed in several battles before Cornwallis moved northward into Virginia, toward the small harbor town of York.

ens, a 41-year-old Presbyterian warrior who appeared so taciturn that, it was said, he only spoke after he had put his words "between his fingers and examined them." A veteran Indian fighter, Pickens had been captured at Ninety Six after the siege of Charleston, and paroled when he gave his word not to pick up arms again. He had kept that promise until ravaging Tories plundered his Long Cane Creek plantation in South Carolina. Then Pickens once again reached for his saber, although, true to his upbringing, he first rode to the nearest British outpost and personally informed the commander of his intention to take back his parole.

Greene was less successful with another famous partisan, prickly 46-year-old Thomas Sumter, whose nom de guerre was the Carolina Gamecock. Rivaling the Swamp Fox in reputation, Sumter had also learned to fight like an Indian in the Cherokee expedition and had served with the South Carolina militia. But he had been in retirement when the present hostilities commenced. After Tarleton's legion burned down his plantation, the Gamecock moved into the field, raised a militia, and began a series of retaliatory raids, with mixed success. Indeed, his strategic sense appeared to be not much better than a gamecock's, and his career suffered a disaster just before the Camden battle, when Tarleton gave him a bad beating at Fishing Creek. A second skirmish in November had ended bloodily in a tie; a third run-in on November 20 at Blackstocks had left him badly wounded, although his men fought Tarleton to a standstill. When Greene asked him to join his forces, however, Sumter declined, preferring to conduct his own war against the British.

Having brought in the partisans who would come, Greene pondered his most pressing problem: how to get out of Charlotte without bringing Cornwallis baying at his heels. He discussed strategy with his top advisers, then made his decision. Even as the enemy gathered strength, Greene explained to his staff and General Washington, he would split his small, weary force in two. Roughly two-thirds of it, under his command, would march east to the Pee Dee, to a spot named Hick's Creek, and await the arrival of Light-Horse Harry Lee. Morgan would move west across the Catawba with the remaining third—320 light infantry, 200 riflemen, and 80 cavalry under Colonel William Washington, the commander in chief's second cousin.

Greene was painfully aware that in dividing his inferior force he violated one of the fundamental tenets of classical warfare. But this tactic was not all desperation. Greene had shrewdly calculated that, if he diluted his own strength, he forced the same, and worse, upon Cornwallis. In the foreground of Greene's mind was a map not of his immediate campaign front but of the entire southern theater of battle. On that larger backdrop he could see the enemy's fatal weakness. Aside from Cornwallis's forces, and their main supply base at Charleston, British troops were strung like red beads across Savannah, Charleston, Beaufort, Georgetown, Camden, Ninety Six, Winnsboro, Augusta. The thinly spread force was the perfect target for fast-moving partisans, and splitting the American army caught Cornwallis in a fork move. "He cannot leave Morgan behind him to come at me," Greene observed, "or his posts of Ninety Six and Augusta would be exposed. And he cannot chase Morgan far, or prosecute his views upon Virginia, while I am here with the whole country open before me."

On December 16, barely two weeks after his arrival, Greene issued marching orders. Walls of rain began to fall, delaying his departure for the banks of the Pee Dee until December 20. The next day, Morgan and his small troop marched off for the Catawba.

Cornwallis watched the American maneuvers through the eyes of scouts and spies from his headquarters in Winnsboro. He had known when Greene took up his command, and had an excellent idea of his strength. Now word reached him of Greene's latest move. The aristocratic Briton and

The Swamp Fox, Francis Marion, travels the Pee Dee River with his ragged band of fighters in the 19th-century painting below. Marion's successful hit-and-run tactics against the enemy impressed even British colonel Banastre Tarleton: "Mr. Marion, by his zeal and abilities, shewed himself capable of the trust committed to his charge."

the merchant-class American embodied all the differences between the two sides in this war—Cornwallis was an heir to a great fortune, Eton educated, trained at Turin's incomparable military academy, a veteran of combat in the Seven Years' War, a well-placed member of the world's most powerful colonial elite. He was all that Greene was not. If they had something in common, it was a taste for the bold, unexpected gambit, a willingness to risk everything on a daring stroke. The difference was that Cornwallis was a tactician, Greene a strategist; the American saw the forest, the Briton, only trees.

The American tactic suggested that Greene acted without any real idea of the force arrayed against him—a force that would soon include 1,500 of Leslie's troops, who had arrived in Charleston on December 13. That was a blind—in actuality Greene knew what he faced. Cornwallis poked further into his enemy's intentions and at last saw what Greene was up to. By dividing the American army, Greene had effectively divided Cornwallis's forces as well.

But, reassured by Leslie's reinforcements, Cornwallis decided to divide his own force into three parts. One would be left to guard Camden under Lieutenant Colonel Lord Francis Rawdon. Tarleton and his 1,100 cavalry and foot soldiers would become a fast-moving hammer that would pursue Morgan and finally crush him against an anvil—Cornwallis's third force, which would hover in North Carolina and intercept the rebels as they fled from Tarleton's onslaught.

A British victory of that magnitude, like the win at Camden, would attract the region's Tories to fight for the British Crown, an essential element in the strategic calculations of Sir Henry Clinton, Cornwallis, and the ministers watching from London. Despite abundant evidence to the contrary, they all still believed in the myth that a vast population of

Fearing that his entire garrison at Ninety Six might be in jeopardy, Cornwallis let slip the Green Dragoons. On January 1, 1781, the 550-man legion and 200 kilted Scots Highlanders of the 71st Infantry Regiment moved briskly toward the Broad River, along with a Royal Artillery squad dragging a pair of three-pounders, called grasshoppers because they hopped when fired. Another 250 men soon joined them. Their aim: to cross the Broad, then push Morgan back to the north toward Kings Mountain, where the combined forces of Cornwallis and Leslie—the anvil—would be waiting.

Tarleton's were not the only dragoons riding across South Carolina. Five days after the Loyalist troop set out on its search-and-destroy mission, Light-Horse Harry Lee and his troop cantered into Nathanael Greene's camp on the Pee Dee, spurs jin-

"I received intelligence that a body of Georgia tories, about two hundred and fifty in number, had advanced as far as Fair Forest.... I dispatched Lieut.-Col. Washington, with his own regiment and two hundred militia horse ... to attack them.... One hundred and fifty were killed and wounded, and about forty taken prisoners. What makes this success more valuable, it was attained without the loss of a man."

BRIGADIER GENERAL DANIEL MORGAN, CAMP ON PACOLET CREEK, DECEMBER 31, 1780

southern Tories would leap at the chance to fight alongside British troops.

Before either hammer or anvil could be emplaced, however, Morgan made his presence known. A week after his small, footsore band had headed west, the Virginia commander heard that some 250 Georgia Loyalists had crossed the Savannah River and were torching American homesteads along Fair Forest Creek, north of Ninety Six and Winnsboro. Morgan wasted no time. William Washington and his dragoons, supported by units of South Carolina and Georgia mounted militia, thundered after the raiders and caught up with them at a small cluster of dwellings called Hammond's Store. In the screaming, smoke-misted melee, 150 Tories were sabered out of their saddles and another 40 captured.

gling and plumed helmets glinting in the sun. The grimy army could only stand and gape at this dashing new weapon. The young Virginian—Lee was only 24——stayed for a week while Greene instructed him on the tactics he wanted the horsemen to use, and contacted the man with whom Lee would join forces: Francis Marion. In mid-January, Lee and his men vanished into the swamps to join the Fox.

The Green Dragoons' quarry, somewhat revived by the successful ambush of the Loyalist raiders from Georgia, still faced hard times. Morgan had managed to reinstill some of the old fighting spirit into his small band of men, but his very presence in the region had antagonized Thomas Sumter, the militia brigadier who considered himself to be the commander of the region around Pacolet Creek, where Morgan had settled into camp. Sumter resented the newcomer's reputation so much that he ordered his men not to help the intruders forage without his personal say-so. Before the end of the summer, the Carolina Gamecock's tactical blunders would, as Harry Lee put it, make his name "almost universally odious" and end Sumter's career.

For the moment, however, Sumter was principally a pebble in Morgan's boot, for the old wagoner had more pressing problems to deal with. Hundreds of militia volunteers were swarming in from the surrounding countryside to join Morgan's troop, and the Virginian found it was becoming increasingly difficult to feed either his men or his horses. Morgan informed Greene that he must either advance or retreat, but as December turned into January, he was himself not sure which. "Col. Tarleton is said to be on his way to pay you a visit," Greene wrote Morgan. "I doubt not but he will have a decent reception and a proper dismission." Of course, retreat was out of the question.

Waiting did not suit Morgan's temperament; it made him depressed and let him dwell upon his physical agony. The all-enveloping dampness of the Carolina winter was seeping into his bones, reigniting his acute sciatica. His joints were stiffening so severely that he could barely mount a horse. He began toying with the idea of a quick strike into Georgia, just to keep the enemy off-balance—and his own internal fires burning. But his orders were to stay in place, like a tethered goat waiting for a tiger.

On January 15, camped at a spot called Burr's Mills on Thicketty Creek, Morgan began a mournful letter to Greene. "My force," he wrote, "is inadequate to the attempts you have hinted at." He asked to come back to the main force, leaving the harassment of the British to mounted militia forces. Be-

Although the number of men he commanded was small, American brigadier general Daniel Morgan's military skill and resourcefulness posed a severe threat to the British. On January 2, 1780, Cornwallis urged his dragoon commander, Lieutenant Colonel Banastre Tarleton, to pursue the American and "push him to the utmost."

fore Morgan finished the letter, he got news that altered its conclusion. Tarleton had just crossed the nearby Tyger River and was moving as fast as he could in a heavy downpour. He was just 10 miles distant, looking for ways to cross the Pacolet.

Morgan's doleful letter was put aside, along with the discomfort of his sciatica and rheumatism. The bad news fired him with energy. But it was necessary for him to move quickly. His troops were scattered up and down Pacolet Creek, guarding its many fords.

Tarleton marched upstream toward Wofford's ironworks, where he had his men make a silent, fireless bivouac. But it was a ruse. At night, the British troops stole back down the Pacolet and made their crossing six miles below Morgan's rear guard, tantalizingly close to the prey: His men discovered still-burning fires with half-cooked breakfasts on them.

Morgan had sent word up and down the waterway: fall back fast. His soaking huddle of Continental regulars, militia, and riflemen, encumbered with heavy, wooden-wheeled wagons, had quickly formed ranks before dawn on January 16 and began moving toward Cherokee Ford, the best place for them to cross the Broad. Keenly aware of these implacable British hounds on his fresh trail, Morgan pushed his men another dozen miles. Finally, he stopped for the night in a swath of sparsely treed meadow called Hannah's Cowpens; a local Tory farmer had owned extensive cattle enclosures there.

Morgan waited for his force to regroup. Some of his men were still quick-marching in from their upstream positions, and Pickens was due to arrive with 150 newly inducted militia. "Many a hearty curse had been vented against Gen. Morgan," recalled one soldier, "for retreating, as we thought, to avoid a fight." Hunted by a mobile force they had reason to fear, they had been marched out of a strong defensive position moated by a swollen creek, in favor of

Brutal and relentless, Banastre Tarleton, commander of the British Legion in America, earned the nickname Bloody Tarleton after slaughtering Americans who were surrendering in battle. Vengeful rebels at the Battle of Cowpens, yelling "Tarleton's quarter," would have struck down British prisoners had American officers not intervened.

this ominously open place—this place that looked like a killing ground.

When dusk fell on that first day of retreat, Morgan was still seven miles from the Cherokee Ford on the Broad River. In classical military terms, his position was disastrously bad, opening toward a voracious enemy but with a wide, rain-swollen river barring his line of retreat to the north and east. There was no swamp or thicket on either of Morgan's flanks to protect him from an enveloping charge by the dragoons. The only advantage Cowpens offered the Americans was the vantage point of two small hills toward the northern edge of the clearing, with a dip about 80 yards long between the smaller and the larger. Behind the second hill was open meadow all the way to the river. Tarleton himself would write, "Certainly as good a place for action as Lt. Col. Tarletone could desire. America does not produce any more suitable for the nature of the troops under his command."

Morgan saw it differently. "My situation at the Cowpens," he explained afterward, "enabled me to improve any advantage I might gain, and to provide better for my own security should I be unfortunate. These reasons induced me to take this post at the risk of its wearing the face of a retreat." He considered the river at his back an advantage, because it gave his militia—notoriously prone to run from a determined attack by British soldiers—no way to retreat. "Men fight as much as they find necessary and no more," he would laconically observe. "When men are forced to fight, they will sell their lives dearly." He bade his soldiers, whose numbers were still swelling as militia units joined them, to set up camp, light fires, and enjoy what might be their last dinner.

Having decided to take a stand, Morgan became the legendary warrior chieftain of earlier days. As his men hunkered down around their fires, he ordered the supply wagons to safety five miles away and led off his mounted militia's horses, to remove the temptation of flight. Then he sat down to devise a plan that would avoid the perennial problem of the American forces: how to keep the militia units from collapsing, as they had at almost every juncture—as they had with Gates at Camden.

Militia aside, some of the troops under Morgan's command were among the best the Continental army had to provide: 300 blooded veterans of the Maryland and Delaware line. Another group of 140 Virginia riflemen, and a company of Georgians, had seen nearly as much action: Many of them were Continental army vets eager to take another crack at the enemy. They were all under the command of Lieutenant Colonel John Eager Howard, "as good an officer," Greene observed, "as the world affords." These would be the backbone of his force, and Morgan put them 150 yards ahead of the crest of the first, lower hill at the south end of the pasture.

Then he turned to some 300 North and South Carolina militia under Colonel Pickens. Many were armed with long rifles, which would give them an edge over the British regulars in terms of accuracy. Morgan placed them 150 yards down the slope from his main line, where they would fire only two volleys at nearly point-blank range before turning and marching left across the field of battle, at which point they would swing behind the main battle line, re-form, and wait to return to the fight. In effect, Morgan was meeting Tarleton's strength with his least reliable troops, then moving the men out of the action before they were panicked by the proximity of cold steel. Another 150 yards below them, in the grass and trees at the bottom of the hill, he put 150 Georgia and North Carolina sharpshooters under the command of Major Joseph McDowell and Major John Cunningham. Both the riflemen and the Carolinians had instructions

"If warfare allow me, I shall give these disturbers of the peace no quarter. If humanity obliges me to spare their lives, I shall convoy them close prisoners to Camden."

BANASTRE TARLETON, AUGUST 5, 1780

A menacing skull and crossbones decorates the front of this plumed helmet, worn by a rider of the 17th Light Dragoons. The detachment under Tarleton in the South wore white turbans across the back instead of the red one seen here.

to take aim in particular at the stripes and epaulettes—the British officers and noncoms.

Finally, Morgan prepared another surprise for the attacking dragoons. Half a mile behind the hill where he had placed his main line, he stationed Lieutenant Colonel Washington and his seasoned cavalry, bolstered with another 45 of the mounted Georgia infantry, armed with sabers and seated on the best remaining horses available.

As the night deepened, Morgan limped from campfire to campfire, bellowing encouragement, explaining his strategy, and putting spirit into his men. He told and retold his old story about the missing 500th lash on his back, pulling up his shirt as he did so, and promised to deliver the missing welt to Ben Tarleton with their help. Then he let his men get a good night's sleep.

At around 6 a.m., American scouts told Morgan that Tarleton was five miles away, and coming on fast. "Boys, get up, Benny is coming!" he shouted. The men ate a hurried breakfast and formed their lines. Morgan moved back and forth, giving fiery speeches. He finally stopped in front of Colonel Howard's line atop the hill. "My friends in arms, my dear boys," he cried, pounding his fist into his palm. "I request you to remember Saratoga, Monmouth, Paoli, Brandywine, and this day you must play your parts for your honor and liberty's cause."

At around 7 a.m., green coats showed through the woods at the bottom of the pasture, as about 50 dragoons and their supporting light infantry moved into the open field. Behind them were the 250 or so members of the legion infantry. Then came the dull shine of bronze as the grasshopper cannon moved up. Red coats flickered through the trees farther back: 200 men of the Seventh Regiment of Foot and 200 Scots from the 71st Highlanders, followed by 50 members of the

17th Light Dragoons. Then the bulk of Tarleton's cavalry emerged. The British commander had ordered his troops back into the saddle at 3 a.m., hoping to catch his prey against the swollen stream; he left his baggage and wagons behind with orders to move up at daybreak. But even traveling light, he slogged on after first light without any pause for breakfast—his men would fight on an empty stomach. But Tarleton was a confident hammer, buoyed by his low opinion of the rebel forces and the certainty that Cornwallis and Leslie were moving their anvil into position east of the trapped Americans.

The young dragoon was dead wrong on both points. He would find a potent foe at Cowpens, but he would not find an anvil. Cornwallis had delayed the march, believing that Tarleton was still blocked by flooding rivers.

The British soldiers began shedding their excess equipment and stacking it where it could be retrieved after the fight, then formed up for battle about 400 yards in front of the American sharpshooters. Tarleton placed his light infantry on the right and the legion infantry to the left of them, in the center. To their left he put the Seventh Regiment—a regiment of raw recruits. The small cannon were placed in the left and right of center, and 50 dragoons on each flank. The kilted Highlanders and 200 dragoons were kept in reserve.

Puffs of smoke rose suddenly from the grass and nearby trees: Morgan's riflemen were firing. Tarleton sent two troops, 50 cavalrymen, to chase them away. The Americans retreated slowly, firing as they moved backward, and 15 of the attackers toppled from their saddles. The other horsemen drew back.

Nettled by this unexpected reversal, Tarleton ordered his cannon to fire before his lines were fully formed, to drive back the marksmen. Then, cadenced by fife and drum, his men advanced. One American officer wrote admiringly, "It was the most beautiful line I ever saw." The soldiers started slowly, then accelerated into a trot, giving a loud shout.

"They gave us the British halloo, boys! Give them the Indian halloo, by God!" shouted Morgan, gallop-ing along the line of nervous militia, urging them to hold their fire until ordered to pull the trigger. The British trotted closer: 150 yards, 125. Then: "Fire!"

Pickens's militia unleashed its lead at a deadly 100 yards, aiming as they had been ordered at the glint of gold braid. Officers in unusual numbers fell—they composed some 40 percent of British dead—and the line began to resemble a pushed piece of string. The militia fired again, then began their prepared retreat, while the staggered British re-formed, fixed bayonets, and prepared to charge. For the last of the militia line, it was a long trip across the hill as the sharp steel moved toward them. They had only reached the center when they had a shock. Waving sabers and screaming for blood, 50 cavalry on the British right were after them. The citizen-soldiers began to run.

To the rest of the British line, the retreat smelled like the disastrous militia failure at Camden. They sprinted forward, baying defiance, pulling out of formation as they charged up the hill toward the main battle line; the soldiers there held their fire as the demoralized final segment of the militia line fled across their front. As the militia cleared the line of fire, the Americans blasted away in unison and the charge collapsed like an ox beneath a butcher's hammer. Still, as their casualties mounted, they kept marching, braving the storm of lead to put their bayonets to work.

The terrified militia regained something like good order as they marched behind the second of the two Cowpens hills, then moved full circle around to support the American line on the right. Their help was badly needed. Tarleton had called up his reserve Highlanders on his left, and the attacking British lines extended farther to their foes' right than the defenders' lines. The Highlanders were on the verge of outflanking them. Colonel Howard hastily ordered the Virginians on the right of his line to face about and meet the enemy. The command was misunderstood. The company turned 180 degrees as commanded—but then started to march off the battlefield. Other officers on the line saw the withdrawal and followed. Ever the fierce opportunist, Morgan kicked his horse hard and galloped in front of the retreating line. Over his shoulder, he could hear the British cheer as they saw an apparent retreat. Tarleton, whose ardor was always inflamed by the sight of his enemies' backs, threw his remaining cavalry into the battle, and the attackers broke ranks, advancing at a run.

Then Washington, waiting with his cavalry on the right, sent word to Morgan: "They're coming on like a mob. Give them one fire and I'll charge them." Morgan bellowed at his infantry to halt. "Give them one fire and the day is ours!"

The British were within 50 yards when the Continentals turned on their heels and fired a devastating volley from the hip. Then they leveled their own bayonets and charged back at the stunned enemy.

sparingly. The Continentals pivoted to face them, and Pickens's militia rushed in to engage them hand to hand. The Highlander commander, Major Archibald McArthur, was taken prisoner and the Scotsmen finally grounded their arms.

Tarleton himself was suddenly in a dangerous predicament. As he tried to make his own escape, William Washington spotted him and rushed in pursuit, alone. Galloping into close quarters, Washington slashed at one of the two officers with Tarleton, but he parried the blow—and broke Washington's blade in the middle. Before Tarleton's man could finish off his disarmed foe, Washington's 14-year-old bugler, a boy named Collins, rode up and put a pistol ball through the British officer's shoulder. Another officer struck at Washington, but the blow was parried by an American sergeant ma-

"The enemy's great superiority in numbers and our distance from the main army, will enable Lord Cornwallis to detach so superior a force against me as to render it essential to our safety to avoid coming to action." BRIGADIER GENERAL DANIEL MORGAN, JANUARY 15, 1781

Now it was Pickens's turn. He wheeled his militia back into the line and fired on the Highlanders. Washington also sprang into action, crashing into the British cavalry that had joined the charge up the hill. He and his troopers burst through the British horse, re-formed, and charged back again, smashing the Green Legion a second time. The cavalry quailed, and about 200 of them bolted from the battlefield. Washington was now behind the British regulars of the Seventh Regiment, who had no stomach for bayonets at their front and sabers at their back. Most of them threw down their muskets and fell facedown on the ground. The remaining British forces turned and began to run, scattering ammunition boxes as they fled. "An unaccountable panic," Tarleton mused later, "extended itself along the whole line." Before long, most of the fleeing soldiers were prisoners.

The only fighting remained on the American right, where the stubborn Highlanders gave ground

jor, who wounded the British dragoon with his saber. When Tarleton tried his blade on Washington, the American parried with the stump of his sword. After a second and third blow failed to maim Washington, the frustrated Tarleton fired his pistol into his enemy's horse and made good his escape with a band of 14 officers and 40 horsemen—all that remained of his 550 legionnaires.

To Daniel Morgan, the day must have seemed to be more like a miracle than an armed skirmish. In all, the American side lost only 12 dead and 60 wounded, whereas the British suffered 100 killed, 39 of whom were officers, as well as 229 wounded and about 600 taken prisoner. Morgan also picked up 800 muskets, 2 cannon, much baggage, and "all the enemy's music"—the British bagpipes, fifes, and drums. A few days later an elated Morgan wrote a friend, William Snickers, that they had given Tarleton "a devil of a whipping, a more compleat victory never was obtained."

"Colonel Washington's cavalry was among them like a whirlwind, and the poor fellows began to keel from their horses," wrote American James Collins of William Washington's charge against the British at Cowpens. Washington's actions saved a group of retreating militia, among them Collins, who had thought "my hide is in the loft" until that moment.

Lord Cornwallis and Leslie had marched their forces only as far as the settlement of Turkey Creek before the first straggling survivors of the Green Dragoons began to arrive with their disheartening report: The avenging hammer of the counterrevolution had been shattered. Perhaps even more unsettling was the attribution of blame. Many of the British officers disliked the arrogant Tarleton—a "rash, foolish boy," in the words of the Highlander major Archibald McArthur—whose close relationship with their chief apparently counted for more than experience and judgment.

The British leader penned a letter to Sir Henry Clinton that put the best face possible on the Cowpens disaster. Scrawling quickly, he exculpated Tarleton from any charges of negligence or bad judgment. Then, briefly betraying his emotion in a letter to Lord Rawdon, he confessed, "The late affair has almost broke my heart."

But as he paced around his tent at Turkey Creek, Cornwallis felt less sorrow than rage. Rain drizzled outside, and he could hear the cursing, shouted commands and creaking of heavy equipment as his army of some 3,000 men arrayed themselves for another fitful rest.

Beneath the sheets of rain, the British general railed against his condition. He had no interest in becoming the caretaker of obscure provincial garrisons in the backwoods of a savage colony, as Clinton evidently desired. If he stayed where he was, the

partisans could nibble away at his forces with relative impunity. But if he carried the fight into Virginia, he could end the war in a matter of months.

For the moment, however, there was the matter of his fury, and its authors, the damnable Nathanael Greene and Daniel Morgan. They had to be crushed and their British prisoners retrieved. With Leslie's men now in his column, Cornwallis could begin hounding Morgan through the Carolina winter.

Of course, the old wagoner had not waited to be caught. After Cowpens, Morgan headed east across the Broad River, then northeast across the North Carolina border toward the settlement of Ramsour's Mills near the Little Catawba River. The trek had been brutal. Even after leaving 60 wounded at Cowpens, two-thirds of Morgan's entourage were British prisoners, and the column was burdened by the weight of all the guns and other booty captured in the battle. Rain had poured down on the grunting, slipping men as they pushed across the Carolina Piedmont. Behind them, tributaries of the Broad were fattening up with mountain runoff, and the Catawba flooded ahead of them, making things steadily more difficult for the pursuing British. As a precaution, Morgan sent his prisoners on ahead; even if Cornwallis overtook and whipped him, he would not get back those men.

In fact, the British general and his long line of wagons, cannon carriages, and gear reached Ramsour's Mills just two days after the Americans had crossed the Catawba. Cornwallis had already ditched some of his heaviest baggage—along with the army's camp followers—in order to speed up the advance, but Morgan was still 20 miles away, and although he covered only about 10 miles a day, likely to maintain that separation.

Desperately looking for greater mobility, Cornwallis had the kind of brainstorm that few of his colleagues—Clinton, for one—would have considered. He would get rid of almost all his baggage—supplies, extra clothing, tents, all but such essentials as salt and ammunition—and turn his entire force into the equivalent of a light infantry. Like the ancient Greeks burning their boats before besieging Troy, he would make this place his point of no return.

The soggy North Carolina woods became the scene of a bizarre rite, as horse carts, food, clothing, and the personal effects of a European army on the march went up in smoke amid the loblolly pines. The air filled with the scent of officers' cologne, hair powder, and—saddest of all, for the men—rum, as even the store of British grog was sacrificed to speed.

But while Cornwallis was lightening his load, he was not moving. For two precious days the bonfires blazed and heavy rains soaked the Catawba watershed. By the time Cornwallis was ready to cross the swollen river, it was dark and ugly, its waters choked with dirt and fallen logs.

Nathanael Greene soon heard of the British commander's strange bonfires in the woods, and when he did, a thin smile doubtless played across his lips. All the effort Greene had invested in surveys of the Carolina countryside had been for this moment. It was time to bring the two halves of his army back together, and there was reason now for speed. Morgan had written Greene to say that his sciatic condition was nearly unendurable, then that he was stricken by an outbreak of painful hemorrhoids. The Virginian had asked to retire, urging that the dour Colonel Pickens, along with North Carolina militia commander Brigadier General William Davidson, take his place. But no sooner had Greene received the proposal than Morgan wrote twice on January 25 saying he intended "to move towards Salisbury" because the enemy was rapidly approaching, "destroying all before them."

Greene ordered his main army under General Isaac Huger to be ready to proceed upriver, past the point where the Pee Dee becomes the Yadkin, and then march west to Salisbury. He also ordered Lieutenant Colonel Carrington to begin assembling flatboats on the Dan River. Greene was planning a long retreat. The farther he could lure Cornwallis from his supply base in Charleston, the more vulnerable the Briton would become. Leaving his main

American officers wielded the spontoon, usually six to seven feet in length and topped by a lethal blade, as both an effective weapon and a badge of office easily identified during battle. At Cowpens, however, one enterprising American captain, racing a fellow officer to claim an abandoned enemy cannon, used it to pole-vault atop the gun and win the prize.

force with Huger, Greene sped off on January 28 with only a couple of aides to join Morgan, who was stationed 125 miles away.

En route, he sent a message to Huger. In it he ordered Huger to go immediately to Salisbury, and his supplies to a little settlement called Guilford Court House. Then Greene ordered his roving cavalry commander, Light-Horse Harry Lee, to Salisbury. "Here is a fine field," Greene wrote, "and great glory ahead." Finally, he sent a note to one of the tough mountain men who had led the successful American attack at Kings Mountain. In it Greene asked him to bring 1,000 sharpshooting riflemen to Guilford Court House.

The carefully choreographed withdrawal began. As the Catawba subsided, Cornwallis made moves to cross, and the Americans fell back toward yet another water barrier, the Yadkin, where flatboats were waiting, leaving behind a militia force of 500 men under the command of Davidson in order to delay the British as long as possible. It was not very long. As the dripping redcoats marched ashore, they met a hail of rifle fire that killed a few, and shot Cornwallis's horse from under him, but the crimson line surged ahead.

Although the British did not know it, Greene was just 16 miles away on the Salisbury road, waiting for Davidson and the militia at the house of David Carr. At midnight, word came that Davidson had died in the fight, and the militia had fled; Cornwallis had crossed the Catawba. Greene moved on to Salisbury, where he took breakfast at a hostel known as Steele's Tavern. The mistress of the place gave him two purses of hard cash that Greene immediately declared to be his entire military treasury. Before he left the inn, the Rhode Island general reached above the roaring fireplace to turn a staring portrait of King George III to the wall. Then he wrote across the back of the picture in charcoal "O George, hide thy face and mourn."

The British commander tossed the dice again, and burned even more of his dwindling supply train. Still, the Americans managed to cross the rain-flooded Yadkin River ahead of him, leaving no boats behind. Cornwallis's vanguard could not see their camp on the far side of a high ridge along the turbulent waterway, but they lobbed a few cannonballs at the roof of a small cabin—Greene's headquarters. Boards splintered and shingles flew, but the imperturbable commander ignored the commotion; he had letters to write, after all.

As Cornwallis bulled on, Greene moved again—this time across the Dan River into Virginia, on a squadron of flatboats that he had presciently ordered Carrington to have ready there some weeks before. Along the way he stopped at Guilford Court House, to be rejoined by General Huger, Carrington, Lee, and Davie, along with the sickly Morgan, whose leave of absence from the Continental army Greene finally granted. Huger's men had set a kind of record. They had marched 100 miles with few shoes and with only a single blanket for four men, possessing little food and no liquor, over terrible roads—without a single desertion.

Greene sent Washington's cavalry and Lee's legion, and a contingent of Continental infantry and Virginia riflemen, to act as a screen between the British and the main army. They lured Cornwallis toward the upper fords of the Dan but adroitly kept clear of confrontations. Greene feinted Cornwallis in one direction, then crossed the flooded Dan River, continuing his retreat into Virginia.

"All our exertions were in vain," moaned Cornwallis in a letter to Lord George Germain in London. It was February 15, three weeks since he had burned his bridges in the Carolina forest. His opponent was safely on the other side of another rain-swollen river, while he remained 230 miles from the supplies of Winnsboro; many of his men were walking through the freezing mud barefoot. As Greene watched from his carefully maintained distance, the earl retired to the North Carolina town of Hillsborough to rest, try to recruit Loyalist supports, and rethink his strategy. Seeing the British go to ground, the American general decided they should have no chance of regaining their strength.

In just over a week, he was back across the Dan River, teasing Cornwallis into motion, keeping his men on their cracked feet, but still avoiding confrontation. "I have been obliged," Greene mused in a note to Thomas Jefferson, "to effect that by finesse which I dare not attempt by force."

The British army soon chewed through the scarce food supplies of Hillsborough and began killing the Loyalist families' draft oxen. Their welcome exhausted, they had to move on, this time to a new headquarters at Alamance Creek. As they did, Greene's fastest moving light infantry, under Colonel Otho Williams, stayed constantly between Cornwallis and the main American army, probing, harassing, intercepting supplies, while Greene built his militia forces to the point where he dared to risk a confrontation.

These fresh forces were not long in coming. As mid-March approached, 400 Continentals from Virginia joined Greene's army, along with 1,693 less experienced militia. Another two militia brigades, with about 1,000 men, marched in from back-country North Carolina. On March 10, Greene recalled his harassing light troops and reorganized his newly bulked out forces. Then he set off for the place he had picked more than a month earlier as the testing ground of his strategy: Guilford Court House.

The British leader and his famished men were by then encamped only 12 miles away, at a Quaker settlement called New Garden. On March 14 they learned of their adversary's move. Cornwallis saw that he had only two choices: fight or retreat, and he had little appetite for the latter.

A Horse of the Same Color

In February 1781, a curious chance of tailoring led to the slaughter of a troop of North Carolina Loyalists. On February 24, Lieutenant Colonel Henry Lee (above) and Brigadier General Andrew Pickens, whose cavalry had been tracking Banastre Tarleton's dragoons, learned the enemy was encamped just across the Haw River, not far from Hillsborough. Riding out to join the famous green-coated British legion were some 350 Loyalists under the command of Colonel John Pyle. Determined to spoil the plans, the rebels crossed the river in pursuit.

Daylight was fading as two of John Pyle's scouts, sent to find Tarleton, spotted a troop of riders in snug green jackets and plumed helmets, whom they hailed. The young scouts soon rode back to Pyle, presenting Tarleton's congratulations and his request that the Loyalists move to the side of the road. Sabers drawn in salute, the green-clad riders began to file past Pyle's waiting men. Suddenly, Loyalists in the rear guard realized their mistake and shouts rang out. But it was too late. Light-Horse Harry Lee's men, whose uniforms were so similar to Tarleton's, rose in their stirrups and swung their sabers. "In ten minutes the whole body of the enemy was routed," wrote one witness, and "the greater part was left on the ground dead and wounded."

The next morning his troops formed up and marched down the Great road between Hillsborough and Salisbury to join in battle. As was so often the case for them, they would fight empty; there was not enough food for breakfast.

The first clash of probing reconnaissance patrols occurred at midmorning. Fittingly enough, it was between the two sets of green jackets—Lee and Tarleton. They exchanged shots and Tarleton took a rifle ball through his right hand, maiming the first and middle fingers. As tough as he was cruel, Tarleton retreated long enough to put on a sling, then returned to his command. He would lead the charge, when the time came, without being able to raise a pistol or sword to defend himself.

Past noon, with a bright sun shining to warm them, the redcoats marched out of a deep, wooded defile onto the open meadow at Guilford. No sooner had they tramped into the field than they heard the whistle and roar of six-pound cannonballs flying overhead. Greene was well emplaced there and waited for them.

As always, he had given the battleground careful thought and preparation. His men had breakfasted, and they had also been served a restorative gill of rum. Invisible to the redcoats, roughly 1,000 North Carolina militiamen were posted behind a picket fence about 900 yards away, on both sides of the Salisbury road. Slightly ahead of the center of their line were two cannon. About 300 yards back from the militia, hidden from view by the woods, were two militia brigades from Virginia, about 1,200 men in all. Greene's Continental regiments, totaling about 1,600, were atop the hill

At Guilford Court House, Lee's legion *(above)* and Tarleton's dragoons clashed, leaving the English colonel maimed. Cornwallis hardly fared better. "Nearly a third of his force slaughtered, many of his best officers killed or wounded," wrote Lee, "and that victory for which he had so long toiled ... bringing in its trail not one solitary benefit."

This contemporary drum, often associated with Guilford Court House, undoubtedly acquired its colorful Revolutionary art— including a solemn white face, French and American flags, siege cannon, and deadly pole arms—after the war.

and to the left of the Salisbury road as the British faced them. Cavalry legions under Lee and William Washington protected the left and right flanks, respectively. Along with a few hundred riflemen, Greene's army counted fewer than 4,500 men.

The 1,900 red-coated regulars who faced them were undeterred by the welcoming cannon fire; they pushed forward two guns and replied, and Cornwallis merely worked out the timing of the salvos, then deployed his troops while the enemy reloaded. For 20 minutes the British filed onto the field with parade ground precision. Light infantry, German jaeger riflemen, and a troop of cavalry were posted back on the Salisbury road. The red lines gleamed against the gray brown grass. Then the fifes sounded and the British drums beat out a quickstep. The advance was on, as the soldiers, muskets outstretched, paced across the fallow cornfields.

Most of the North Carolinian militia loosed a single volley too far away to have much effect; the British line rolled on unhindered. Then, at point-blank range, the regulars unleashed a volley of their own and charged in disciplined order. The North Carolinians took one look—and ran for their lives. They flooded through the second American line, where Brigadier General Edward Stevens cleverly yelled to his waiting troops that the retreat was all part of the battle plan. The Virginia line held.

Light infantry and riflemen deployed on the left and right also managed to hold their ground, pouring fire into the British as they surged ahead. The battle moved toward the woods, immobilizing the cavalry on both sides. A shoving, stabbing melee waltzed clumsily through ravines and gullies. Cornwallis re-formed and advanced on the second line as the Virginians, using trees as cover, took an increasing toll on the redcoats.

But, despite their desperate condition, the tough professional soldiers absorbed the punishment and pushed back the right side of the Virginia line, finally inducing the same kind of panic that inspired the Carolinians. The American militia on the right broke and ran, with the British in disciplined pursuit. On the left, the Americans held until Cornwallis led a charge against them, when they grudgingly gave way.

Teeth chattering, the Maryland Continentals atop the hill on the left, mostly new recruits, were the first American line regiment to break before the charging British Guards, abandoning two cannon and their crews. Their comrades in the First Maryland wheeled and tried to fill the gap, as William Washington's cavalry charged down in support. The air was filled with shouts, screams, and the thud of steel on flesh. One American cavalryman, Peter Francisco, cut down a dozen redcoats by himself—the last after his opponent had pinned his leg to his saddle with a bayonet.

The American counterattack was turning the tables on the British Guards. Seeing this, Cornwallis made a desperate decision. He ordered his cannoneers to load with grapeshot and fire into the struggling crowd of soldiers. The scything metal cut down men and horses on both sides with brutal effect, but the horrifying tactic worked. As the American left staggered, the 71st Regiment and the Guards grenadiers added pressure there. Suddenly Greene's whole army was threatened with encirclement. "I thought it most advisable," the American commander later wrote with characteristic understatement "to order a retreat."

With his artillery horses all dead, Greene had to leave his cannon and ammunition behind. Nonetheless, he fell back in good order to Reedy Fork, then, as good weather gave way again to a soaking rain, he marched 10 miles more that night. When his army was settled in bivouac, the master strategist finally relaxed—and fell over in a dead faint.

In the clearer light of day, Greene took stock of the Guilford Court House fight. Cornwallis had won the battle, but at terrible cost. More than 25 percent of his men lay dead and wounded—532 in all. Another 50 wounded died overnight from exposure. Cornwallis's disastrously wrongheaded campaign, as one Guards general put it, had "totally destroyed the army." The Americans had lost a little

less than half that in casualties—261 killed and wounded. Another 1,046 Continentals and militiamen were missing, but many of them were no doubt unharmed and on their way home.

With the remaining men at his disposal, Greene chased Cornwallis, hoping to bring him to battle. When the British did not stand and fight, the American commander turned back toward Camden and the remaining British forces. The object, he wrote, was much the same as it had been at Charlotte: to "oblige the Enemy to follow us or give up their posts" in South Carolina. The emboldened partisans began to pick off one strongpoint after another. In the months following Guilford, Greene's army would clear much of South Carolina of its British occupiers—without a single decisive win. In his odd but effective logic, the right kind of loss was infinitely more valuable than the wrong kind of victory. Indeed, too many Guilford-style triumphs could destroy an army.

Greene's skill, as he was always too modest to say explicitly, was not to fight masterfully, but to win masterfully. "There are few generals that has run oftener, or more lustily, than I have done," he wrote. "But I have taken care not to run too far, and commonly have run as fast forward as backward, to convince our Enemy that we were like a Crab, that could run either way."

Leaving 70 of his men who were most seriously injured at New Garden, Cornwallis limped southeast, toward the town of Cross Creek, halfway to Wilmington, where a British force had established a new base of supply. Along the way, Cornwallis vainly tried to whip up active Loyalist support. There was virtually none.

The British troops reached the security of Wilmington on April 7, approximately two and a half months after Cornwallis had set out to smash the Americans once and for all. He now knew the true cost of the cold, ruining wars of maneuver in the backwoods. Cornwallis must have turned his thoughts to Sir Henry Clinton, safely holed up in the security of New York, with a British fleet to back him. "If we mean an offensive war in America," he observed in a letter to a colleague, "we must abandon New York and bring our whole force into Virginia; we then have a stake to fight for, and a successful battle may give us America."

Like a heavily indebted gambler, Cornwallis could see no other course than another wager for higher stakes. Whatever his orders from New York, he would march on Virginia. It was all or nothing.

On May 20, Cornwallis reached Petersburg, to join his command to British troops from Norfolk. With this larger force, he believed, he might rip open the exposed underbelly of the colonies.

The man charged with blunting Cornwallis's advance was the Marquis de Lafayette, a 23-year-old Frenchman lusting for renown. But Lafayette's small army could not stand up to the rampaging British. "I am not strong enough," he wrote George Washington, "even to get beaten." He fell back toward the north, and Cornwallis pursued him without success, then turned toward other prey: the Virginia assembly, which was meeting clandestinely in Charlottesville. Cornwallis dispatched his reliable scourge, Lieutenant Colonel Banastre Tarleton, who grabbed seven assembly members and just missed Governor Thomas Jefferson, who managed to flee the dragoons. But while Cornwallis relished his successful raid, Lafayette's force was being reinforced by western Virginia militia and by another 1,000 Pennsylvania regulars under General "Mad Anthony" Wayne. This beefier American army trailed Cornwallis southward and eastward, in the direction of Williamsburg.

But here British strategy took a most peculiar turn. Sir Henry Clinton abruptly ordered Cornwallis to send some of his regiments to New York, which Clinton believed was under threat from George Washington. Enraged, Cornwallis had no choice but to follow this direct order, and on July 4 he left Williamsburg for Portsmouth to board ships. Then Clinton had second thoughts and ordered his general to find a strongpoint along the Chesapeake

THE WAR'S MOST FAMOUS PRIVATE

In 1776, at age 15, six-foot-six-inch, 260-pound Peter Francisco joined the rebel forces, where his great strength and bravery made him a legendary figure. Among his feats: At the Battle of Camden, Francisco fought on as his comrades fled; attacked by a dragoon, he bayoneted the rider from his saddle, leaped on the horse, and escaped through enemy lines by shouting, "Huzzah, my lads, let's go after the rebels." Spying his colonel, William Mayo, on foot, Francisco gave him the horse. Legend claims he then carried off a 1,100-pound cannon, a story celebrated 200 years later by a U.S. postage stamp.

In the summer of 1781, Francisco, on a special mission in Virginia, was caught by nine British dragoons. When eight disappeared inside a nearby house, he grabbed his guard's sword and killed him. Alerted, a second man rushed out, jumped on a horse, and tried to shoot the rebel. Francisco lunged for the gun and wounded his adversary *(above)*. Then he yelled to imaginary comrades, "Come on, my brave boys, now's your time; we will soon dispatch these few." Alarmed, the remaining seven fled to the nearby army, and the American legend escaped.

and fortify it. Still in a fury, Cornwallis sent out his engineers, and they settled on the decaying Chesapeake Bay tobacco port of Yorktown.

Clinton's change of strategy may have been based on reports that a French fleet of 20 ships of war was on its way to the West Indian garrison at Santo Domingo. It sailed under the command of François-Joseph-Paul, Comte de Grasse, a tough, combative officer whose sailors liked to say stood six feet two on regular days, and six feet six on fighting days. The fleet would sail north with some 3,300 French soldiers commanded by the Marquis de Saint-Simon and about 1.2 million francs for the allied war chest. It would join with the eight French ships of the line and their entourage of frigates and transports sailing under Comte de Barras. For a brief interval, at least, the British naval superiority that had defined the war might be reversed in favor of the allied French and Americans. For them, it was the first good news in a long time.

Jean-Baptiste-Donatien de Vimeur Rochambeau, lieutenant general in the army of His Majesty Louis XVI of France, considered the fateful journey of Cornwallis to his lair inside Yorktown's fortified walls to be one of the war's profound puzzles. It had been so unnecessary—and would prove so fatal.

On this early morning in late September of 1781, Rochambeau inhaled with a vast amount of pleasure the harsh bustle and clamor of an army preparing to fight. White-coated French soldiers and dark-frocked members of the Continental Army of the United States marched in formation down the road from the colonial capital of Williamsburg toward Yorktown. Deep-throated sergeants barked orders in French and English as the baggage of a siege army were dragged into position. Even though it was not yet dawn, the air was already thick with dust, the smell of animals and sweating men, the occasional whiff of gunpowder. Such a hubbub was music to Rochambeau's soul. This was the kind of war he knew and loved—a classical siege that was derived from the European blueprint.

The French general was 56 years old; he had been a warrior from the age of 16. "To live and die a gallant knight," the motto on his family's coat of arms proudly proclaimed, and so far he had lived up to it. He had been a soldier's soldier: formerly inspector general of the infantry of France, an innovative tactician who had redesigned the battle formations of 18th-century warfare, an impeccable planner and ceaseless drillmaster. One of his close friends liked to joke that Rochambeau was forever maneuvering soldiers: in the field, on the table in his room, or even on the cover of a snuffbox if you offered him a pinch of the pungent stuff.

In fact, only a soldier's soldier or a gallant knight would have taken his current job as head of the French expeditionary force—the embodiment of France's three-year-old alliance with the American Revolutionaries. Rochambeau had been on the verge of returning to the family estates in the Vendôme on an indefinite leave of absence from the army when fate, in the guise of a royal order, had ordered him to America. Instead of the expected reunion with his beloved wife, Jeanne-Therese, he had found himself in July of 1780 in the Rhode Island town of Newport, ensconced in a roomy clapboard house at Mary and Clark Streets, which until recently had been his headquarters.

But this very private man was not just a soldier. He was also a modest, thoughtful pragmatist who preferred facts to rhetoric or speculation. When he walked the streets of Newport, it was in an unadorned blue frock coat, without medals or gold braid; his subordinates called him Papa. Curiously, this was Rochambeau's first independent command—and perhaps not so very independent at that. His orders had made clear that he should consider himself subordinate to the Americans, although not so subordinate as to acquire their habit of losing.

It was entirely possible, however, that Rochambeau's allies had at last shaken that addiction. After all, he stood where a brilliantly coordinated land and sea operation had put 16,000 French and American troops in a ring around Yorktown, while 36

French ships of the line rocked at anchor in the surrounding bay. And inside the ring, like a moribund spider at the center of a tattered web, was Charles, Lord Cornwallis and his 8,885 men, reduced to formidable desperation.

As he mused on the road to Yorktown, Rochambeau cast a frequent eye at the tall, grave American commander who would be his partner in the coming siege. Until Rochambeau and the other French commanders had come to America, they had known George Washington chiefly through the enthusiastic reports of their young colleague, the impetuous Lafayette. Of course, the boy adored Washington, who seemed to have surrogate sons everywhere among his officers. (The Frenchman's own son had come to America as second in command of a Bourbonist regiment.) But over the course of the past year, although he and Washington had met only a few times, Rochambeau had come to share his compatriot's admiration for the American commander in chief. Later he would write in his memoirs that "our hearts will remain united in life and in death"—although he would also excise the emotional outburst before publication.

Washington had been one of the joys of Rochambeau's time in Newport, but also one of the trials, for the great man had a fixation on New York and a deplorable knack for designing the most impossibly complex strategies—perhaps, one had to concede, because the American general rarely knew whether he would have enough money, troops, or matériel to accomplish an objective. Washington had put the case to him at their first meeting, on September 20, 1780, in the Connecticut capital of Hartford. Rochambeau had been astonished by the intensity of Washington's belief that only an attack on New York would end the war. Without forgetting that he was, after all, the subordinate, he had coaxed the American commander away from that point of view, arguing that they could not carry New York without control of the sea and a two to one superiority of troops. Rochambeau had brought only 4,000 men with him to Newport. To defeat

TAKING THE FIGHT TO THE BRITISH

American naval hero John Paul Jones wears the ribbon and cross of France's Ordre du Mérite Militaire, awarded for his victory over HMS *Serapis*. During battle Jones wore an 11-pound corselet *(below)*, made of sheet iron lined with canvas and stuffed with horsehair, as a protection against small-arms fire and flying splinters.

"I have not yet begun to fight."

JOHN PAUL JONES ABOARD *BONHOMME RICHARD*, APRIL 23, 1779

Not content to harass British shipping off the American coast, a handful of American sea captains took the war into British waters. The most famous among them was Scottish-born captain John Paul Jones. Early on the afternoon of September 23, 1779, the 32-year-old Jones's crew spotted a convoy of 41 ships off the chalky cliffs of Flamborough Head, which juts into the North Sea from Yorkshire. The convoy was escorted by HMS *Serapis,* a fast new 50-gun frigate, and the 20-gun HMS *Countess of Scarborough.* Jones commanded a small squadron that included his flagship, the 40-gun *Bonhomme Richard,* and three ships with French captains: *Alliance, Pallas,* and *Vengeance.*

The outgunned *Richard* soon engaged *Serapis* in what would become the most famous naval battle of the war. During the first hour of combat the two ships maneuvered around each other until the *Serapis* became entangled in *Richard*'s lines. They continued the fight grappled together bow to stern *(above).*

While *Richard* and *Serapis* struggled in a death grip, *Pallas* captured *Scarborough,* and *Vengeance* stayed out of the fight. But traitorous *Alliance,* whose captain later admitted that he wanted to capture the *Serapis,* blasted *Richard* three times.

Despite *Richard*'s desperate condition—she was on fire, sinking, and without working cannon—Jones's determination and the deadly marksmanship of his French sharpshooters forced *Serapis* to surrender after more than three hours of bitter fighting. Two days later, after he and his crew had abandoned his ship for *Serapis,* the shattered *Bonhomme Richard* sank into the North Sea.

Clinton's 15,000 redcoats, 30,000 allied troops were needed, and Washington had no way of making up the deficit. Indeed, the American ranks were not merely thin—they had no shoes or ammunition and served without pay.

Yet the obsession with invading New York would not go away. On May 21, the day after Cornwallis reached Petersburg, the two commanders had held their second summit meeting at Wethersfield, a few miles south of Hartford. Again Washington had put forward his favorite plan. Captured letters from Lord George Germain to Clinton had made explicit what Washington had suspected: The British were concentrating on a southern strategy. New York's defenses would be weakened, he argued, making the time ripe for his attack, which, if it succeeded, would neutralize any British successes in the South. Finally, a thrust

Chesapeake campaign. But the British had intercepted Washington's plain-language report, corroborating Clinton's belief that New York was the American target. This accidental intelligence foreclosed on the possibility that Clinton would commit a large force to help Cornwallis at Yorktown. Because there was now little hope of pushing the British out of New York, the American plan was deferred. As the white-coated French soldiers marched off to join their allies at Dobbs Ferry, Clinton reinforced his intention to stand pat by ordering Cornwallis to send troops to reinforce New York.

Then, in mid-August, Rochambeau and Washington had heard from de Grasse that his fleet was headed not for Sandy Hook, but for Virginia. With this help from the admiral, Washington felt the attraction of a southern strategy. Immediately,

"I shall take the liberty of repeating that if offensive war is intended, Virginia appears to me to be the only Province in which it can be carried on.... But to reduce the Province and keep possession of the country, a considerable army would be necessary, for with a small force the business would probably terminate unfavourably, tho' the beginning might be successful."

GENERAL CORNWALLIS, MAY 26, 1781

at New York might draw troops away from the South, and ease pressure on Lafayette.

Like a good lieutenant, Rochambeau had remained politely skeptical, but Washington would not be deterred. In a letter summarizing the conference he declared that "the West India Fleet should run immediately to Sandy Hook," a point of land jutting into Raritan Bay outside New York harbor. Meantime, Washington had urged, the French and American forces, headquartered at Newport and at Morristown, New Jersey, respectively, would join forces at Dobbs Ferry, on the Hudson River. These plans had been part of Washington's unciphered report on the Wethersfield meeting.

They had been saved from the New York scheme by fate, or so it must have seemed to Rochambeau. Writing privately and in code, he had mentioned to the French minister to America the chance of a

the American headquarters outside New York had exploded into a planning frenzy. Given de Grasse's itinerary—he had to be back in the Indies by mid-October—the allied forces had just two months to travel some 450 miles by land and sea to the Chesapeake, surround their foe, and force his surrender. Their objective lay on the far side of a veritable forest of ifs: if de Grasse ran past the British navy into the Chesapeake, if their troop movements were not apprehended by Clinton's forces, if Cornwallis remained in Yorktown, they might prevail.

The first uncertainty had been resolved with the inadvertent assistance of crusty Admiral Sir George Rodney, one of the most gifted and aggressive commanders in the Royal Navy. Rodney was now 62 years old, ailing, and anxious to go home. His usual tough mind fogged with infirmity, Rodney had done nothing when he learned that de Grasse's fleet had reached the Indies in late April. At worst, the French commander might send a dozen or so ships northward. Rodney had then handed over command to his deputy, Rear Admiral Sir Samuel Hood, and sailed for London with his flagship and a frigate. Hood, with 14 ships, cruised north, looking for Frenchmen.

Rodney had also alerted the naval commander at New York, Rear Admiral Thomas Graves, of de Grasse's presence in the Indies. But Graves was looking for a French troop convoy in the vicinity of Boston. By the time he got back to New York harbor on August 28, he had missed both Rodney's message and the French fleet bottled up at Newport. Under the command of Vicomte de Barras, those ships had set sail for the Chesapeake, carrying Rochambeau's heavy cannon and all the soldiers they could take on board.

Washington took this opportunity to strengthen his hand with a clever ruse. Hoping to sustain Clinton's belief that the rebels intended to besiege New York, Washington ordered the French stationed near the town of Chatham, New Jersey, to begin building large bake ovens at their encampment. There could be no clearer signal to British spies that the enemy planned to stay near New York for a long time. Meanwhile, the French and American forces still stationed close to New Jersey ostentatiously broke camp and headed in the direction of the baking bread, a long file of white uniforms, baggage wagons, and brave banners. If the Americans' step was jauntier than usual, it was because of another Washington touch. "A little hard money would put them in a proper temper," he had opined to Robert Morris, his chief financier. Morris had come up with $30,000—$20,000 of it borrowed from Rochambeau—to pay the troops.

On August 30, the French and American forces surprised the British by turning suddenly southwest, toward Trenton and Princeton. The long race to the Chesapeake was on.

Rochambeau had arrived at the Delaware estuary town of Chester, Pennsylvania, in early September, having decided to sail downriver from Philadelphia.

He was astonished to see, waiting for him on the dock, the commander in chief himself, waving his hat in one hand and a white kerchief in the other. When Rochambeau debarked, Washington grabbed the Frenchman in his arms. He had the most amazing news: de Grasse was already in the Chesapeake.

Indeed, the French admiral's luck had attained mythic proportions. He had taken an indirect route through the difficult Bahama Channel, hoping to conceal his movement as long as possible. This put him behind Hood, who followed a direct route. Hood had reached the Chesapeake well before the French, but finding nothing had proceeded north to meet Graves, who now hurried south with five ships of the line; de Grasse entered the bay and disgorged his thousands of soldiers.

On the morning of the same day that Washington and Rochambeau embraced on the Chester quay, one of de Grasse's seaward patrols sighted topsails. It was the combined fleet of Graves and Hood—19 ships against 24 that the French were able to muster. The British were steering on a southwest course for the entrance to the bay's main channel, with the wind behind them, in full line of battle. The French, with the wind in their teeth, were not advantageously placed to counter an attack. They had straggled into the open sea around Cape Henry, with dangerous gaps opening up between the foremost ships in their line. To a commander as aggressive as Sir Samuel Hood, they would have been easy prey.

But Hood had deferred to Admiral Graves and watched in tight-lipped amazement as Graves, on the 98-gun *London,* slowed down, allowing the French to repair their battle line; then he had maneuvered the British fleet so that it approached the French at an oblique angle. In that formation, as everyone was exquisitely aware, the French were able to fire full broadsides at the British, while the British could only bring some of their guns to bear. As the broadsides began to roll, the first British ships suffered a brutal mauling. By nightfall, some 350 British seamen were dead or wounded, and seven ships savaged. After that, in a kind of nautical minuet, the two fleets had sailed around each other for several days, until de Grasse returned to the safety of the Chesapeake. Graves had dithered for a few days before heading for home.

Ranging far ahead of their main forces on September 14, Washington and Rochambeau had galloped their lathered horses into the camp near Williamsburg where Lafayette was headquartered with Saint-Simon's soldiers. After Washington dismounted, Lafayette had rushed toward him, arms extended. He grabbed his commander in a bear hug, and, as one awed observer wrote: "absolutely kissed him from ear to ear once or twice, as well as I can recollect, with as much ardor as ever an absent lover kissed his mistress on his return." French military men poured out of their tents to see the arrival of the American hero.

Now, at last, with Rochambeau happily registering the scents and sounds of an army on the march, the long-awaited assault had begun. At 5 a.m. on September 28, Washington gave the order to march on Yorktown, his light-infantry regiments in the vanguard. "The General particularly enjoins the troops," he wrote, "to place their principle reliance on the Bayonet, that they may prove the Vanity of the Boast which the British make of their particular prowess in deciding Battles with that Weapon."

Events seem to have proved too much for Lord Cornwallis, at the center of the constricting circle of French and American forces. While disaster, in the form of Comte de Grasse and his artillery and troops, had sailed toward him from the Indies, Cornwallis had been preoccupied by a bickering battle with Clinton about what to do at Yorktown. He had avoided confrontations with Lafayette and temporized over building the Yorktown defenses. Cornwallis was not entirely to blame. None of the information from Clinton had suggested that he would soon be under attack—a September 2 letter

A CURE FOR THE REVOLUTION

Lafayette set out for France in October 1778 to persuade Louis XVI to send America more military aid. En route from Philadelphia to Boston, he caught pneumonia, falling gravely ill. A concerned George Washington asked his personal physician, John Cochran, to drop all other duties and make the marquis his exclusive charge. Upon his recovery, the grateful patient presented his own brace of pistols (above)—engraved with his arms and coronet—to Cochran. Lafayette finally reached France, where he successfully persuaded Louis to send soldiers to America. Those Frenchmen, under the command of Jean-Baptiste-Donatien de Vimeur Rochambeau, would fight beside Washington at Yorktown.

warning of the allied advance did not catch up with Cornwallis until September 16. Instead Clinton reassured him, explaining that he would provide Cornwallis with "all the troops that can possibly be spared consistent with the security of this important post." Clinton also urged him to bring reinforcements from South Carolina. Curiously desultory, Cornwallis seemed not to care.

When Clinton learned of de Grasse's arrival in the Chesapeake, he had sent Cornwallis further reassurance: "The best way to relieve you is to join you as soon as possible, with all the Force that can be spared from hence. Which is about 4,000 men." After that there was nothing.

Cornwallis had belatedly turned to building his Yorktown defenses. Three of his outermost strongpoints lay near the head of a ravine gouged by Yorktown Creek, which ran from the York River to just south of town. To the southeast of Yorktown lay smaller works that were situated behind the nearly impassable swamps surrounding Wormley Creek and its upper extension, called Mill Pond. Between these water obstacles lay an open space of about half a mile containing the main road to Williamsburg and a second road leading to Hampton. This area was covered by fire from the redoubts along Yorktown Creek and a smaller work near the Hampton road. On his extreme right, near the riverbank, he built a fourth, star-shaped redoubt and staffed it with hard-fighting Royal Welsh Fusiliers. Meantime, around the town itself, he had begun to raise a number of earthworks that covered the town on the right along the Williamsburg road, to the left down the riverside, and at the rear. Two additional redoubts, numbered 9 and 10, protected the left flank. The strongpoints were armed with 65 cannon in 14 batteries—none of them bigger than 18-pounders.

When he learned that the British fleet had been defeated, Cornwallis had hundreds of trees chopped down and houses destroyed in order to give his troops a clear field of fire in front of the earthworks. But even at this juncture, he had clung to the hope that Clinton would ultimately rescue him, and that all the work was unnecessary. It was the same futile belief that had helped destroy John Burgoyne at Saratoga.

At no point had Cornwallis tried to fight. "If I had no hopes of Relief," he wrote Clinton on September 16, "I would rather risk an Action than defend my half-finished Works. But as you say Admiral Digby is hourly expected, and promise every Exertion to assist me, I do not think myself justifiable in putting the fate of the War on so desperate an Attempt." In a postscript written the next day, Cornwallis added: "This place is in no State of defense. If you cannot relieve me soon, you must be prepared to hear the Worst." The worst, he reckoned, was less than a month away.

Washington (center), Rochambeau (right), and Lafayette (left), accompanied by an aide and fellow officers, survey the devastation on the York River in a painting by James Peale. Executed shortly after the siege, the picture shows the masts of sunken British ships jutting from the water and the carcasses of several horses littering the beach.

Once, Cornwallis seemed to revive. When de Grasse bottled up the mouth of the York River with two frigates and a ship of the line, Cornwallis had deployed fire ships against them. At midnight on September 22, British seamen aboard five small ships in the Yorktown harbor cut their cables and drifted silently toward the French pickets. Their vessels reeked of tar and sundry other combustibles. As the ships slipped close to the French, one of the British commanders unaccountably torched his vessel too soon. Warned of the fire ship assault by this sudden blaze, the French cut their own cables and retreated, firing wildly at the flaming apparition. Quick seamanship and some powerful broadsides kept that menace away—barely. But nothing impeded the allied advance.

Soon rifle balls were screaming past the helmets of Cornwallis's outlying pickets. By the second day, the Americans were moving on the right, in the direction of the York River. On the left, the French began to fire on the fusiliers' redoubt. Outside rifle range, the British could see French and American officers conferring over the best way to crack their strong outer defenses. But the defenses held firm—until at one o'clock in the morning, the officers received an order to fall back.

Yet another surreal communication had arrived from Clinton aboard a courier packet that slipped past the French patrols. Some 5,000 men, he informed Cornwallis, were about to embark on 23 ships of the line and head for Yorktown to break the siege. "There is every reason to hope we start from hence the 5th October," Clinton wrote. That could put relief in sight within days. Buoyed by a fresh swell of false hope, Cornwallis made a fateful decision. If his vulnerable outer defenses were enveloped, as they easily could be, by the superior allied force, he would have even fewer soldiers to defend the inner line. Better to bring them all within the inner earthworks and wait.

Cornwallis might have chosen another course had he known that help, if any came, was weeks, not days, away. Nor did the British commander seem to be aware that the recently arrived French ships of Admiral de Barras had brought all the heavy siege guns from the French post in Newport.

The morning after Cornwallis's withdrawal, an eerie silence hung over the British defenses. Not until noon did the cautious allies send scouts forward to discover the bizarre truth. Washington asked Colonel Timothy Pickering about moving the troops up closer to the enemy works now that Cornwallis had brought in his outer defenses. Pickering thought they were "near enough."

Washington disagreed. "Well, but we must invest the place," he protested.

Colonel Pickering then compared the object of investment with the present disposition of allied troops and concluded, "So I think, Sir, the place is already invested."

As the siege unfolded, Washington's famed carelessness in the face of enemy fire began to reassert itself. On October 1, he strolled within 300 yards of

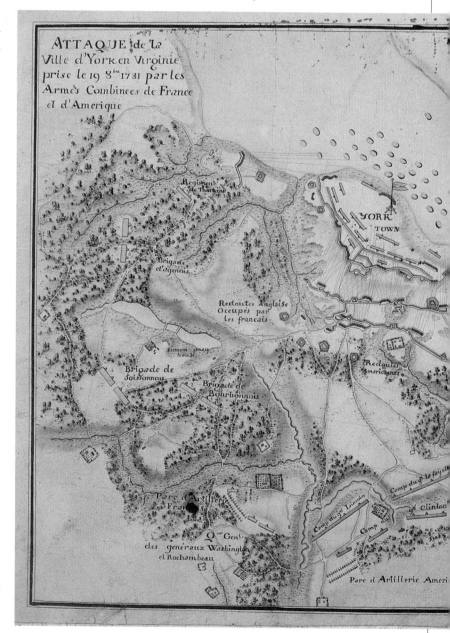

A contemporary French map displays the American and French siege works and the defensive redoubts built by the British during the Battle of Yorktown. The headquarters of Generals Washington and Rochambeau can be seen in the lower left corner.

the main British defenses to take their measure. One artillery round came whizzing close enough that most of his aides scrambled for cover. Washington, field glass to his eye, did not move. Two days later, as he stood by one of the captured British redoubts, a cannonball plowed into the dirt a few feet away. A light-infantry chaplain who had been showered with dirt pointed to the mess on his clothes. Washington smiled and indicated the cannonball.

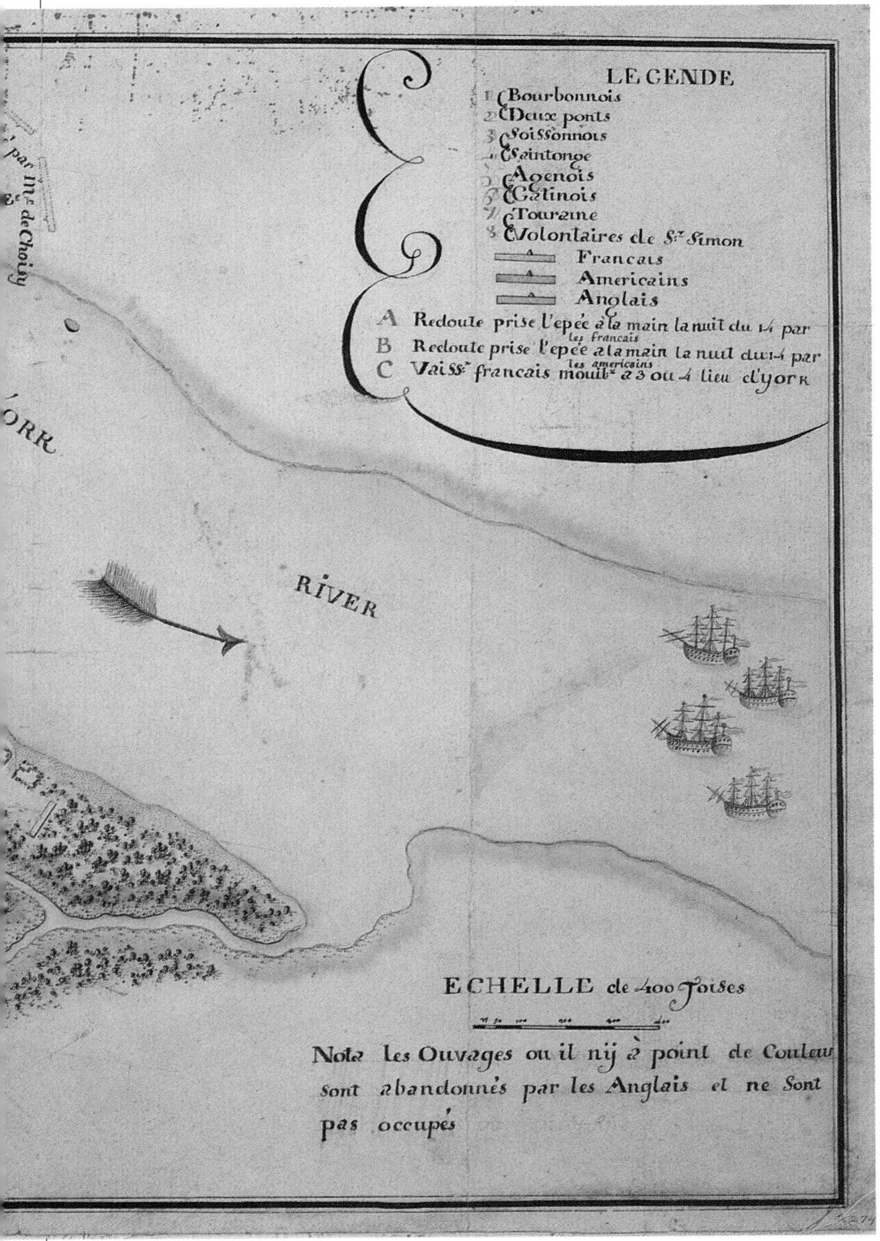

"Mr. Evans," he said. "You had better carry that home and show it to your wife and children."

The Americans had yet to fire a cannonade in reply, however, because Brigadier General Henry Knox, Washington's talented artillery commander, had not yet been able to manhandle the powerful siege guns into the battlefield area and build positions for them. According to siege doctrine, the barrage could not get under way until trenches had been dug for the cannon emplacements.

The chosen evening was October 6, and out in the darkness and rain, soldiers in a detachment of sappers and miners—soldiers charged with digging what the French called *saps,* or trenches—began digging frantically into the sandy soil, directed by siege-wise French engineers. Suddenly, a lone figure cloaked in a civilian surtout appeared in the darkness, asking which troops they were, then cautioning them against saying anything if taken prisoner. "We were obliged to him for his kind advice," one of the sappers would write, "but we considered ourselves as standing in no great need of it. For we knew as well as he did that sappers and miners were allowed no quarters, at least are entitled to none, by the laws of warfare." The stranger vanished, then reappeared with the French engineers; one of them called the man "Your Excellency." It was George Washington in mufti, making his nocturnal rounds.

Over the next several nights, thousands of sweating men dug a trench 2,800 to 3,200 feet from the British defenses, and only 1,920 feet on the left. Near British redoubts 9 and 10 the distance dwindled to about 1,800 feet. The entire ditch was close to a mile long, with two redoubts on each flank.

A nearby group of French soldiers cut another trench on the left for the artillery battery that would cover the York River and block Cornwallis's only escape route. The workers moved quickly and quietly, until one of the French soldiers deserted. He told the British that the French were moving against the fusiliers, and their artillerymen opened up on the York River trench. Eight men were injured, but the noise of the British barrage served an-

LEGENDE

1 Bourbonnois
2 Deux ponts
3 Soissonnois
4 Saintonge
5 Agenois &
6 Gatinois
7 Touraine
8 Volontaires de S.t Simon

Francais
Americains
Anglais

A Redoute prise l'epée à la main la nuit du 14 par les francais
B Redoute prise l'epée à la main la nuit du 14 par les americains
C Vaiss.r francais mouill.s à 3 ou 4 lieu d'York

YORK

RIVER

ECHELLE de 400 Toises

Nota les Ouvrages où il n'y à point de Couleur sont abandonnés par les Anglais et ne sont pas occupés

other purpose—it cloaked sounds from the much bigger trench spreading around them.

At noon, the Americans, led by Lafayette's division, began filing into the trenches under the British guns. So well constructed were the berms of dirt and timber, one officer reported, that "we did not lose a man in relieving, though the enemy fired much." Then, Alexander Hamilton, a hot-tempered young colonel of light infantry, hopped onto a parapet and ordered his entire regiment to follow. He put the men through the manual of arms, while the British watched in silent astonishment.

As siege guns up to 24-pounders were dragged into position all along the line, the British mistook the intervening silence for a lack of firepower. At 3 p.m. on October 9, such delusions dissolved in flame. On the far left of the French line, cannon shots boomed out toward the handful of British ships in Yorktown harbor. At 5 p.m., the American battery joined in. Washington himself sent the first 24-pound shell roaring toward Cornwallis. One American colonel later recalled that he "could distinctly hear the ball strike from house to house" in town. The booming, battering attack continued for the rest of the day, and all night, with sputtering mortar shells creating brilliant parabolas in the dark sky.

Next morning the French Grand Battery of a dozen cannon went into action along with three others. The allies now had 46 guns in more or less continuous action, and poured roughly 4,600 rounds of shot and shell into an area of a few thousand square yards. The house where Cornwallis had made his headquarters was soon a smoking shell. The beleaguered general retreated into a riverbank cave.

As the unrelenting fire continued, French soldiers let out a shout. A half-dozen boats of British soldiers were spotted on the river, apparently probing the strength of the enemy. They were cannon-

Twenty-six-year-old American colonel Alexander Hamilton, seen at right amid the siege works, hotly protested Lafayette's appointment of another officer to lead the storming of British redoubt 10. Washington supported Hamilton, who proved his worth by securing the redoubt in a matter of minutes.

aded back to shore. That night, the French heated cannonballs nearly molten hot and fired them at the remaining British ships on the river. Three vessels, including the frigate *Charon,* burned to the water line. The others beat a retreat.

Under cover of darkness on October 11, allied navvies began to dig a second trench that was located closer to Yorktown: the so-called second parallel 300 yards from the British defenses. When it was finished, the guns would be moved forward, and fire at virtually point-blank range. Work on the trench continued for several nights, without any sign of a British sortie to interrupt it. "Lord Cornwallis' conduct," observed a bemused Washington, "has hitherto been passive beyond conception; he either has not the means of defence, or he intends to re-

ing were blocked by British redoubts 9 and 10. If it was possible for those two mini-forts to be taken, the allies would have a clear field of fire into the enemy camp. Washington ordered 400 American light infantry to get ready to move on redoubt 10. "Papa" Rochambeau gave a similar order for preparations on his side, telling the members of his Gatinais and Royal Dieux Ponts regiments, "My children, I have great need of you tonight."

The signal came: six mortar shells. With fearsome yells, the attackers leaped forward, hacking their way through an abatis—a barricade of tree trunks and branches—and a fraise, or defense, consisting of sharpened wooden stakes set at an angle in the earthwork, all under a hail of British musketry. Flashes of gunfire stabbed through the dark,

"The rapidity and immediate success of the assault are the best comment on the behaviour of the troops.... There was not an officer nor soldier whose behaviour, if it could be particularized, would not have a claim to the warmest approbation."

ALEXANDER HAMILTON, YORKTOWN, OCTOBER 1781

serve his strength until we approach very near him."

Cornwallis had little strength to conserve. Inside Yorktown, life had become a screaming hell. Most houses had been battered into rubble. On October 11, a German soldier reported, some 3,600 cannon shots were fired at the town, the defenses, and the ships in harbor. "One saw men lying nearly everywhere who were mortally wounded and whose heads, arms and legs had been shot off." Some cannonballs skipped all the way across the York River and wounded soldiers in Gloucester.

Yet the men remained at their posts, and Cornwallis moved constantly among them, offering encouragement. But his heart was sinking. On October 11 he wrote to Clinton, "Nothing but a direct move to York river, which includes a successful naval action, can save me." He added a postscript: "Since my letter was written we have lost 90 men."

By October 14, the allied second parallel had been nearly completed, but the 400 yards remain-

then bayonets ripped into bellies. Within only 10 minutes, the fort in the American sector was taken. The French suffered heavy casualties before the Hessian mercenaries and British troops they faced pleaded for surrender.

By the next morning two howitzers had been dragged into the strongpoints and trenches dug connecting with the American lines. With the entire British line of defense now open to fire, the allies began moving larger batteries of heavy guns and mortars into position. At 5 p.m., the guns and howitzers began spitting shells.

Cornwallis wrote to Clinton, who was now two days behind his promised schedule, "The safety of the place is therefore so precarious that I cannot recommend that the fleet and army should run great risk in endeavoring to save us."

The dispirited British general tried one last combative gambit: a sortie by 350 men under the command of Lieutenant Colonel Robert Abercromby to spike as many of the enemy cannon as possible. The men slipped into the captured redoubts on both sides, took the guards by surprise, and stabbed their bayonet tips into the touchholes of a few cannon before they were driven out. It was a brave deed, but it accomplished little; the cannon were working again within a few hours.

The British now prepared to play a final desperate card. After dark, the troops would pull back to the river and cross quietly in boats; it would take three trips to bring the army over. Tarleton, whose dragoons had been trapped in Gloucester, and the other British forces there would fling themselves at the French and American besiegers. Then, seizing as many horses as possible, the British army would begin a march toward Maryland. Those remaining at Yorktown—the sick and wounded—would surrender.

Before midnight on the 16th, the retreat began as planned. Sixteen flatboats filled with veteran Foot Guards and Royal Welsh Fusiliers—the best troops Cornwallis had. The first contingent made it safely to the other side. Then the boats began their second attempt at the two-hour crossing. But only 10 minutes into the passage a screaming gale began to blow. The boats turned back. The storm did not blow over until 2 a.m.—too late for the rest of the defenders to escape. Cornwallis ordered back his best forces. As dawn broke, a few boats were still on the river, and the sharp-eyed French and American gunners opened up. Somehow, only a few wet, frozen soldiers lost their lives.

On the morning of October 17, the firing resumed from the second parallel. A Hessian defender said it seemed to him "as though the heavens should split." One of Cornwallis's aides was struck by a hissing shot and fell at the general's feet, headless. Over their battered parapet, the defenders could see more cannon being heaved into position. More than 100 cannon poured death on the British walls, where no British guns were left to reply. At 7 a.m. on October 17, Cornwallis called his officers into conclave. They were outnumbered perhaps five to

one. They had virtually no ammunition left. Cornwallis already knew what their advice would be. He dictated a letter to his enemies: "Sir, I propose a cessation of hostilities for 24 hours, and that two officers may be appointed by each side to meet at Mr. Moore's house to settle terms for the surrender of the posts at York and Gloucester."

At about 9 a.m. a small red-coated figure beating steadily on a drum appeared on the blasted parapet at the center of the British defenses. "Had we not seen the red coat when he first mounted," American lieutenant Ebenezer Denny recalled, "he might have beat till doomsday." The roar of cannon fire erased the puny pounding. Then a British officer appeared waving a white flag. He began walking toward American lines. Everything went silent, except the drum's tapping. "I thought I never heard a drum equal to it, the most delightful music to us all," said Denny. An American ran to the British officer, blindfolded him with the white kerchief, then led him to the trenches to deliver the Cornwallis note. "An Ardent Desire to

spare the further Effusion of Blood," Washington replied by courier, inspired him to listen to terms. At 2 p.m., the cannon ceased firing.

The next day at dawn, Washington's terms were delivered to Cornwallis. The defenders would lay down their arms, and be treated as prisoners. Cornwallis had two hours to accept or reject.

The beaten British commander concurred, with the proviso that one British sloop be allowed to sail free with his dispatches and unspecified passengers—a way out of America for Loyalists. There was haggling over a strange detail. Under the normal articles of war, a surrendering army was allowed to march out with colors flying, and playing one of the victor's national airs. The Americans would not allow it, for it had not been allowed them at Charleston. The British would march out with colors cased, drums beating a British or German air.

Through the night, the negotiators worked through their differences. The surrender terms then went to Washington for approval. He balked at one

Its colors cased, according to the terms of surrender, the defeated British army marches through a gantlet of American (foreground) and French soldiers on October 19, 1781. Artist Louis-Nicolas van Blarenberghe based this 1785 painting of the Yorktown surrender on eyewitness accounts, maps, and documents in the French War Office as well as on sketches by an engineer in Rochambeau's army.

in particular that would have granted immunity to Americans who had joined the British forces. Then the commander in chief sent the Articles to Cornwallis, advising him that the garrison was expected to march out at 2 p.m.—and went to have his breakfast.

By 11 a.m., Cornwallis had signed. Two hours later, the allied armies formed up facing each other along opposite sides of the York-Hampton road, about a half-mile from the smoking ruins of Yorktown. The Americans wore tattered blue uniforms, or even civilian clothes. The French wore their best whites, decorated where appropriate with gold braid. At the head of the two lines, Washington and Rochambeau waited. Then, in the distance, they heard a muted, slow beat and the trilling of a British air. A file of red coats appeared, headed by a resplendent officer on horseback. It was not Cornwallis but his deputy, General Charles O'Hara; the commander had decided to spare himself the humiliation, claiming illness. Nor was O'Hara inclined to be shamed by rebels. He asked a French officer to point out General Rochambeau and extended his sword toward him. Then, as one French observer reported, O'Hara "urged his horse forward to present his sword to the French general." Rochambeau shook his head, and pointed O'Hara toward Washington.

But a commanding general did not accept a deputy's sword. Washington refused to accept the British surrender at Yorktown from anyone but Cornwallis. Instead, he pointed toward his own deputy, General Benjamin Lincoln, and O'Hara handed over his weapon, which was received to mark the surrender, and immediately returned. Then the British grounded their arms in a circle of French hussars and returned to Yorktown.

By 3 p.m. the surrender at Yorktown had been concluded; across the river in Gloucester, it had just begun but was soon completed. In the fashion of the day the enemies were now social equals. Washington entertained O'Hara. The British enlisted men got fiercely drunk. The next day, the British sloop *Bonetta* sailed, crammed with Americans who had deserted the Continental army for the British.

A few did not make it aboard. When they were later discovered they were tried and hanged.

The British surrender at Yorktown on October 19, 1781, was not simply another defeat for the Royal Army—it was a decisive and resounding victory for the allied French and American forces. Washington might fret about the British army in Charleston, where Nathanael Greene would soon have them bottled up, or brood about Clinton's large force in New York. With so many men still in the field, more battles might reasonably be expected. In fact, the war would not formally be concluded until 1783, with the signing of the Treaty of Paris. And yet the fateful day at Yorktown was immediately perceived from Newport to Savannah as a final American triumph.

October 24 Lieutenant Colonel Tench Tilghman, Washington's hard-riding personal envoy, delivered the general's account of his victory to the congress in Philadelphia. Cannon boomed from the State House and from American ships anchored in the harbor. In Fishkill, New York, according to one newspaper account, "French and American colors were displayed, cannon fired, and in the evening, illuminations, bonfires, rockets, and squibs gave agreeable amusement." Up the Hudson toward West Point, the victory was celebrated somewhat more pointedly, by burning Benedict Arnold in effigy—without quite denying him his due as a former hero of the Revolution. The leg crippled at Quebec was duly amputated from the effigy and "safely laid by" as the remainder was committed to the flames.

On that same day, the flagship of the British fleet—it had finally sailed to relieve Cornwallis—was hailed by a small boat containing three men, who told Admiral Graves and Sir Henry Clinton they had left Yorktown on the eve of surrender. The fleet cruised off the Virginia coast for five more days before accepting the bleak news and turning for home.

Not until late November did word of the defeat cross the sea to London. "Oh God," cried the prime minister, Lord North, "it is all over!" And, on the battlefield at least, it was. ◆

PRIVATE YANKEE DOODLE

BEING A NARRATIVE OF SOME OF THE ADVENTURES, DANGERS AND SUFFERINGS OF A REVOLUTIONARY SOLDIER

BY JOSEPH PLUMB MARTIN

A contemporary German etching of an American rifleman and a brown-coated member of the Pennsylvania infantry shows the two soldiers dressed in far nattier attire than that worn by most Revolutionary troops.

In 1776, at the tender age of 15, Joseph Plumb Martin, a young farm boy from Milford, Connecticut, signed up for a six-month hitch in a state regiment. After this brief taste of soldiering, he reenlisted the following spring in the Eighth Connecticut Continental Regiment. Later assigned to the Corps of Sappers and Miners—builders of fortifications and heavy-gun emplacements—Martin rose in rank from private to sergeant.

His charming, witty account of his wartime experiences, which were written when he was nearly 70 years old, first appeared in 1830, to negligible acclaim. By then Martin had married and fathered five children and was eking out a living working as a laborer and town clerk in the small community of Prospect, Maine. Largely self-taught, he read widely all his life, did some sketching, and composed hymns. Martin died in 1850, at the age of 89. His headstone is inscribed, fittingly, with a simple tribute: "A Soldier of the Revolution."

Soldiers were at this time enlisting for a year's service. I did not like that; it was too long a time for me at the first trial; I wished only to take a priming before I took upon me the whole coat of paint for a soldier. However, the time soon arrived that gratified all my wishes. In the month of June, this year, orders came out for enlisting men for six months from the twenty-fifth of this month. The troops were styled new levies [state troops]. They were to go to New York. And notwithstanding I was told that the British army at that place was reinforced by fifteen thousand men, it made no alteration in my mind; I did not care if there had been fifteen times fifteen thousand,

I should have gone just as soon as if there had been but fifteen hundred. I never spent a thought about numbers; the Americans were invincible in my opinion. If anything affected me, it was a stronger desire to see them. . . .

. . . I one evening went off with a full determination to enlist at all hazards. When I arrived at the place of rendezvous I found a number of young men of my acquaintance there. The old bantering began—come, if you will enlist I will, says one; you have long been talking about it, says another—come, now is the time.

In a typical scene at the war's outset, a recruiter exhorts able-bodied townsmen to enlist and rally around the cause, as an eager youth signs up to join the fight.

"Thinks I to myself" . . . what did I come here for tonight? Why, to enlist. Then enlist I will. So seating myself at the table, enlisting orders were immediately presented to me; I took up the pen, loaded it with the fatal charge, made several mimic imitations of writing my name, but took especial care not to touch the paper with the pen until an unlucky wight who was leaning over my shoulder gave my hand a stroke, which caused the pen to make a woeful scratch on the paper. . . . And now I was a soldier, in name at least, if not in practice; but I had now to go home, after performing this, my heroic action. How shall I be received there? . . . [Martin's grandfather] proceeded, "I suppose you must be fitted out for the expedition, since it is so." Accordingly, they [his grandparents] did "fit me out" in order, with arms and accouterments, clothing, and cake, and cheese in plenty, not forgetting to put my pocket Bible into my knapsack. . . .

I was now what I had long wished to be, a soldier. I had obtained my heart's desire; it was now my business to prove myself equal to my profession.

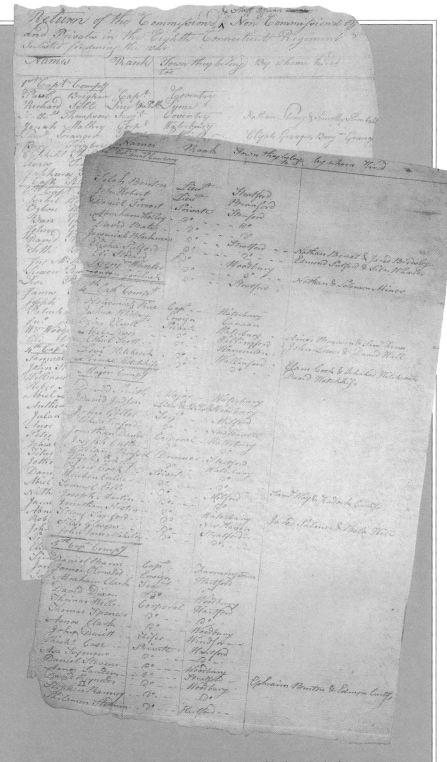

Preserved for posterity, Joseph Plumb Martin's name, with his rank of private, appears halfway down this 1779 roster of officers and men in the Eighth Connecticut Regiment.

We soon landed at Brooklyn, upon the [Long] Island, marched up the ascent from the ferry to the plain. . . .

. . . By the time we arrived, the enemy had driven our men into the creek, or rather millpond . . . where such as could swim got across; those that could not swim . . . sunk. The British, having several fieldpieces stationed by a brick house, were pouring the canister and grape upon the Americans like a shower of hail. . . . There was in this action a regiment of Maryland troops . . . all young gentlemen. When they came out of the water and mud to us, looking like water rats, it was a truly pitiful sight. Many of them were killed in the pond, and

more were drowned. Some of us went into the water after the fall of the tide, and took out a number of corpses and a great many arms that were sunk in the pond and creek. . . .

. . . The next day, . . . [a] few of our men . . . went over the creek upon business that usually employed us, that is, in search of something to eat. There was a field of Indian corn at a short distance from the creek . . . [where] they were fired upon by about an equal number of the British . . . our people took to the hay, and the others to the fence, where they exchanged a number of shots.

Caught in the middle of British crossfire, the Americans suffered a major defeat at the Battle of Long Island, which resulted in the loss of more than 1,000 men.

We marched from Valentine's Hill for the White Plains in the night. There were but three of our men present. We had our cooking utensils (at the time the most useless things in the army) to carry in our hands. They were made of cast iron and consequently heavy. I was so beat out before morning with hunger and fatigue that I could hardly move one foot before the other. I told my messmates that I could not carry our kettle any further. They said they would not carry it any further. Of what use was it? They had nothing to cook and did not want anything to cook with. We were sitting down on the ascent of a hill when this discourse happened. We got up to proceed when I took up the kettle, which held nearly a common pailful. I could not carry it. My arms were almost dislocated. I sat it down in the road and one of the others gave it a shove with his foot and it rolled down against the fence, and that was the last I ever saw of it. When we got through the night's march, we found our mess was not the only one that was rid of their iron bondage.

The cast-iron kettle was the most common piece of cookware in camp. Because of its weight, it was also the most frequently discarded; hundreds of roadside pots frequently marked an army's route of march.

In the latter part of the month of June, or the beginning of July, I was ordered off in a detachment of about a hundred men . . . to the lines near King's Bridge, to join two regiments of New York troops which belonged to our brigade.

. . . We arrived upon the lines and joined the other corps. . . . No one who has never been upon such duty as those advanced parties have to perform, can form any adequate idea of the trouble, fatigue and dangers which they have to encounter. Their whole time is spent in marches, especially night marches, watching, starving, and, in cold weather, freezing and sickness. . . .

We were once on one of those night marches, advancing toward the enemy and not far from them, when, towards the latter part of the night, there came on a heavy thundershower. We were ordered into some barns near by . . . when we were informed that we were discovered by the enemy, and that two or three thousand Hessians were advancing upon, and very near us. We were immediately hurried out, the shower being then at its height. We were then marched across fields and fences, pastures and brooks, swamps and ravines, a distance of two or three miles, and stationed upon a hill. . . . Here we waited for [Hessians] till the sun was two hours high, but no one coming to visit us, we marched off, and left the enemy to do the same, if they had not already done it.

To protect their legs, Hessian dragoons donned thick leather boots, weighing up to 12 pounds a pair, over their regular footgear. Equally encumbered by heavy coats and long swords, such overequipped troops plodded toward the battlefront.

About daybreak our advanced guard and the British outposts came in contact. . . . Our brigade moved off to the right into the fields. We saw a body of the enemy drawn up behind a rail fence on our right flank; we immediately formed a line and advanced upon them. Our orders were not to fire till we could see the buttons upon their clothes, but they . . . hid their clothes in fire and smoke before we had either time or leisure to examine their buttons. They soon fell back and we advanced, when the action became general. The enemy were driven quite through their camp. They left their kettles, in which they were cooking their breakfasts, on the fires, and some of their garments were lying on the ground, which the owners had not had time to put on.

Affairs went on well for some time. The enemy were retreating before us, until the first division that was engaged had expended their ammunition. Some of the men unadvisedly calling out that their ammunition was spent, the enemy were so near that they overheard them, when they first made a stand and then returned upon our people, who, for want of ammunition and reinforcements, were obliged in their turn to retreat, which ultimately resulted in the rout of the whole army.

In October 1777 several American columns attacked the British encampment at Germantown but were repulsed by enemy troops holed up in the Chew house *(below, right).*

Almost every one has heard of the soldiers of the Revolution being tracked by the blood of their feet on the frozen ground. This is literally true, and the thousandth part of their sufferings has not, nor ever will be told. . . . For on our march from the Valley Forge, through the Jerseys . . . a fourth part of the troops had not a scrip of anything but their ragged shirt flaps to cover their nakedness, and were obliged to remain so long after. . . .

. . . But we never received what was allowed us. Oftentimes have I gone one, two, three, and even four days without a morsel, unless the fields or forests might chance to afford enough to prevent absolute starvation. Often, when I have picked the last grain from the bones of my scanty morsel, have I eat the very bones . . . and then have had to perform some hard and fatiguing duty, when my stomach has been as craving as it was before. . . .

. . . How often have I had to lie whole stormy, cold nights in a wood, on a field, or a bleak hill, with such blankets and other clothing like them, with nothing but the canopy of the heavens to cover me. All this too in the heart of winter, when a New England farmer, if his cattle had been in my situation, would not have slept a wink from sheer anxiety for them.

Washington and his tattered troops head to Valley Forge. During the bitterly cold winter, the ill-clothed army endured starvation, mud, filth, lice, smallpox, and pneumonia.

By this time the British had come in contact with the New England forces at the fence, when a sharp conflict ensued. . . .

. . . We were immediately ordered from our old detachment and joined another, the whole composing a corps of about five hundred men. We instantly marched towards the enemy's right wing, which was in the orchard, and . . . into the open fields and formed our line. . . . As I passed through the orchard I saw a number of the enemy lying under the trees, killed by our field-piece. . . . They were retreating in line, though in some disorder. I singled out a man and took my aim directly between his shoulders. (They were divested of their packs.) He was a good mark, being a broad-shouldered fellow. What became of him I know not; the fire and smoke hid him from my sight. . . .

. . . The first shot they gave us from [a small piece of artillery]

. . . cut off the thigh bone of a captain, just above the knee, and the whole heel of a private in the rear of him. . . . We then laid ourselves down under the fences and bushes to take a breath, for we had need of it. I presume everyone has heard of the heat of that day, but none can realize it that did not feel it. Fighting is hot work in cool weather, how much more so in such weather as it was on the twenty-eighth of June, 1778.

After the action in our part of the army had ceased, . . . I found [a] wounded captain . . . lying on the ground and begging his sergeant . . . to help him off the field or he should bleed to death. . . . I then offered to assist . . . in carrying him to a meetinghouse a short distance off, where the rest of the wounded men and surgeons were. . . . I . . . tarried a few minutes to see the wounded and two or three limbs amputated.

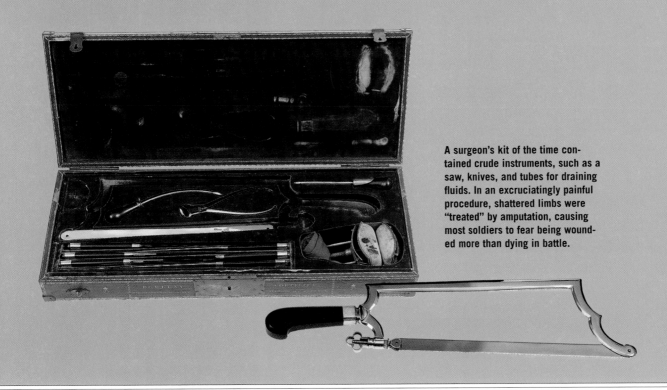

A surgeon's kit of the time contained crude instruments, such as a saw, knives, and tubes for draining fluids. In an excruciatingly painful procedure, shattered limbs were "treated" by amputation, causing most soldiers to fear being wounded more than dying in battle.

About the middle of this month (December) we crossed the Hudson at King's Ferry, and proceeded into New Jersey, for winter quarters. The snow had fallen nearly a foot deep. Now I request the reader to consider what must have been our situation at this time, naked, fatigued and starved, forced to march many a weary mile in winter, through cold and snow, to seek a situation in some (to us, unknown) wood to build us habitations to starve and suffer in. . . .

. . . We arrived on our wintering ground in the latter part of the month of December, and once more, like the wild animals, began to make preparations to build us a "city for habitation." . . .

We encamped near our destined place of operation and immediately commenced. It was upon the southern declivity of a hill; the snow, as I have already observed, was more than a foot deep, and the weather none of the warmest. We had to level the ground to set our huts upon; the soil was a light loam. When digging just below the frost, which was not deep, the snow having fallen early in the season, we dug out a number of toads, that would hop off when brought to the light of day as lively as in summertime.

A contemporary sketch of the winter encampment at Morristown, 1779-1780, depicts the small wooden huts, housing 12 soldiers each, and the larger officers' quarters. The crudely constructed buildings provided little protection from the wind and cold.

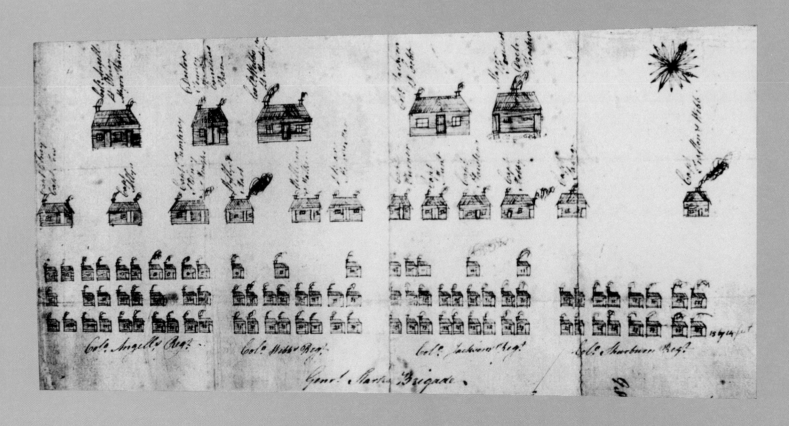

*W*e passed on to West Point. The Connecticut forces crossed the river to the eastern side and encamped opposite to West Point, upon what was called Nelson's Point. It was now very hot weather. . . . Here, for a considerable length of time, our rations, when we got any, consisted of bread and salt shad. This fish, as salt as fire, and dry bread, without any kind of vegetables, was hard fare in such extreme hot weather as it was then. . . .

Soon after we were encamped here I was sent off with a working party to work upon some fortifications on Constitution Island, a mile or two higher up the river. We . . . were to remain there a week. Our duty was, chiefly, wheeling dirt upon a stone building intended for a magazine. . . .

. . . [T]he weather became so hot that it was difficult to breathe. The rays of the sun reflected from the bare rocks . . . was stifling in the extreme, and to complete a bad business there was not a drop of water on the island, except the brackish water of the river. . . . There was no shade, and we had no tents. We could get no refreshment but in a place where were two high points of rocks butting upon the shore, which caused a small draught of wind . . . from the river. Here we repaired two or three hours, in the heat of the day, and then went to work again till dark.

To a soldier, the wooden canteen served a vital purpose. It could hold his water or his ration of rum—which was often a less risky beverage than contaminated stream water.

YORKTOWN, VIRGINIA, OCTOBER 1781

t coming on to rain hard, we were ordered back to our tents [at Yorktown], and nothing more was done that night. The next night, which was the sixth of October, the same men were ordered to the lines that had been there the night before. We this night completed laying out the works. The troops of the line were there ready with entrenching tools and began to entrench, after General Washington had struck a few blows with a pickax, a mere ceremony, that it might be said, "General Washington with his own hands first broke ground at the siege of Yorktown." . . .

. . . I was in the trenches the day that the batteries were to be opened. All were upon the tiptoe of expectation and impatience to see the signal given to open the whole line of batteries, which was to be the hoisting of the American flag in the ten-gun battery. About noon the much-wished-for signal went up. I confess I felt a secret pride swell my heart when I saw the "star-spangled banner" waving majestically in the very faces of our implacable adversaries. It appeared like an omen of success to our enterprise, and so it proved in reality. A simultaneous discharge of all the guns in the line followed, the French troops accompanying it with "Huzza for the Americans!"

On October 14, American troops captured one of the last British-held redoubts at Yorktown and proudly hoisted aloft the flag of the new United States. Their lightning attack had taken only five minutes and opened the way for the final assault on the enemy's forward trenches.

At length the eleventh day of June, 1783, arrived. "The old man," our captain, came into our room, with his hands full of papers, and first ordered us to empty all our cartridge boxes upon the floor (this was the last order he ever gave us). . . . He then handed us our discharges . . . permission to return home. . . .

. . . I confess, after all, that my anticipation of the happiness I should experience upon such a day as this was not realized; I can assure the reader that there was as much sorrow as joy transfused on the occasion. We had lived together as a family of brothers for several years, setting aside some little family squabbles, like most other families, had shared with each other the hardships, dangers, and sufferings incident to a soldier's life; had sympathized with each other in trouble and sickness; had assisted in bearing each other's burdens or strove to make them lighter by council and advice; had endeavored to conceal each other's faults or make them appear in as good a light as they would bear. In short, the soldiers, each in his particular circle of acquaintance, were as strict a band of brotherhood as Masons and, I believe, as faithful to each other. And now we were to be . . . parted forever. . . . I question if there was a corps in the army that parted with more regret than ours did. . . . Ah! It was a serious time.

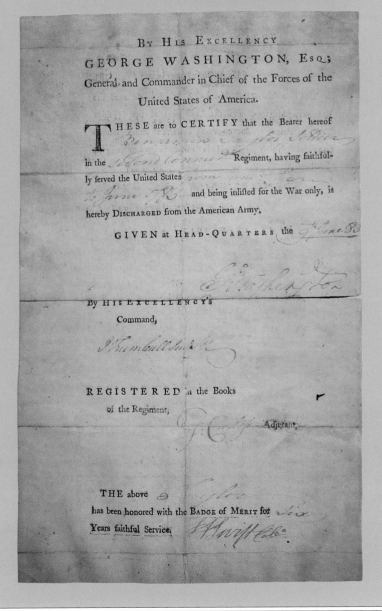

At war's end, thousands of honorable discharges such as this one, belonging to a Connecticut soldier, were signed by General Washington and given to his victorious troops.

Although the curtain came down on the drama of America's fight for independence in 1783, many among its rich cast of characters lived on. These brief accounts describe what happened to a few of them in the years after the war.

✦ **ABIGAIL AND JOHN ADAMS** During the decade John served the congress in Philadelphia, Abigail and her five children—including John Quincy, who would become the sixth president of the United States—kept to their Quincy, Massachusetts, home, where Abigail honed her skills as an avid and colorful correspondent. The family moved to Philadelphia in 1789 when John assumed the new nation's first vice presidency. He became the second president of the United States in 1797. Abigail died in 1818. John died on July 4, 1826, the 50th anniversary of the Declaration of Independence—but not quite alone. His old friend and occasional adversary Thomas Jefferson died on the same day.

✦ **BENEDICT ARNOLD** A pariah in England after the war, America's hero-turned-traitor moved back to New Brunswick in 1786, returned to trade, and helped suppress a 1794 slave revolt in Martinique. Awarded 13,400 acres in Canada, Arnold was too ill to profit from them. He died in London, deeply in debt and suffering from gout and dropsy, in 1801.

✦ **JOHN BURGOYNE** Censured in England for the British defeat at Saratoga, Burgoyne was also hounded by the United States, whose prisoner he technically remained until the end of the war. Although he was made commander in chief in Ireland during 1782 and 1783, his military career had ended. Burgoyne then struck up a career as a playwright and, at age 60, took a married actress as his mistress; she bore him four children before his sudden death in 1792.

✦ **CHARLES, LORD CORNWALLIS** His reputation somehow surviving Britain's ruinous defeat at Yorktown, in 1786 Cornwallis became governor general of India, where his incorruptible civil service became the cornerstone of successful British rule. Cornwallis went to Ireland as viceroy in 1798 but resigned in 1801, after King George III denied Irish Roman Catholics their political rights. He died in 1805 in India.

✦ **MARGARET AND THOMAS GAGE** Widely blamed for the loss of the American colonies, Gage held the title of Royal Governor of Massachusetts even after they had won their independence. He was promoted to full general in 1782, but his health had begun to decay. So had his marriage to New Jersey-born Margaret Kemble Gage. He died in London in 1787 after a decade of suffering; Margaret died in 1824 at the age of 90.

✦ **HORATIO GATES** Having intrigued against Washington and lost ignominiously at Camden, the hero of Saratoga saw no further action, although some said he participated in a postwar conspiracy of restive officers. Three years after a long illness killed his first wife, he married a wealthy English-born widow, sold his Virginia plantation, and moved to Rose Hill Farm, three miles north of New York. He was a member of the state legislature before his death in 1806.

✦ **NATHANAEL GREENE** The Revolutionary War made Greene a conquering hero to his fellow Rhode Islanders, but it had so ruined the once-wealthy foundryman financially that he was forced to sell off all his holdings. For the second time in his life, Greene abandoned New England for the South. In 1785 he and his family moved to Georgia, where he died the following year of sunstroke.

✦ **ALEXANDER HAMILTON** The young attorney served as New York's delegate to the Constitutional Convention and as the nation's first treasury secretary under George Washington. In 1800 Hamilton helped Thomas Jefferson break a tie for the presidency with Aaron Burr, whom Hamilton later helped defeat in the New York governor's race. Soon after, in 1804, the implacably angry Burr lured Hamilton into a pistol duel and killed him.

✦ **JOHN HANCOCK** The first to sign the Declaration of Independence, Hancock was elected the first governor of Massachusetts in 1780 and was returned to office at every election until his death in 1793.

✦ **JOHN PAUL JONES** In France after the Continental navy was decommissioned, Jones was made a chevalier by King Louis XVI, and in 1787 he received the only American gold medal awarded to a naval officer. But he had "not yet begun to fight," serving the Russian navy of Catherine the Great against Turkey in the Black Sea. He died in Paris in 1792.

✦ **HENRY KNOX** After George Washington stepped down in 1783, Knox became commander in chief, then secretary of war under the Articles of Confederation and the first secretary of war under the Constitution, during Washington's administration. He died in 1806 from a chicken bone lodged in his intestines.

✦ **MARIE-JOSEPH-PAUL-YVES-ROCH-GILBERT DU MOTIER, MARQUIS DE LAFAYETTE** A hero at home by virtue of his American exploits, Lafayette urged the establishment of a constitutional monarchy in France. On July 15, 1789, a day after the storming of the Bastille by Revolutionary forces, he was named commander of the newly created national guard of Paris. Sent to command the Army of the North in Metz (succeeding Rochambeau), Lafayette entered a war with Austria, to which, fearing Jacobin radicals at home, he fled in 1792, when the French monarchy was overthrown. Repatriated by Napoleon in 1797, he lived the rest of his life as a gentleman-farmer, with occasional forays into politics, and died in Paris in 1834.

✦ **CHARLES LEE** Court-martialed for disobedience after the New Jersey campaign of 1776, Lee was suspended from the army for a year, at the end of which he sent the congress such an offensive letter that the lawmakers ejected him from the service altogether. The famous eccentric retired to his estate in the Shenandoah Valley of Virginia, where he died in 1782. Not until the middle of the 19th century was it known that Lee, while he was a captive in 1776, had treasonously offered the British a strategy that might have defeated the colonists—a strategy that General Sir William Howe evidently rejected.

✦ **HENRY (LIGHT-HORSE HARRY) LEE** Although he served a term as Virginia's governor and wrote what many consider the best account of America's war of independence by a participant, Henry Lee was troubled by depression and financial failure—he spent 1809 in debtor's prison. He and his wife had one child, a son who would do more to sunder the United States than Light-Horse Harry Lee had done to join them: Robert E. Lee, who was born in 1807. The intrepid horseman died at his Virginia home in 1818.

✦ **FRANCIS MARION** Like so many war heroes, the former Swamp Fox faded into civilian life, protesting the continued persecution of Tories after the war and urging education as an antidote for tyranny, to little avail. He served sporadically in state offices until his death in 1795.

✦ **DANIEL MORGAN** Although still plagued by ill health, the resilient wagoner fought against the Whiskey Rebellion of 1794, served in the congress, and outlived many of his peers, including George Washington and Benedict Arnold, before succumbing in July of 1802 at his Virginia home, Saratoga. "Doctor," Morgan reputedly told his physician just before his death, "if I could be the man I was when I was 21 years of age, I would be willing to be stripped stark naked on the top of the Allegheny Mountain, to run for my life with a pack of dogs at my heels."

✦ **THOMAS PAINE** Rewarded with a confiscated Loyalist estate in New York, Paine returned in 1787 to England, where his *Rights of Man* brought a British charge of libel. Still following the tides of revolution, he went to France in 1792 and was elected to the revolutionary assembly—until, a year later, the radical Jacobins threw him into prison, where he wrote *The Age of Reason*. Back in the United States after he was released, Paine was reviled as a deist; he died in 1809, as impoverished and obscure as he had been before the first shots of the Revolutionary War were fired at Lexington and Concord.

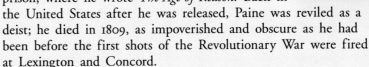

✦ **LORD HUGH PERCY** Although the young brigadier helped Britain win in New York in 1776, he became increasingly disenchanted by his side's prosecution of the war. In 1777 he resigned his commission and returned to England, where, on his father's death, he became the powerful Duke of Northumberland. Long plagued by gout, he died in 1817, one of Britain's wealthiest—and most irascible—men.

✦ **PAUL REVERE** Admitted to the Massachusetts militia as a lieutenant colonel commanding Boston Harbor's Castle William, the erstwhile messenger hungered for a post with the Continentals but remained trapped in the militia, where he participated in two abortive campaigns. Although his failed military career never ceased to rankle, Revere turned his postwar talents to his flourishing silver shop, casting bells, and metallurgy. He died in May 1818, 43 years after his greatly mythologized midnight ride.

✦ **JEAN-BAPTISTE-DONATIEN DE VIMEUR, COMTE DE ROCHAMBEAU** First named commander of Calais and later of Alsace after his 1783 return to France, Rochambeau commanded the Army of the North in 1791, during the French Revolution, but, disenchanted, resigned before the fight with Austria began. Arrested for treason during the Reign of Terror, Rochambeau barely escaped the guillotine. Made a marshal of France in 1803, he was pensioned off by Napoleon, and died at Vendôme in 1807.

✦ **BANASTRE TARLETON** His reputation tarnished but not destroyed by the Cowpens defeat, Tarleton returned to England and entered Parliament in 1790. He was promoted to full general in 1812, became a baronet in 1815, and was knighted in 1820. Despite his ascent in rank and privilege, the hot-blooded warrior who had given no quarter never fought on a battlefield again, and he died uneventfully in 1833.

BRITISH CANADA

NOVA SCOTIA

Quebec

Halifax

Montreal • Saint Johns

LAKE CHAMPLAIN

N.H.

Ticonderoga

Concord
Lexington

Oswego

Saratoga

MASS.

Boston

Oriskany • Albany

NEW YORK

CONN.

R.I.

Newport
New London

LAKE SUPERIOR

LAKE MICHIGAN

LAKE HURON

LAKE ONTARIO

LAKE ERIE

Saint Lawrence River

Hudson River

Mississippi River

PENNSYLVANIA

New York
Morristown

Princeton
Germantown
Valley Forge
Brandywine

Monmouth Court House
Trenton

Philadelphia

NEW JERSEY

SPANISH LOUISIANA

Sandusky •

Pittsburgh •

MD. • Baltimore

DELAWARE

Mount Vernon

Potomac R.

CHESAPEAKE BAY

Chillicothe •

Ohio River

Williamsburg •

Yorktown

Missouri River

Vincennes •

VIRGINIA

Appalachian Mountains

Kaskaskia •

Guilford Court House •

NORTH CAROLINA

Kings Mountain •

Charlotte •

Cowpens •

Ninety Six •

SOUTH CAROLINA

Camden •

Augusta •

Eutaw Springs •

GEORGIA

Charleston •

Savannah •

Wilmington •

Mississippi River

ATLANTIC OCEAN

SPANISH FLORIDA

GULF OF MEXICO

Miles

0   50   100   150   200

ORIGINAL 13 COLONIES

U.S. EXPANSION BY 1783

1,600,000	Population in 1760
2,780,000	Population in 1780
42	Percentage growth in population, 1760-1780
500,000	Approximate population of black slaves, 1763-1774
34,000	Population of largest city (Philadelphia)
6.3	Average number of children per family
26.7	Average age of marriage for males
23.7	Average age of marriage for females
5.2	Percentage of males never marrying
20.8	Percentage of females never marrying
33.3	Percentage of births out of wedlock
90	Percentage of work force engaged in agriculture
17	Percentage of population that belonged to church, 1776
270	Number of students at Yale, largest of any college, in 1783.
5	Number of days it took to travel from Philadelphia to Baltimore
160	Gallons of alcohol passed out by George Washington to 391 potential voters when running for his first political office, 1758
150,000	Barrels of rice exported to Britain by Carolina and Georgia, 1770
$36,500,375	National debt, 1783
$134,645,177	Total cost of Revolutionary War

LIFESTYLE

• Five students organized a social fraternity at the College of William and Mary in 1776 known as Phi Beta Kappa. In 1831 it became an honorary society for academic distinction.

• New England's use of the scarlet letter A for adulterers was abandoned in 1782.

• A typical colonial curriculum for wealthy young southern males included Latin, Greek, Hebrew, the Grecian and Roman Histories and Antiquities, reading, writing, arithmetic-vulgar, decimals and duodecimal geometry, planometry, trigonometry, surveying, gauging, Italian bookkeeping, and navigation.

• Education for women emphasized practical learning, including spelling and writing.

• Women got the vote in New Jersey in 1776 but lost it in 1807, when laws restricted the electorate to free white males.

• *A Pretty Story,* a 16-page satire of British rule by "Peter Grievous, Esquire, ABCDE, Velunti in Speculo," was published by Francis Hopkinson of Williamsburg, Virginia, in 1774 for the amusement of a friend's children—the first American "novel."

• One of the most popular American cookbooks in 1761 was Mrs. E. Smith's *The Complete Housewife; or Accomplished Gentlewoman's Companion; Being a Collection of Several Hundred of the Most Approved Receipts in Cookery, Pastry, etc.*

• After independence, works formerly protected by British copyright could be printed in the United States, among them America's first Bible in English, published in Philadelphia in 1782.

• Philadelphia publisher Benjamin Towne began the *Pennsylvania Evening Post,* America's first daily newspaper, in 1783.

• At a town meeting in Worcester, Massachusetts, a state liquor excise was opposed on the grounds that it ran contrary to the genius of free people. Indeed, it was argued that spirits were an absolute necessity for the morale of farmworkers.

• According to legend, the cocktail was invented by Elmsford, New York, barmaid Betsy Flanagan, who decorated her bar with rooster plumes. When an inebriated client asked for "some of those cocktails," she stuck a feather in his drink—and coined the term.

• Nocturnal deer hunting in the Carolinas was made a misdemeanor in 1784 because of the accidental slaughter of many cows and horses.

CHRONOLOGY OF EVENTS

THE WAR FROM PROLOGUE TO PEACE TREATY

1760 British capture Montreal and Detroit from French, see victory in the Seven Years' War (in America, the French and Indian War).

1760 George III crowned King of England.

1761 James Otis makes first public speech against British rule, denouncing Writs of Assistance before the Massachusetts Supreme Court.

1762 France secretly cedes the Louisiana Territory to Spain to keep it away from the British.

1763 Indian forces, led by an Ottawa chief named Pontiac, besiege Detroit and destroy British garrisons west of Niagara; although defeated at Fort Pitt, Chief Pontiac continues his resistance for another two years.

1763 Treaty of Paris ends Seven Years' War.

CHIEF PONTIAC OF
THE OTTAWA

1764 Britain enacts the Sugar Act to help pay war debt, and the Currency Act to prevent colonies from issuing their own money.

1765 Britain enacts the Stamp Act, requiring the purchase of tax stamps, to be affixed to numerous goods.

1765 Britain enacts the Quartering Act, forcing colonists to provide room and board to British soldiers.

TOOLED LEATHER BOX FOR
STORING TAX STAMPS

1766 Stamp Act is repealed as London businesses cite decreased colonial demand for their goods.

1766 Britain enacts the Declaratory Act, asserting its right to make laws for the colonies.

1767 Townshend Acts are passed, requiring colonists to pay import duties on tea and other products.

1768 Colonists refuse to abide by Quartering Act, denying rooms to British troops in Boston.

1769 Chief Pontiac murdered in Illinois by a Kaskaskia Indian.

1769 British governor of Virginia dissolves assembly because of its resolutions against British taxes.

1769 Colonial seaports draw up nonimportation agreements against British.

1770 Tensions over Townshend and Quartering Acts erupt in Boston Massacre as jittery British soldiers fire into angry crowd.

1770 Britain repeals the Townshend Acts but retains tax on tea. Colonists end embargo on British goods, temporarily improving relations with Great Britain.

1771 British suppress uprising of North Carolina farmers protesting excessive taxes.

POLITICS, SCIENCE, AND THE ARTS

1760 Tired of carrying two pairs of spectacles, Benjamin Franklin invents bifocal lens.

1760 Tobacco prices in England drop sharply, forcing many colonists to farm corn and wheat instead.

1761 Philadelphia-based "Corporation for the Relief of Poor and Distressed Presbyterian Ministers and of the Poor and Distressed Widows and Children of Presbyterian Ministers" issues first American life insurance policy, to Francis Alison.

1761 George Washington begins experimenting with crop rotation and livestock breeding.

1762 Ethan Allen establishes an ironworks and blast furnace in Connecticut that will produce cannon for the Revolutionary War.

1763 Henry Williams tests first steam-powered boat on Conestoga Creek near Lancaster, Pennsylvania.

1763 George Washington's Mississippi Company asks Crown for 2.5-million-acre grant at confluence of Ohio and Mississippi Rivers, to reward militia service in French and Indian War.

1764 *Connecticut Courant*, which as the *Hartford Courant* would become the oldest continuously published newspaper in the United States, begins as a weekly.

1765 First medical school is established as the College of Philadelphia Department of Medicine (now the University of Pennsylvania Medical School), graduating its first class of 10 doctors in 1768.

1765 Scottish scientist James Watt invents a more efficient steam engine.

AMERICAN STAGECOACH
WITH ELLIPSOIDAL DESIGN
FOR HIGH-SPEED TRAVEL

1766 New stagecoach, a "flying machine," cuts the trip between New York and Philadelphia to two days.

1767 Daniel Boone makes first exploration west of the Appalachian Mountains, traveling along the present-day border of Kentucky and West Virginia.

1767 Harvard professor John Winthrop publishes study on density of comets.

1768 A commemorative silver bowl by Paul Revere is presented to Massachusetts legislators, who protested trade restrictions and taxation to King George III.

1768 First edition of the *Encyclopaedia Britannica* appears in Scotland.

1769 Wesley Chapel, America's first Methodist church, is dedicated in New York.

1770 Thomas Jefferson designs and builds first house at Monticello, beginning a project that will remain a work in progress for the rest of his life.

1770 Public Hospital for Persons of Insane and Disordered Minds opens in Williamsburg, Virginia.

1771 Benjamin Franklin begins his autobiography, intended for his son, Tory New Jersey governor William, but never finished.

LEATHER PURSE CARRIED BY
A CONCORD MINUTEMAN

1772 Rhode Islanders attack and burn British revenue cutter *Gaspee* in Narragansett Bay.

1772 Samuel Adams leads the Committees of Correspondence in revolt against the British.

1773 Britain enacts the Tea Act to fund the foundering British East India Company and to reassert its right to tax the colonies. Colonists respond with the Boston Tea Party.

1774 Britain passes the Intolerable Acts.

1774 First Continental Congress meets in Philadelphia.

1775 Patrick Henry delivers his "Give me liberty or give me death" speech.

1775 Minutemen and militia confront redcoats at Lexington and Concord.

1775 Benedict Arnold and Ethan Allen capture Fort Ticonderoga.

1775 British win costly Battle of Bunker Hill.

1775 Second Continental Congress in Philadelphia appoints George Washington commander in chief of the Continental army.

SILVER CAMP CUP MADE FOR
GEORGE WASHINGTON

1776 Congress adopts the Declaration of Independence, drafted by Thomas Jefferson.

1776 British evacuate Boston, ending siege.

1776 General Howe defeats colonists in New York.

1776-1777 Washington crosses Delaware to surprise British and Hessians at Trenton and Princeton.

1777 Howe wins at Brandywine and Germantown, Pennsylvania, giving British control of Philadelphia. Washington retreats to hard winter at Valley Forge.

1777 John Burgoyne recaptures Ticonderoga from colonists but is decisively beaten at Saratoga, New York.

1777 Congress adopts the Articles of Confederation and Perpetual Union.

1778 Reassured by Saratoga victory, France signs treaty of alliance with America, entering the war against Britain.

1778 Washington defeats British at Monmouth, New Jersey; British capture Savannah, Georgia.

1778 Henry Clinton replaces General Howe, evacuates Philadelphia, fearing blockade by French ships.

1779 General "Mad Anthony" Wayne defeats British at Stony Point, New York.

1779 John Paul Jones wins naval battle against British frigate *Serapis* off east coast of England.

1779 Spain declares war on Britain but does not form alliance with American rebels.

1780 French general Rochambeau and his troops arrive at Newport, Rhode Island.

1780 British capture Charleston and score heavily at Camden, to control much of South Carolina.

1780 Discovered about to surrender West Point to British, turncoat general Benedict Arnold defects to other side.

1780 Britain declares war on the Netherlands.

1781 Colonials win at Cowpens, South Carolina, and lure Cornwallis to a costly victory at Guilford Court House, North Carolina.

1781 Allies surround British at Yorktown, Virginia, where General Cornwallis surrenders to Washington.

1782 Benjamin Franklin, John Adams, and John Jay negotiate peace treaty with British in Paris.

1782 British troops evacuate Savannah and Charleston.

1783 Treaties of Paris and Versailles are signed, formally ending the war.

ARRIVAL OF
ROCHAMBEAU'S FORCES
AT NEWPORT

1772 Crisis in British banking system cuts credit to colonies, depressing American economy until 1776 war boom.

1772 Charles Willson Peale, the most important painter of the Revolutionary period, completes a life-size portrait of George Washington.

1773 Using the current from six Leyden jars, Benjamin Franklin experimentally electrocutes several chickens, a 10-pound turkey, and a lamb.

1773 The first public museum in America is organized and opened in Charleston, South Carolina, by the Charleston Library Society.

1774 Thomas Jefferson's *A Summary View of the Rights of British America* asserts the right to independent rule.

1775 Postal system established, with Ben Franklin first postmaster.

1775 Freemasons of Boston initiate their first black member at an army lodge under General Thomas Gage. But when African Lodge No. 1 is formed a year later, American Masons will not recognize it.

1775 Forks of Tar, North Carolina, becomes the first of many American towns to be called Washington.

1776 The term "United States," as opposed to "United Colonies," is authorized by the Second Continental Congress.

1777 The first American flag, the "Betsy Ross flag," is adopted by Congress. A 15-star version adopted in 1795 will be immortalized by Francis Scott Key as the "star-spangled banner" during the War of 1812.

1777 Thanksgiving Day is first celebrated nationwide on December 18, commemorating Burgoyne's October surrender near Saratoga, New York. But it will not become an annual holiday until 1863.

1778 The Headquarters Secret Service—today's Secret Service—is formed under Aaron Burr.

1779 Congress issues more than $10 million in paper money, bringing the total issued since mid-1775 to more than $240 million.

1779 British Peace Commission arrives in Philadelphia with offers the congress will reject.

$2 BILL FROM 1775, THE FIRST YEAR
THE CONGRESS ISSUED MONEY

1780 The congress passes the Forty to One Act, which deflates continental paper money to one-fortieth face value.

1780 The Massachusetts constitution is ratified with a bill of rights declaring that "all men are born free and equal," including African slaves.

1781 Bank of North America established to fund federal government, since the congress had no power to levy taxes under the Articles of Confederation.

1782 James Watt patents a piston-driven engine.

1782 Virginia emancipation law pressed by Jefferson permits the liberation of slaves in last wills and testaments.

1783 Society of the Cincinnati, a fraternal order of former Continental army officers, is founded by Henry Knox, with George Washington as president.

The editors wish to thank the following individuals and institutions for their valuable assistance in the preparation of this volume: Amy Fleming, Historical Society of Pennsylvania, Philadelphia; Carol Haines, Concord Museum, Concord, Mass.; Emmie Lapsansky, Haverford College, Haverford, Pa.; Nancy Moses,

ACKNOWLEDGMENTS

Atwater Kent Museum, Philadelphia; Paul Okey, Saratoga National Historical Park, Stillwater, N.Y.; Jeffrey Ray, Atwater Kent Museum, Philadelphia; Richard Raymond, Colonial

National Historical Park, Yorktown, Va.; Douglas P. Sabin, Minuteman National Historical Park, Concord, Mass.; Jane Sundberg, Colonial National Historical Park, Yorktown, Va.; Brent W. Tharp, Jamestown-Yorktown Foundation, Williamsburg, Va.; David Wood, Concord Museum, Concord, Mass.

PICTURE CREDITS

The sources for the illustrations that appear in this volume are listed below. Credits from left to right are separated by semicolons; credits from top to bottom are separated by dashes.

Cover: Valley Forge Historical Society. 8: Painting by John Singleton Copley, gift of Joseph W., William B., and Edward H. R. Revere/courtesy Museum of Fine Arts, Boston. 10: Courtesy John Carter Brown Library at Brown University. 12, 13: Courtesy Concord Museum, Concord, Mass., photograph by David Bohl. 15: Painting by John Singleton Copley, Yale Center for British Art, Paul Mellon Collection. 16: Courtesy Concord Museum, Concord, Mass., photograph by Chip Fanelli. 17: Courtesy American Antiquarian Society. 18: The Putnam Foundation, Timken Museum of Art, San Diego. 19: Courtesy Massachusetts Archives (SC 1, 45x). 20: Map by Maryland CartoGraphics, Inc. 21: Paintings by John Singleton Copley, deposited by the City of Boston, courtesy Museum of Fine Arts, Boston. 22: Lexington Historical Society, photograph by David Bohl—courtesy Concord Museum, Concord, Mass., photograph by David Bohl. 23: Chicago Historical Society 1973.I, gift of William McCormick Blair. 24: Courtesy American Antiquarian Society. 25: Concord Free Public Library, photograph by David Bohl. 26, 27: Courtesy Concord Museum, Concord, Mass., photograph by David Bohl. 28, 29: Courtesy Concord Museum, Concord, Mass., photograph by David Bohl; Bedford Free Public Library. 30: Chicago Historical Society 1973.IC, gift of William McCormick Blair. 31: Courtesy American Antiquarian Society. 32: Mark Sexton, courtesy Acton Public Library, Acton, Mass. 33: Lexington Historical Society. 34: Chicago Historical Society 1973.Id, gift of William McCormick Blair. 35: Courtesy John Carter Brown Library at Brown University. 36, 37: Library of Congress; Miriam and Ira D. Wallach Divisions of Art, Prints, and Photographs/New York Public Library, Astor, Lenox, and Tilden Foundations; Historical Society of Pennsylvania. 38: Historical Society of Pennsylvania; Library Company of Philadelphia. 39: Historical Society of Pennsylvania. 40: Historical Society of Pennsylvania—Collection of New-York Historical Society. 41: Historical Society of Pennsylvania—Old Dartmouth Historical Society, New Bedford Whaling Museum; Free Library of Philadelphia. 42: From *Getreue Darstellung und Beschreibung der in der Arzneykunde Gebräuchlichen Gewächse* by Dr. Friedrich Gottlob Hayne, 1809 Auf Kosten des Verfassers, Berlin—Brad Trent/DOT. 43: Brad Trent/DOT, Mercer Museum of Bucks County Historical Society—courtesy Atwater Kent Museum. 44:

Historical Society of Pennsylvania—courtesy Atwater Kent Museum. 45: © Breton Littlehales/National Geographic Society Image Collection; Historical Society of Pennsylvania. 46: Library of Congress, neg. no. USZ262-7708. 47: Courtesy Atwater Kent Museum. 48: Washington/Custis/Lee Collection, Washington and Lee University, Lexington, Va. 50: Courtesy The Bostonian Society/Old State House. 51: *Attack on Bunker's Hill, with the Burning of Charles Town,* gift of Edgar William and Bernice Chrysler Garbisch, © 1996 Board of Trustees, National Gallery of Art, Washington, D.C. 54: National Museum of American History, Smithsonian Institution, no. 76-3259. 55: Library of Congress, neg. no. USZ262-40054. 56: Courtesy Fort Ticonderoga Museum. 57: Anne S. K. Brown Military Collection, Brown University. 58: Yale University Art Gallery, Trumbull Collection. 60: Deposited by the city of Boston, courtesy Museum of Fine Arts, Boston. 61: American Philosophical Society. 62: Boston Public Library. 63: The British Museum, London. 65: Anne S. K. Brown Military Collection, Brown University Library. 67: Lafayette College Art Collection, Easton, Pa. 68: From *The American Revolution: A Picture Sourcebook*, by John Grafton, © 1975 Dover Publications, Inc., N.Y. 71: Independence National Historical Park Collection, Philadelphia. 73: Courtesy Morristown National Historical Park. 75: Independence National Historical Park Collection, Philadelphia. 76: Trinity College, Hartford, Conn.—courtesy American Antiquarian Society. 77: New York Public Library, Astor, Lenox, and Tilden Foundations. 78: Courtesy Boston Athenaeum; Chicago Historical Society. 79: National Portrait Gallery, Smithsonian Institution/Art Resource, N.Y. 80: Library of Congress—National Museum of American History, © 1995 Smithsonian Institution. 81: Independence National Historical Park Collection, Philadelphia; American Philosophical Society. 82: National Portrait Gallery, Smithsonian Institution/Art Resource, N.Y. 83: Library of Congress. 84, 85: Yale University Art Gallery, Trumbull Collection. 86: Deposited by the city of Boston, courtesy, Museum of Fine Arts, Boston—Independence National Historical Park Collection, Philadelphia. 87: National Archives. 88: Yale University Art Gallery, Trumbull Collection. 90: Map by Maryland CartoGraphics, Inc. 91: New York Public Library, Astor, Lenox, and Tilden Foundations. 92: Pennsylvania Academy of the Fine Arts, Philadelphia, gift of Maria McKean Allen and Phebe

Warren Downes through the bequest of their mother, Elizabeth Wharton McKean. 93: National Museum of American History, Smithsonian Institution. 94: Library of Congress. 95: First Troop Philadelphia City Cavalry Museum. 96: Historical Society of Pennsylvania. 98: Yale University Art Gallery, Trumbull Collection, John Hill Morgan, B.A. 1893 Fund. 99: American Philosophical Society—Library of Congress, neg. no. USZ62-C4. 100: Painting by Mather Brown, courtesy Mrs. Sharon Molin, photograph by Henry Groskinsky. 101: Jamestown-Yorktown Educational Trust, photograph by Katherine Wetzel. 102: Saratoga National Historical Park, photograph by Michael L. Noonan. 103: Frick Collection. 105: Board of Trustees of the Royal Armouries, London. 106: Map by Maryland CartoGraphics, Inc. 107: Collection of the Maryland Historical Society, Baltimore. 108: Courtesy Director, National Army Museum, London. 109: William L. Clements Library, University of Michigan. 111: Saratoga National Historical Park, photograph by Michael L. Noonan. 112, 113: Fort Ticonderoga Museum. 114: Dr. Hubertus Riedesel, Freiherr zu Eisenbach, Wartenburg, Germany. 116, 117: Yale University Art Gallery, Trumbull Collection. 119: American Numismatic Society. 120: Collection of New-York Historical Society—collection of the Albany Institute of History & Art. 121: *Colonel Guy Johnson and Karonghyontye,* Andrew Mellon Collection, © 1995 Board of Trustees, National Gallery of Art. 122: Hamilton College. 123: Yale University Art Gallery, Trumbull Collection—New York Public Library, Astor, Lenox, and Tilden Foundations. 124: British Library, London. 125: National Gallery of Canada, Ottawa; Rochester Museum and Science Center, Rochester, N.Y., photograph by Brian D. Fox. 126: Chicago Historical Society. 127: Collection of New-York Historical Society; New York State Museum, Albany, N.Y., cat. no. 36700. 128: Independence National Historical Park Collection, Philadelphia. 129: Buffalo and Erie County Historical Society. 130: Independence National Historical Park Collection, Philadelphia. 133: Library of Congress, neg. no. USZ262-45217. 134: Frank & Marie-Thérèse Wood Print Collections, Alexandria, Va.—New York State Library, photograph by Ann Aronson—© James L. Stanfield/National Geographic Society Image Collection; Yale University Art Gallery, gift of Ebenezer Baldwin, B.A. 1808. 135: Anne S. K. Brown Military Collection, Brown University Library. 136: Courtesy National Portrait Gallery, London. 137: National Park Service, Colonial National Historical Park, Yorktown, Va., photograph by

Charles Ledford. 138: Map by Maryland CartoGraphics, Inc. 139: *Swamp Fox* by W. Ranney, Authenticolor, Inc., courtesy C. Burt. 141: Independence National Historical Park Collection, Philadelphia. 142: National Gallery, London. 143: Courtesy Musée de L'Emperi, Salon-de-Provence, France. 146: Yale University Art Gallery, Mabel Brady Garvan Collection; The George C. Neumann Collection, a gift of the Sun Company to Valley Forge National Historical Park, 1978. 149: Independence National Historical Park Collection, Philadelphia. 150: Prints Collection, New York Public Library, Astor, Lenox, and Tilden Foundations—National Park Service. 152: Colonial Williamsburg Foundation and Abby Aldrich Rockefeller Folk Art Center, Williamsburg, Va. 154: Painting of John Paul Jones by C. W. Peale, courtesy American Philosophical Society—courtesy U.S. Naval Academy Museum, photograph by Richard Bond Jr. 155: Courtesy U.S. Naval Academy Museum. 158: Yorktown Victory Center Museum, photograph by Katherine Wetzel. 159: Colonial Williamsburg Foundation. 160, 161: William L. Clements Library, University of Michigan. 162: Museum of the City of New York. 164, 165: Photo R.M.N./Phillip Bernard. 167: Anne S. K. Brown Military Collection, Brown University Library. 168: Munson-Williams-Proctor Institute, Museum of Art, Utica, N.Y., gift of T. Proctor Eldred. 169: Connecticut State Archives, Connecticut State Library, Hartford, photograph by Gus Johnson. 170: Brooklyn Historical Society. 171: Jamestown-Yorktown Educational Trust, photograph by Katherine Wetzel. 172: Jamestown-Yorktown Educational Trust, photograph by Katherine Wetzel. 173, 174: Valley Forge Historical Society. 175: Jamestown-Yorktown Educational Trust, photograph by Katherine Wetzel. 176: Courtesy Morristown National Historical Park. 177: Jamestown-Yorktown Educational Trust, photograph by Katherine Wetzel. 178: State Capitol, Commonwealth of Virginia. 179: Connecticut State Archives, Connecticut State Library, Hartford, Main Vault 973.3 D93wd, photograph by Gus Johnson. 180: Frick Collection; Collection of the Maryland Historical Society, Baltimore. 181: Independence National Historical Park Collection, Philadelphia; Chicago Historical Society—Independence National Historical Park Collection, Philadelphia. 182: Map by Maryland CartoGraphics, Inc. 184: Granger Collection, New York; National Museum of American History, Smithsonian Institution—courtesy DuPont Museum, Winterthur. 185: Courtesy Concord Museum, Concord, Mass., photograph by David Bohl; National Museum of American History, Smithsonian Institution, no. 78-5815-A; American Antiquarian Society; Library of Congress, neg. no. 262-19422.

BIBLIOGRAPHY

BOOKS

Abbatt, William. *The Crisis of the Revolution: Being the Story of Arnold and André.* New York: William Abbatt under the Auspices of the Empire State Society, Sons of the American Revolution, 1899.

Abbott, Shirley. *The National Museum of American History.* New York: Harry N. Abrams, 1981.

Alden, John Richard. *General Gage in America: Being Principally a History of His Role in the American Revolution.* Baton Rouge: Louisiana State University Press, 1948.

Billias, George Athan (ed.). *George Washington's Generals.* New York: William Morrow, 1964.

Boatner, Mark Mayo. *Encyclopedia of the American Revolution.* New York: David McKay, 1966.

Brandt, Clare. *The Man in the Mirror: A Life of Benedict Arnold.* New York: Random House, 1994.

British Library. *The American War of Independence 1775-83.* London: British Library Board, 1975.

Brown, Marvin L., Jr. (trans.) *Baroness von Riedesel and the American Revolution.* Chapel Hill: University of North Carolina Press, 1965.

Buchan, William. *Domestic Medicine or a Treatise on the Prevention and Cure of Diseases by Regimen and Simple Medicines.* Boston: n.p., 1793.

Carruth, Gorton. *The Encyclopedia of American Facts & Dates.* New York: Harper & Row, 1987.

Carter, Clarence Edwin. *The Correspondence of General Thomas Gage with the Secretaries of State, 1763-1775* (Vol. 1). New Haven, Conn.: Archon Books, 1969.

Chase, Ellen. *The Beginnings of the American Revolution* (Vol. 3). New York: Baker and Taylor, 1910.

Clark, Ronald W. *Benjamin Franklin: A Biography.* New York: Random House, 1983.

Crane, Elaine Forman (ed.). *The Diary of Elizabeth Drinker* (Vol. 1). Boston: Northeastern University Press, 1991.

Cresswell, Donald H. (comp.). *The American Revolution in Drawings and Prints.* Washington, D.C.: Library of Congress, 1975.

Davis, Burke. *The Cowpens: Guilford Courthouse Campaign.* Philadelphia: J. B. Lippincott, 1962.

Fischer, David Hackett. *Paul Revere's Ride.* New York: Oxford University Press, 1994.

Fleming, Thomas J.:
The Battle of Yorktown. New York: American Heritage Publishing, 1968.
Beat the Last Drum. New York: H. Wolff, 1963.
Now We Are Enemies. New York: St. Martin's Press, 1960.
1776: Year of Illusions. New York: W. W. Norton, 1975.

Flexner, James Thomas:
The Face of Liberty: Founders of the United States. New York: Clarkson N. Potter, 1975.
George Washington in the American Revolution (1775-1783). Boston: Little, Brown, 1968.
The Traitor and the Spy: Benedict Arnold and John André. Boston: Little, Brown, 1975.
Washington: The Indispensable Man. Boston: Little, Brown, 1969.

Foner, Eric, and John A. Garraty (eds.). *The Reader's Companion to American History.* Boston: Houghton Mifflin, 1991.

Forbes, Esther. *Paul Revere & the World He Lived In.* Cambridge, Mass: Riverside Press, 1942.

Freeman, Douglas Southall. *George Washington: A Biography* (Vols. 3 and 4). New York: Charles Scribner's Sons, 1951.

French, Allen. *The Day of Concord and Lexington: The Nineteenth of April, 1775.* Boston: Little, Brown, 1925.

Frost, J. William. *The Quaker Family in Colonial America.* New York: St. Martin's Press, 1973.

Galvin, Major John R. *The Minute Men.* New York: Hawthorn Books, 1967.

Gilpin, Thomas. *Exiles in Virginia.* Philadelphia: n.p., 1848.

Gottschalk, Louis. *Lafayette Joins the American Army.* Chicago: University of Chicago Press, 1937.

Graham, James. *The Life of General Daniel Morgan.* Bloomingburg, N.Y.: Zebrowski Historical Services, 1993.

Graymont, Barbara. *The Iroquois in the American Revolution.* Syracuse, N.Y.: Syracuse University Press, 1972.

Hakim, Joy. *From Colonies to Country* (Vol. 3). New York: Oxford University Press, 1993.

Hatch, Robert McConnell. *Major John André: A Gallant in Spy's Clothing.* Boston: Houghton Mifflin, 1986.

Higginbotham, Don:
Daniel Morgan: Revolutionary Rifleman. Chapel Hill: University of North Carolina Press, 1979.
The War of American Independence. New York: Macmillan, 1971.

Kane, Joseph Nathan. *Famous First Facts.* New York: H. W. Wilson, 1981.

Ketchum, Richard M.:
Decisive Day: The Battle for Bunker Hill. Garden City, N.Y.: Doubleday, 1974.
The World of George Washington. New York: American Heritage Publishing, 1974.

Ketchum, Richard M. (ed.). *The American Heritage Book of the American Revolution.* New York: American Heritage Publishing, 1958.

Lancaster, Bruce. *The American Revolution.* (The American Heritage Library series). New York: American Heritage Press, 1985.

Lee, Henry, Jr. *The Campaign of 1781 in the Carolinas.* Chicago: Quadrangle Books, 1962.

Lefferts, Charles M. *Uniforms of the American, British, French, and German Armies in the War of the American Revolution 1775-1783.* Edited by Alexander J. Wall. Old Greenwich, Conn.: WE Inc., 1971.

Lopez, Claude-Anne. *Mon Cher Papa Franklin and the Ladies of Paris.* New Haven, Conn.: Yale University Press, 1966.

Lumpkin, Henry. *From Savannah to Yorktown: The American Revolution in the South.* Columbia: University of South Carolina Press, 1981.

Malone, Dumas. *The Declaration of Independence.* New York: Oxford University Press, 1975.

Martin, Joseph Plumb. *Private Yankee Doodle.* Edited by George F. Scheer. Boston: Little, Brown, 1962.

Mekeel, Arthur J. *The Relation of the Quakers to the American Revolution.* Washington, D.C.: University Press of America, 1979.

Miller, John C. *Origins of the American Revolution.* Stanford, California: Stanford University Press, 1979.

Miller, Lillian B. *The Dye Is Now Cast: The Road to American Independence, 1774-1776.* Washington, D.C.: Smithsonian Institution Press, 1975.

Mintz, Max M. *The Generals of Saratoga: John Burgoyne and Horatio Gates.* New Haven, Conn.: Yale University Press, 1990.

Mitchell, Broadus. *Alexander Hamilton: The Revolutionary Years.* Edited by North Callahan. New York: Thomas Y. Crowell, 1970.

Moon, William Arthur. *Peter Francisco: The Portuguese Patriot.* Pfafftown, N.C.: Colonial Publishers, 1980.

Morison, Samuel Eliot. *John Paul Jones: A Sailor's Biography.* Boston: Little, Brown, 1959.

Morpurgo, J. E. *The Treason at West Point: The Arnold-André Conspiracy.* New York: Mason/Charter, 1975.

Morris, Richard B., and the Editors of Time-Life Books. *The Making of a Nation 1775-1789* (Vol. 2) (The Life History of the United States series). New York: Time-Life Books, 1963.

Neumann, George C., and Frank J. Kravic. *Collector's Illustrated Encyclopedia of the American Revolution.* Harrisburg, Pa.: Stackpole Books, 1975.

Onuf, Peter S. (ed.). *The New American Nation: 1775-1820, Volume 11: American Society 1776-1815.* New York: Garland, 1991.

Paine, Thomas. *Common Sense.* Edited by Isaac Kramnick. New York: Penguin Books, 1986.

Peabody, James Bishop (ed.). *The Founding Fathers, Volume 1:*

John Adams: A Biography in His Own Words. New York: Newsweek Books, 1973.

Peterson, Harold L. *The Book of the Continental Soldier.* Harrisburg, Pa.: Promontory Press, 1968.

Purcell, L. Edward, and David F. Burg (eds.). *The World Almanac of the American Revolution.* New York: World Almanac, 1992.

Randall, Willard Sterne:

Benedict Arnold: Patriot and Traitor. New York: William Morrow, 1990.

A Little Revenge: Benjamin Franklin and His Son. Boston: Little, Brown, 1984.

Rice, Howard C., Jr., and Anne S. K. Brown (eds. and trans.). *The American Campaigns of Rochambeau's Army, 1780, 1781, 1782, 1783, Volume 1: The Journals.* Princeton, N.J.: Princeton University Press, 1972.

Saffron, Morris H. *Surgeon to Washington: Dr. John Cochran, 1730-1807.* New York: Columbia University Press, 1977.

Scheer, George F., and Hugh F. Rankin. *Rebels and Redcoats: The American Revolution through the Eyes of Those Who Fought and Lived It.* New York: World Publishing, 1957.

Skemp, Sheila L. *Benjamin and William Franklin: Father and Son, Patriot and Loyalist.* Boston: Bedford Books of St. Martin's Press, 1994.

Smith, Carter (ed.). *The Revolutionary War: A Sourcebook on Colonial America.* Brookfield, Conn.: Millbrook Press, 1991.

Smith, Samuel Stelle:

The Battle of Princeton. Monmouth Beach, N.J.: Philip Freneau Press, 1967.

The Battle of Trenton. Monmouth Beach, N.J.: Philip Freneau Press, 1965.

Stone, William L. *Life of Joseph Brant, (Thayendanegea)* (Vol. 1). Albany, N.Y.: J. Munsell, 1865.

Tarleton, Banastre. *A History of the Campaigns of 1780 and 1781 in the Southern Provinces of North America* (The Eyewitness Accounts of the American Revolution series). New York: Arno Press, 1968.

Thane, Elswyth. *The Fighting Quaker: Nathanael Greene.* New York: Hawthorn Books, 1972.

Thayer: Theodore:

Nathanael Greene: Strategist of the American Revolution. New York: Twayne Publishers, 1960.

Yorktown: Campaign of Strategic Options (The America's Alternatives series). Edited by Harold M. Hyman. Philadelphia: J. B. Lippincott, 1975.

Tolles, Frederick B. *Meeting House and Counting House: The Quaker Merchants of Colonial Philadelphia 1682-1763.*

Chapel Hill: University of North Carolina Press, 1948.

Treacy, M. F. *Prelude to Yorktown: The Southern Campaign of Nathanael Greene 1780-1781.* Chapel Hill: University of North Carolina Press, 1963.

200 Years: A Bicentennial Illustrated History of the United States (Vol. 1). Washington, D.C.: U.S. News & World Report Books, 1973.

Urdang, Laurence (ed.). *The Timetables of American History.* New York: Simon & Schuster, 1981.

Wallace, Willard M. *Traitorous Hero: The Life and Fortunes of Benedict Arnold.* New York: Harper & Brothers, 1954.

Ward, Christopher. *The War of the Revolution* (Vol. 2). Edited by John Richard Alden. New York: Macmillan, 1952.

Whitridge, Arnold. *Rochambeau.* New York: Macmillan, 1965.

Wickwire, Franklin, and Mary Wickwire. *Cornwallis: The American Adventure.* Boston: Houghton Mifflin, 1970.

Wolf, Edwin. *Philadelphia: Portrait of an American City.* Harrisburg, Pa.: Stackpole Books, 1975.

Wright, Esmond (ed.):

Benjamin Franklin: His Life As He Wrote It. Cambridge, Mass.: Harvard University Press, 1989.

The Fire of Liberty. New York: St. Martin's Press, 1983.

Young, Alfred F., Terry J. Fife, and Mary E. Janzen. *We the People: Voices and Images of the New Nation.* Philadelphia: Temple University Press, 1993.

PERIODICALS

Bishop, Morris. "The End of the Iroquois." *American Heritage,* October 1969.

Cook, Fred J. "Francisco the Incredible." *American Heritage,* October 1959.

Flexner, James Thomas. "Benedict Arnold: How the Traitor was Unmasked." *American Heritage,* October 1967.

Lomask, Milton. "Benedict Arnold: The Aftermath of Treason." *American Heritage,* October 1967.

OTHER SOURCES

Fleming, Thomas J. "Downright Fighting: The Story of Cowpens." Handbook. Washington, D.C.: U.S. Department of the Interior, National Park Service, 1988.

"Morristown: A History and Guide." Handbook. Washington, D.C.: U.S. Department of the Interior, National Park Service, 1983.

Sabin, Douglas P. "April 19, 1775: A Historiographical Study." Concord, Mass.: n.p., 1987.

"1776: The British Story of the American Revolution." Catalog. London: Times Books, 1976.

TIME® Time-Life Books is a
LIFE division of Time Life Inc.
BOOKS

TIME LIFE INC.
PRESIDENT AND CEO: George Artandi

TIME-LIFE BOOKS
PRESIDENT: John D. Hall
PUBLISHER/MANAGING EDITOR: Neil Kagan

THE AMERICAN STORY

The Revolutionaries

EDITOR: Russell B. Adams Jr.
DIRECTOR, NEW PRODUCT DEVELOPMENT:
Curtis Kopf
MARKETING DIRECTOR: Pamela R. Farrell

Design Director: Dale Pollekoff
Administrative Editor: Philip Brandt George
Deputy Editor: Jane Coughran
Text Editor: Carl Posey
Associate Editors/Research-Writing: Jacqueline L. Shaffer,
Jarelle S. Stein
Copyeditor: Judith Klein
Picture Coordinator: Catherine Parrott
Editorial Assistant: Patricia D. Whiteford

Special Contributors: Rita Thievon Mullin (editor); Thomas
A. Lewis, Eliot L. Marshall, George Russell (text);
Claudia Bedwell, Patricia Cassidy, Elizabeth P. Schleichert,
Elizabeth Thompson, Gerald P. Tyson, Barry N.
Wolverton, (research-writing); Barbara Fleming, Ann-
Louise G. Gates, Ellen C. Gerth, Barbara F. Quarmby,
Karen Sweet, Jennifer Veech (research); Jennifer Rushing-
Schurr (index).

Correspondents: Christine Hinze (London), Christina
Lieberman (New York), Maria Vincenza Aloisi (Paris).
Valuable assistance was also provided by Angelika
Lemmer (Wachtberg).

Vice President, Director of Finance: Christopher Hearing
Vice President, Book Production: Marjann Caldwell
Director of Operations: Eileen Bradley
Director of Photography and Research: John Conrad Weiser
Director of Editorial Administration: Judith W. Shanks
Production Manager: Marlene Zack
Quality Assurance Manager: James King
Library: Louise D. Forstall

The Consultant
Don Higginbotham has taught history for 40 years and is
currently Dowd Professor of History at the University of
North Carolina. Dr. Higginbotham has written numerous
articles and books about the American Revolution, in-
cluding *Atlas of the American Revolution, Daniel Morgan:
Revolutionary Rifleman, George Washington and the American
Military Tradition, War and Society in Early America: The
Wider Dimensions of Conflict,* and *The War of American
Independence: Military Attitudes, Policy, and Practice,* 1763-
1789. He is also a former president of the Society for
Historians of the Early American Republic and of the
Southern Historical Association.

Library of Congress Cataloging-in-Publication Data
The revolutionaries / by the editors of Time-Life Books.
    p.   cm.—(American story)
    Includes bibliographical references and index.
    ISBN 0-7835-6250-O
    1. United States—History—Revolution, 1775–1783.
2. United States—History—Revolution, 1775–1783—
Pictorial works. I. Time-Life Books. II. Series.
E208.R46 1996
973.3—dc20   96-18598
                                                          CIP

Other Publications

HISTORY
The American Story
Voices of the Civil War
The American Indians
Lost Civilizations
Mysteries of the Unknown
Time Frame
The Civil War
Cultural Atlas

SCIENCE/NATURE
Voyage Through the Universe

COOKING
Weight Watchers® Smart Choice Recipe Collection
Great Taste-Low Fat
Williams-Sonoma Kitchen Library

DO IT YOURSELF
The Time-Life Complete Gardener
Home Repair and Improvement
The Art of Woodworking
Fix It Yourself

TIME-LIFE KIDS
Family Time Bible Stories
Library of First Questions and Answers
A Child's First Library of Learning
I Love Math
Nature Company Discoveries
Understanding Science & Nature

For information on and a full description of any
of the Time-Life Books series listed above, please
call 1-800-621-7026 or write:

Reader Information
Time-Life Customer Service
P.O. Box C-32068
Richmond, Virginia 23261-2068

On the cover: Through the falling snow, George
Washington and his officers watch weary soldiers
of the Revolutionary army trudging toward Valley
Forge in this detail from William B. T. Trego's
19th-century painting. Despite severe weather and
a lack of basic supplies, Washington's troops survived the 1777-1778 winter encampment, keeping
the fight for independence alive.